HERE'S WHAT FOLKS HAVE TO SAY ABOUT *SAVAGE LOVE*

"*Savage Love* deals in sex and relationships, with side excursions . . . [His] tone is funny, and confrontational, although Mr. Savage can be wise and kind."

—*New York Times*

"The far-out drag queen's unabashed sex-advice column ["Savage Love"] in the free weekly *The Stranger* propelled that paper to must-read status."

—*Newsweek*

" 'Savage Love' has everything I want in a column: it's funny, addictive, smart, and naughty."

—Tim Keck, publisher of *The Stranger*

"Sex is a complicated subject for most of us, full of anxiety and woe. In Savage's hands, sex is a playground full of wonder and laughs."

—Doug Simmons, managing editor of the *Village Voice*

DAN SAVAGE's column, "Savage Love," is a nationally syndicated sex-advice column read, loved, and despised by more than 3.5 million people each week. For six years it has run in 16 newspapers in the United States and Canada, including the *Village Voice* and the *San Francisco Weekly*. Savage is the associate editor of *The Stranger* and a regular contributor to National Public Radio. He lives in Seattle. *Savage Love* is his first book.

SAVAGE LOVE

STRAIGHT
ANSWERS
FROM
AMERICA'S
MOST
POPULAR
SEX
COLUMNIST

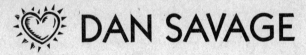 DAN SAVAGE

A PLUME BOOK

PLUME
Published by the Penguin Group
Penguin Putnam Inc., 375 Hudson Street,
New York, New York 10014, U.S.A.
Penguin Books Ltd, 27 Wrights Lane,
London W8 5TZ, England
Penguin Books Australia Ltd, Ringwood,
Victoria, Australia
Penguin Books Canada Ltd, 10 Alcorn Avenue,
Toronto, Ontario, Canada M4V 3B2
Penguin Books (N.Z.) Ltd, 182–190 Wairau Road,
Auckland 10, New Zealand

Penguin Books Ltd, Registered Offices:
Harmondsworth, Middlesex, England

First published by Plume, an imprint of Dutton NAL,
a member of Penguin Putnam Inc.

First Printing, October, 1998
10 9 8 7 6 5 4 3 2 1

The selections in this book first appeared in *The Stranger*, Seattle, Washington.

Ⓟ REGISTERED TRADEMARK—MARCA REGISTRADA

LIBRARY OF CONGRESS CATALOGING-IN-PUBLICATION DATA:

Savage, Dan.
Savage love : straight answers from America's most popular sex columnist / Dan Savage.
    p.   cm.
  ISBN 0-452-27815-5
  1. Sex—Miscellanea.   2. Man-woman relationships—Miscellanea.   3. Love—
Miscellanea.   I. Title.
HQ21.S264   1998
306.7—dc21
                                                            98-20611
                                                              CIP

Printed in the United States of America
Set in Futura Book
Designed by Leonard Telesca

*For Ann Landers, Abigail Van Buren,
and Xaviera Hollander*

ACKNOWLEDGMENTS

I've been aided and abetted every step of the way, and would like to thank the following people for their help with *Savage Love*:

Tim Keck, Christine Wenc, William Bennett, Robert Fikso, Nancy Hartunian, Judy Sobiesk, Kevin Patnik, Terry Hecker, D. J. Elliott, Ken Starr, David Schmader, Mary Martone, Peri Packroo, Matt Cook, Emily White, Danny Clark, Sara DeBell, Jennifer Hattam, Anna Woolverton, Rebecca Pellman, George Will, Joel Schraufnegal, Elizabeth Wales, Kurt Timmermeister and the staff of Cafe Septieme, Scott Spear, Jack Daniels, Carole DeSanti, Alexandra Babanskyj, M. L. Lyke, Doug Simmons, Tom Flint, Mark Finley, Alison True, Kyle Shaw, Christine Oreskovich, Catherine Salisbury, Ian Hanington, Andrew O'Hehir, Vince Bielski, Jim Rizzi, Heather Kinney, Yeun Littlefield, Crow Boudro, Tom Bianchi, Ellen Forney, everyone who has ever worked at *The Stranger*, Mark Mitchell, Mark Van-S, Donald Wildmon, everyone who has ever taken the time to send me a letter—even if you wrote to call me names, everyone who has ever served as a guest expert in my column, and finally, my good friend Isadora Alman.

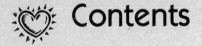 # Contents

SAVAGE LOVE

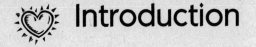 # Introduction

In Which I Tell the Incredible True Story of How a Nice Catholic Boy Like Me Wound Up Giving Sex Advice to Breeders for a Living.

I'm a sex advice columnist. My column, "Savage Love," appears in straight weekly newspapers across this glorious North American continent of ours, from sea (Atlantic: New York City; Philadelphia; Halifax, Nova Scotia) to shining sea (Pacific: Seattle; San Francisco; Vancouver, British Columbia). Mostly I give advice to breeders—eating pussy for boys, sucking dick for girls, buttfucking for everybody—which is an odd job, considering I'm one of those boys who doesn't sleep with girls. Thanks to my advice column, I enjoy a lifestyle my famished Irish ancestors could never have imagined: indoor plumbing, off-the-floor beds, guilt-free sodomy, and a refrigerator full of see-through beer.

By way of introduction to this collection of my columns, I would like to answer a few of the questions people typically ask me. Let's start with the fourth most commonly asked question, right after What's a cock ring? Is this normal? and Will sex kill me? How did you get this job?

Well, George Bush was in the White House, Saddam Hussein was in Kuwait, and I was in a video store in Madison,

Wisconsin. I was the night manager, and one night when I was watching the Gulf War on television, Joel, one of the guys who rented action videos to frat boys five nights a week, gave his two weeks' notice. He was moving to Seattle with some friends to start a weekly newspaper. I couldn't understand why anyone would move to Seattle to do anything—this was just before Nirvana, Starbucks, and Microsoft ate the world—but I wished Joel luck, and told him I'd heard it rains there a lot. Then I made the offhand comment that forever altered my life: "Make sure your paper has an advice column—everybody claims to hate 'em, but everybody seems to read 'em."

I always did. My grandfather was a sportswriter at two of Chicago's biggest daily newspapers, both of which, like my grandfather, are now dead. An honorary Harlem Globetrotter, my grandfather got all the Chicago dailies (some places you "take" dailies, in Chicago you "get" them). When my parents married, they moved into the second floor of my grandparents' two-flat. Newspapers were everywhere, and reading papers was a grown-up thing to do, so all of us kids wanted to read the papers. First, I mastered the funnies; then I graduated to the advice columns: "Dear Abby" in the *Chicago Tribune* and "Ask Ann Landers" in the *Chicago Sun Times* (now in the *Chicago Tribune*). At five, I preferred Ann to Abby; she was more accessible, direct, and brassy. I loved Ann Landers.

Until I was 12. Then, about the time hair started growing on my balls—plucked until their numbers overwhelmed me—I discovered two other advice columns. These two new columns combined my long love of the form with my newest love—anything to do with sex: "The Happy Hooker," by Xaviera Hollander, which ran in *Penthouse* magazine for several years, and *Playboy*'s "Advisor."

Around the first of every month, I would sneak into my older brother's bedroom and head straight for his stash, knowing the latest issues of *Penthouse* and *Playboy* would be waiting for me. I invested long hours ransacking and restoring my older brother's bedroom; if he was coming home, or if he was somewhere in the house, I was capable of making a surgical strike: get in, get porn, get out. If I got his mags back in his hiding place before he, um, *required* them, he never even knew I'd borrowed them.

I preferred *Penthouse* to *Playboy*. First, Xaviera was so much more interesting than the "Advisor." Xaviera wrote about down & dirty sex things she had actually done herself—sometimes for money, sometimes for fun—and she never stooped to giving advice about stereo equipment and bachelor-pad decorating tips, à la *Playboy*'s "Advisor." *Penthouse* also had a letters section that did much to inspire the brand loyalty of this budding young homo. It was 1978 when I began reading *Penthouse* carefully, the sexual revolution was still in full swing (no one knew at the time that it was the final swing, what with the twin disasters of AIDS and Ronald Reagan only two-ish years off), and everyone was experimenting—if not in practice, at least in theory. The *Penthouse* "Forum" featured letters ostensibly written by "actual" readers about their true-life experiments. Less adventurous readers—and underage readers—could experiment vicariously by reading these letters, and there was one experiment frequently written up in circa '78 "Forums" that I found especially involving: the bisexual experiment. One letter every other month was from a guy who'd just participated in his first-ever, and usually last-ever, bisexual experiment—always in the exonerating presence of a wife or girlfriend, and it was always her idea, but still! Here were boys doing it with boys!

Stealing porn from your older and larger siblings is a dangerous game—ask any younger sib who lived to tell the tale. Even the few times Billy beat me senseless after catching me ducking out of his room with one of his mags—or ducking back in to return one—were no deterrent: there were dirty letters to read, and there was Xaviera. I would have risked pretty much anything to get at Xaviera's page—a picture of a woman's already bright red lips having yet more color applied with a lipstick shaped to look like a penis. Whatever beatings I received were worth the education I was getting from Xaviera. She answered questions about blow jobs, about kinky sex, about women doin' it with women, and men doin' it with men, anal sex, eatin' pussy, porn actresses—there didn't seem to be anything she hadn't done, anything that could fluster her, or anything she wouldn't write about! As I had fallen in love with Ann years before, I was now in love with Xaviera.

So years later, when Joel asked me at the video store what kind of advice column I thought this new paper should have, I remembered Xaviera and the risks I'd run to get my hands on her column. I told Joel the column should be a dirty one, a sex advice column, as people would risk anything, even physical harm, to get their hands on a publication that featured a sex advice column.

We stood at the counter, ignored the frat boys, and brainstormed up a sex advice column for the '90s. A man should write it—too many advice columns are written by women. And it should be written by someone young—too many advice columns are written by septuagenarians. And it should be written by a fag—too many advice columns are written by straights. But unlike the few fag-generated advice columns out there, this one would be written by a fag for breeders, about breeder sex. After all, who knows more about sex than fags? And wasn't it about time that fags got a chance to tell breeders what to do? It was 1991, ACT UP and Queer Nation were at the height of their cultural resonance—angry fags were marching in the streets telling straight people where to get off; why not tell 'em how to get off? We came up with the perfect name for this new model advice column: "Hey, Faggot." It had the same bounce as "Dear Abby," and like "Dear Abby," "Hey, Faggot" could be both the column's name and the salutation.

But who would write it? Honest to God, I wasn't angling for the gig. I didn't think of myself as a writer then, and even though I've been making a living writing for almost eight years now, I still don't think of myself as a writer (here I have a lot of company). But when, at Joel's suggestion, I went to the back room and banged out a prototype on my bosses' computer (and my bosses' dime), I thought, I could do this: I was a fag, I was rude, I was young, I knew a lot about sex. Rereading that prototype column today makes me want to puke—it's so awful, which is why you won't find it in this collection—but back then I didn't think what I'd banged out was half bad.

And neither did Tim Keck, the publisher-to-be of this new

weekly paper, *The Stranger.* Joel passed my prototype on to Tim, who liked the concept, and my writing. What he didn't like was "Hey, Faggot." We met for lunch at Ela's Deli on State Street in Madison, and Tim suggested "My Gay Friend" as the name for this new advice column. That was not okay with me, as "friendly" was not the posture fags in '91 were assuming. A few minutes later, someone came up with "Savage Love." It was agreed that I could keep "Hey, Faggot" as the salutation, and my column was born. Tim moved to Seattle with a handful of folks from Madison—Nancy, Johnie, James—and started the paper. Sadly, Joel went north to Alaska and never wound up working on the paper.

I didn't head off to Seattle with the rest of the Madison mafia, not right away. I stayed on in Madison for a while, writing the column from the back of the video store. When the column became a hit, along with the *The Stranger,* I quit my job and moved to Seattle, where three of *The Stranger*'s early and brilliant editors—Matt Cook, Peri Pakroo, and especially Christine Wenc—made it their job to teach me how to write.

· Which explains how I got the job, but what prepared me for being one of America's handful of perfessional advice columnists?

My early love of Ann Landers and Xaviera Hollander was an important factor, but millions of people grow up reading Ann Landers and most don't become advice columnists when they grow up; and I can't have been the only gay boy reading *Penthouse* magazine in the '70s who had a bone for Xaviera Hollander, but so far as I'm aware, no other Hollander fans followed in her footsteps and became sex advice columnists (though maybe a few became hookers), so there must have been larger forces at work . . . familial forces.

My family lived on the north side of Chicago, in a neighborhood called Rogers Park. My immediate and extended family is loud, argumentative, and very Catholic. The dozens of aunts and uncles who hung out at my parents' apartment when I was growing up were hippies, though my parents themselves were not—my dad was a Chicago cop. Of my parents' four kids, I was the "sensitive" one, and as sensitive boys were unwelcome at the neighborhood boys' reindeer games, I stayed close to home: in our apartment, on our back stoop, in my grandparents' apartment.

My mother would listen to me talk when we were home alone, which seemed to be all the time, but when the phone rang or one of the friends she'd known all her life from the neighborhood dropped by, I would listen to her talk. My mother mostly talked about other people's problems—she was a one-woman support group. This was the late '60s, before therapists and domestic-abuse hot lines and support groups and Sally and Jenny and Ricki. Before empathy became an industry, every neighborhood had someone like my mom, one woman all the other women in the neighborhood went to with their problems, things they couldn't take to a priest.

Piecing together what a caller's problem was from my mother's advice was a game I got pretty good at; when she got off the phone, I would tell her what I thought the problem was, and who the caller had been. But when someone dropped by for advice, listening in was more complicated. My mom would send me outside, but I'd hide in the next room and listen. No made-up games with awful neighbor boys were as compelling as the real-life dramas being discussed in our kitchen—drunk husbands, rotten kids, impending divorces, bad perms. Grown-up problems were irresistible! My mother didn't mind if I listened, but she couldn't appear not to mind, so if I was caught, she would march me out of the house. Still, my mother would sit with me on the back porch and answer my questions about the woman's problem, swearing me to secrecy, and explain why she'd given her the advice she did.

So I studied under the master advice mongers—Ann, Abby, Xaviera, Mom—but what prepared me to be a *sex* advice columnist?

It pisses straight people off when I mention this, but the simple fact that I'm gay—the blessing of my homosexuality—was all the preparation I needed to give sex advice. Gay people know more about sex than straight people do, have more sex than straight people do, and are better at it than straight people are.

Here's why: since little gay boys can't take their sex questions to parents or teachers or classmates or, God forbid, priests, we have to do our own research. Gay men are often criticized, even by other gay men, for being a little too fascinated by sex—a fascination that in some cases becomes an obsession and then a compulsion—but no one ever seems to stop and consider why this is the case. Sex is the central mystery of a gay man's existence, sex is what sets us apart and makes us different. Sex is what makes gay people *not* straight people. If we don't come to some comprehensive understanding about sex, if we don't work out some unified theory, we can never fully understand ourselves, who we are, why we are, and where we fit in. So we read and think and do more about sex than straight people do—and not just about gay sex, but about sex in general.

To understand who we are as gay people, we have to understand who we are not—you can't understand what it means to be gay if you don't understand what it means to be straight; we have to understand what it means to be straight before we can understand what it means to *not* be straight. Finding information about straight people and straight sex isn't nearly as difficult for the young homo as finding info about gay people and gay sex is. After all, gay people are immersed in heterosexual environments for years and years before we're even aware we're gay. Once we become aware that we're different, we start observing straight people—gay people walk many miles in straight shoes; how many straights can say the same about gay shoes? Few straights are raised by gay couples, spend years believing they're gay, their adolescence praying to be gay, walking gay and talking gay, observing their every move for signs of "straightness" that might give them away, and have gay sex, all in an absurd effort to make themselves gay. Well, gay boys do the reverse of all of that to play it straight; we observe and mimic straights, try to pass ourselves off as straights, are hyperaware of what it means to be straight because we're so painfully aware that we are not straight, and never will be, and that this not-being-straight has serious consequences for us. Gay people are better informed about sex—gay and straight— because we have no choice.

Finally, what makes gay people better at sex is good communication. After all, nothing makes a person better at sex than good communication. All sex therapists, advice columnists, and marriage counselors—serious, mainstream, pop culture, religious—are in agreement on this point. An entire chapter of Dr. Ruth Westheimer's *Sex for Dummies* (1996) is titled "Communicate, Communicate, Communicate!" If Dr. Ruth's book is for dummies, than Michael Morgenstern's *How to Make Love to a Woman* (1982) is for morons. Morgenstern devotes a whole chapter to communication, but doesn't risk baffling his readers with a five-syllable stumper: his communication chapter is simply called "Talking." In *The Family Book About Sexuality* (1989), the authors beg married straight people to communicate, because "one of the most important factors in the successful expression of sexuality between two people is communication—the ability to talk with the other person about sex in simple but honest language."

But most breeders seem to believe the hype about breeder sex—that breeder sex is "natural," and that it should happen "naturally," certainly without unnatural and interfering conversation about what he or she likes to do in bed. Where do likes and dislikes fit in anyway? Breeder sex *is* vaginal intercourse, as all young breeders know. What's to talk about? When there's only one item on the menu, you don't need to say much to the waiter. Communication in breeder sex is almost always over after both participants have said "yes." Tab A, slot B—no mystery.

For gay people, "yes" is just the beginning. Two folks of the same sex climb into bed. Now what? What do you do when you've got a tab and a tab or a slot and a slot? Since who is going to do what to whom can't be assumed, the girl couple or the boy couple have to talk it out, we have to communicate. There are no assumptions. Enlightened, let's-get-everything-on-the-table fuck-and-suck conversations that highly evolved straight people have about sex are the same conversations that gays and lesbians must have the very first time we have sex. Gays and lesbians are compelled to communicate, and as communication makes people better at sex, all that conversing we're required to do makes your average gay person better at sex than your average straight person. And therefore better qualified to give sex advice than your average straight person.

I'm often asked what professional qualifications I have, if any. Well, to be honest, none. In the one psych course I had in college, I got a B, and I somehow managed to avoid taking a single human sexuality class. So besides reading advice columns all my life, listening to my mother give advice, and sucking dick, I can't claim to have any "real" qualifications.

But remember: Ann Landers ain't no shrink either, she's just a bright, brassy, opinionated midwestern gal. She's not always right, and when she messes up, she takes her "fifty lashes with a wet noodle" and moves on. I like to think of myself as a gay Ann Landers. I'm bright, brassy, opinionated, midwestern, and I've been a gal on occasion. And when I'm wrong, I take my lashes. And Xaviera Hollander wasn't a shrink, though she rented by the hour like one. And my mom wasn't a shrink, she was a mom—and a good one. Fact is, only recently has the idea taken hold that someone needs professional qualifications—some stinkin' badge—before he or she can offer another human being a piece of advice. The advice game has been hijacked by a self-appointed class of pointy-headed witch doctors, who jealously guard their "practices" from opinionated interlopers like me. They don't want folks to know that advice is simply one person's opinion about what could or should be done, and that anyone can offer advice to anyone who asks for it, and there's not always a need to call in the "professionals."

Another question I'm commonly asked is what it's like to be an advice columnist. Since this is a collection of columns, I thought it would be kosher to include a column right up here in the introduction, in which I answered career-day questions submitted to me by a sixteen-year-old high school student.

Hey, Faggot:

I'm a high school senior and they're making me do this stupid fucking career packet. I have to research 4 different careers, which is only making me all depressed and bitchy about the fact that I have no fucking idea what I want to do with my life. I have to interview one person of each career. So one career is a writer for a magazine or newspaper, and guess what? That's you. I'm sure you're a busy guy and all, but if you'd take the time to answer these questions, I'd just love you for ever and ever.

Vanessa Lee, Bothell, Washington

What education, experience, and other requirements are needed for this job?

You have to know how to open mail and type. At one time you had to know how to spell, but now computers do that for us.

What is a typical day on the job like?

Today I came to work around noon, read mail. Saved letters with questions I knew the answers to, threw the rest away. Had lunch. Ordered intern to enter letters I wanted to answer. Wrote some answers, showed them to editor, who told me they weren't funny. Looked everywhere for the card of a Navy recruiter who tried to sign me up on the street today when I was coming to work. Added Navy stuff to column, showed editor, who was much happier. Made long-distance phone calls, stole stamps, went home.

What are the pay/benefits like?

Vanessa, dear, it's rude to ask people how much money they make. But I will tell you it's up there in the low three figures. As for benefits, well, we uninsured freelance writers have the benefit of knowing that when we get very sick, we place more strain on our tottering, immoral, for-profit health care system. One day, one of us will have the honor of being the straw that breaks that camel's back.

What is the market like for this job? In a few years?

Until Ann and Abby drop dead, there is no market. Don't even think about becoming an advice columnist, you snot-nosed punk.

What are the biggest advantages? Disadvantages?

Advantages: I don't have to wear a suit to work. I don't have to wear anything to work, actually. I edit the letters of people who disagree with me in such a way to make them seem stupid; I always get the last word. Disadvantages: a lot of straight boys work at newspapers, and straight boys are convinced that farts are funny.

Why, when, how did you pick this career?

I didn't pick this career, it picked me.

When you were 16, did you have any fucking idea what you wanted to do when you grew up; if not, did this cause you any anxiety, or is it just me and my uptight parents?

At 16, I wanted to do Patrick Sullivan. We went to the same high school, and we had swim class together—but as much as I wanted to, and as hard as I tried, I never got to do Patrick Sullivan. The lesson for you in this, Vanessa, is that hardly anyone winds up doing what they thought they wanted to do when they were 16 years old. Not knowing what you want to do at 16 is no handicap, as what you want may change. Tell your parents to chill.

Thinking of changing careers or workplaces soon?

Funny you should ask: I'm thinking of joining the Navy. Mark J. Dosch, EMC (SW), a recruiter for the Navy, approached me today. I thought the guy in the Navy dress whites was trying to pick me up, but before I could say, *"Sir, yes, sir!"* Mark asked me if I'd ever thought about joining the Navy. "Never considered it," I said. "Why not?" asked Mark. "Well, because I'm a fag." "You know, we don't ask questions about that anymore." Mark was very nice, he didn't seem like the kind of sailor who would beat a gay sailor to death by repeatedly slamming his head against a urinal in a bathroom in Japan (which happened: the gay sailor was so badly beaten that his mother could only identify her son's body from the tattoos on his arms). After a few minutes, I convinced Mark that I really wasn't interested in joining the Navy, not even the new promise-not-to-beat-you-to-death Navy. I don't have any tattoos, and I would hate to think that if a bad apple were still lurking on an aircraft carrier somewhere, my mother wouldn't be able to identify my body. But maybe you might be interested in going into the Navy, Vanessa? It could be the answer to your what-am-I-going-to-do-with-my-life questions. Call 1-800-327-NAVY. But get a tattoo first.

Any advice for someone starting out as a writer?

Use the word *fuck* liberally, which you're already doing—keep up the good work.

Alert readers will notice that this collection of columns is not actually a collection of columns, but an assemblage of individual letters and responses culled from columns I've written over the last seven years. At the suggestion of my editor, I busted my columns up, and reorganized letters around broad themes, which became the seven chapters of this collection: "Gettin' Together"; "Doin' Time"; "Almost Everything Breeder Boys Need to Know About Women's Genitals"; "Kink"; "Butt Sex & Blow Jobs"; "Life & Death"; and, finally, "Odds & Ends." Busting up the columns allowed me to include good single letters from whole columns that were not all that good, and allowed for the creation of new and interesting juxtapositions and subject threads.

More alert readers may spot letters that could just as easily have appeared in a section other than the one they were placed in. Take the letter from the woman in a long-term SM relationship who's wondering whether or not the use of tit-clamps is going to hamper her ability to breast-feed when she has kids in the not-too-distant future. Now, where should this letter go? It's a long-term relationship question, so it could go in the "Doin' Time" section; but it's a long-term SM relationship question, so it could just as easily go in the "Kink" section; but it is also a long-term SM relationship question involving children, so it could also go in the "Life & Death" section. What to do?

We made a judgment call: it was my considered opinion that this woman's letter had more to do with kink than the other issues it touched on, so you'll find her letter in the "Kink" section. There were a lot of cases like this: questions with considerable overlap. If you feel the inclusion of someone's question in one particular section was inappropriate, or in the case of my having herded the bisexual questions into the weirdos section, discriminatory and mean-spirited, feel free to rip pages out of this book and rearrange it to suit your own tastes. But buy the book first.

Even more alert readers, especially those who clipped columns when they first appeared, may notice that here and there I have tweaked and trimmed my responses. Truth be told, when I sat down and reread my first two years or so worth of columns, I was struck by just how bad a writer I was in the early '90s. The patriot in me simply couldn't allow this book to go into the Library of Congress without taking the time to repair some of my crappiest early work. It may be dishonest to include a reworked column in a "best of" collection, but Ann Landers does it too, so sue us.

And, while I'm fessing up, I should confess that in a very, very few cases—how do I put this?—I changed my mind. Reading an old column, I would find myself thinking, "How much crack was I smokin' when I gave that advice!" So I threw out my original response and wrote a new one, giving the advice I probably should have given in the first place. It's too late for this new and improved advice to help the person I let down back when their question first appeared in the column, but the new and improved advice can still help people with similar problems. It is those people I was thinking of when, um, when I threw out and rewrote a few of my old answers. So sue me. And, hey, the "best" of "Savage Love" isn't always what I had to say, but often—more often than I'd care to admit—what one of my readers had to say. I wanted to include those letters in this collection, even if it meant the extra work of rewriting my original, slightly defective answers.

Finally, this is not a medical textbook, or a self-help book, or a how-to-fuck manual. This isn't a comprehensive overview of human sexuality, and while we've tried to cover as many bases as we could in selecting columns for this collection, by no means will you learn Everything You Need to Know About Sex by reading this book. If there's a sore on your penis, or you missed your period, or you're hearing voices, you're going to need to go get yourself help—you won't find the answers you need in this book. What you will find are funny and informative Q&A bull sessions I've had over the past seven years with the folks who read and write to "Savage Love." You should read this as if it were a conversation you were overhearing, like those conversations of my mother's I overheard when I was a kid. Most of the conversations in this book are about sex—that's titillating—and all of them are about other people's problems— and that's entertainment.

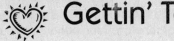 # Gettin' Together

Meeting, Dating, Mating

Beginnings are a good place to start, so we've placed the getting-to-know-you questions right up at the front. Here you'll find straight, bi, and gay men and women beginning new relationships, or confused by the sudden end of what looked like promising relationships, and single folks wondering how on earth they're going to meet someone and get a relationship off the ground. The criteria for inclusion in this section—which, considering it's the first section, is something of an honor—were letters from singles, virgins, the recently dumped, and couples together less than three months.

A few words about meeting people:

People who need people—and what people don't?—are the luckiest people in the world, as we all know. However, for people to successfully meet and hold on to the people they need, well, that requires something more than dumb luck. Getting through those first few crucial weeks—the discovery phase—is a skill, and most of us need practice and good, competent instruction in order to acquire this skill. How much to reveal, and how soon? What can you reasonably demand, and how soon? What are the warning signs, or the good signs? Getting a relationship off the ground is a lot like getting a plane off the ground: it's always at the start of a relationship, like the beginning of a flight, that things are most likely to crash and burn.

I speak from experience—recent experience. I've met plenty of people in my time, and had plenty of what seemed like promising relationships burst into flames. Because I am a fag—have I mentioned that I'm gay?—I didn't start seriously dating until I was in my late teens and early 20s. My two older straight brothers, by comparison, were dating before they had pubic hair. Because most queers can't date until we're well out of high school, we make all the same dating mistakes everyone has to make, gay and straight, but we generally make them when we're older and have access to things like money that can magnify and compound garden-variety trouble. When my brothers started dating, they were living at home and on an allowance and Mom and Dad were there to help and advise them. When I started dating, I had my own apartment, a credit card, and no one to help or advise me—I had to learn by trial and error. Since I had many trials, and made many errors, I learned quite a lot. I got into a lot of trouble early on, and I was getting into trouble when I was old enough to process my dating mistakes fully, remember them more clearly, and use what I'd often recently learned from my mistakes to advise my readers.

I believe the many mistakes I made dating have made me an astute observer of the destructive patterns men and women of all sexual orientations engage in. In the thick of things myself, I've been able to give advice from an informed, practical, centered place, as the shrinks like to say. Despite my sensitive nature, I'm still a man, and men are pigs, and gay men are especially so. When straight people have sex, there's usually only one pig in the room; when gay men have sex, there are at least two, and sometimes more. I started and ended a lot of relationships during my 20s, some of which began and ended on the same weekend. A few on the same night. So, I've had a lot of experience getting to know new people. And this gave me some insight into the "getting to know you" problems my readers were asking me questions about.

Hey, Faggot:

My friends and I have been discussing the finer points of dating, courtship, and the proper way of breaking things off. We have some questions.

If you go on one or two dates with someone—dates being prearranged social engagements attended only by the two parties in question—and things don't work out for whatever reason, do you owe that person a phone call? A written explanation? Lunch? Lunch and a written explanation? Or what? Is it okay to simply not phone them again? What should a person do?

Terry

Hey, T:

Just because someone goes out on a couple of dates does not mean they owe you anything, least of all an explanation, should they decide that they're not interested in pursuing things further. Communication Queens think the healthy, functional thing to do is call, always call, so as not to leave the dumped party hanging. CQs would also have us believe that someone who neglects to call after one or two dates, thus denying you "closure," has somehow abused you.

Well, bullshit. Nonverbal communiqués (no phone call = no thanks) are sometimes just as valid as verbal communiqués ("no thanks" = no thanks). And anyone who's ever gotten a call from a casual date explaining in unnecessary detail just exactly why they don't want to continue dating knows that thanks-but-no-thanks calls are infinitely more aggravating and, in their own underhanded way, more abusive than simply not hearing from the person again.

Hey, Faggot:

I'm a 24-year-old male, and I have developed a female platonic harem. They are like stillborn relationships, once promising love, and then delivering friendship. "Let's just be friends" is a refrain I have heard more than "Stairway to Heaven." Friends are great, but I still sleep alone in my cold, queen-sized bed. When a member of my harem says "goodnight," I hear, "No I won't sleep with you!" Four questions emerge:

1. Why does this keep happening to me?
2. Should I reject friendship when it feels like denial of what I really want?
3. Does each human hair follicle have a limited life span?
4. At what stage should I show my desires?

Joe

Hey, Joe:

Four answers emerge:

1. I don't know.
2. Yes. If hanging out with these women makes you feel bad ("Doctor, it hurts when I go like this!"), don't hang out with them ("Don't go like that"). Why torture yourself? Everyone wants to act like grown-ups after a relationship has ended (or been "stillborn") and remain friends. But for the person who was rejected (in this case, you), remaining friends can be torture. Who wants to have rejection rubbed in their face every day? Spare yourself. Tell the harem your interests are purely prurient and if they're not interested in you *that* way, you aren't interested in them.
3. Don't be cute.
4. Right away. Be up-front from the start. If you find someone attractive and want to ask her out, do it. Be casual, non-threatening, and noncreepy. Try saying "Let's go out on a date . . ." and then invite her to be up-front with you: "If you're not interested in dating me, say so. I'm a grown-up, I can take it." If she rejects you, be thankful that she didn't string you along.

Hey, Faggot:

Recently, I had rigorous sex with a man I met by chance four months ago. I bypassed the dates-then-sex routine and instead used the vibrations I picked up from him to write a prose-poetry porno fantasy with us as its characters [to get him in bed]. While I've expressed agreement to repeat sex, he has not made himself available. So, did I cause his avoidance by:

1. Having read my fantasy to him over the phone?
2. Expecting vaginal, clitoral and oral satisfaction, although not necessarily in that order, during the same experience?
3. Making him think that if he could get an out-of-body (fantasy) and an in-body sex experience with me, surely he could do as well, if not better, with someone else?
4. Not living up to his unexpressed expectations?
5. Not having said "No" to his vibes and to mine when we first met and the weather was too hot for almost everything except a heady sex trip?

EZ

Hey, EZ:

What part of "No, I don't want to fuck you again" don't you understand? Cuz that's what he's telling you, girlfriend, loud and clear. As for your checklist:

1. He had sex with you after you read him the poem, so it wasn't your solo-performance fantasy prose-poetry cycle that scared him off, was it?
2. Why would you want to have "repeat sex" with a guy reluctant to provide you with both vaginal and clitoral stimulation during an encounter? If this is the reason he walked, the question isn't, "Why don't he want more?" but rather, "Why do you?"
3. Don't flatter yourself. Mind-blowingly fabulous sex partners don't get dumped cuz their lovers are convinced that,

if you're that good, there's gotta be someone better out there somewhere. C'mon.

4. This is a possibility, in no way unique to you or your situation—people get dumped every day for not living up to "unexpressed expectations."

5. Maybe it wasn't the sex that turned him off, maybe it was the conversation. You hit on him, he fucked you, and then he decided he didn't wanna fuck you again. It happens. Maybe he didn't like the way your spit tastes, or your apartment looks, or maybe you scared the shit out of him. Find a new muse.

Hey, Faggot:

Most of the sexual experiences I've had have been initiated by the woman. When I meet someone and I start to groove on them and we hang out and this and that, I have a hard time making a move. I just don't know when to do it. I've had women tell me after the fact that they felt I didn't like them, and were hurt that I didn't make a move. I'd like a little guidance in the fine art of seduction.

                    Waiting to Unleash My Hormones

Hey, WTUMH:

When you feel that groove kick in, when you get that love-is-in-the-air buzz, make your move.

By "move" I do *not* mean grab her ass, lunge for her tits, stick your tongue in her mouth, or drop your pants. No, the moves are telling her how you're feeling, and inquiring as to whether the feelings are mutual. Ask, and ask sexy. Say, "Can I kiss you?" or "I'm feeling like we oughta take off all our clothes, grind our genitals together for twenty or so minutes, then hop in the shower for a rinse and some cunnilingus, then jump back in bed, eat some Ben & Jerry's Cherry Garcia and then maybe have another go at it. How are you feeling?"

That people being "good" at seduction means never having to use words is bullshit. Unexpected kisses usually (not always) backfire, while a smoldering "Can I kiss you?" is just as sexy as a sudden kiss, a hell of a lot safer, and you don't have to wait till you're positive you've got a groove going on to make your move. Since it's only a question and not a kiss, you can ask when you merely suspect. *Ask!* Women who want it will say, "Yes! Kiss me already, you asshole!" The ones who don't will say, "Not yet," or "Never."

Hey, Faggot:

I'm a twenty-eight-year-old breeder female. About two years ago, I went through an extended painful breakup with my live-in lover of five years. For the last year I've been dating half-heartedly and recovering from the breakup.

A few months ago, I found a great three-bedroom apartment and moved into it with two men. One, "Oscar," is the ex–best friend of my ex-lover.

One night, Oscar and I confessed our mutual attraction and became lovers. We're both very happy, but I have a number of concerns. I'm uneasy about our romance beginning in a room-mate situation. Who, if anyone, should tell my ex about Oscar and me? It's certain to be a shock. How do you date someone you live with? Will I miss out on romance? Should I move out?

Double Bunking

Hey, DB:

Let your ex find out about you and Oscar the usual way; through the grapevine. It's not really any of his business who you're dating these days, even if you're boffing his ex–best friend. If you're uncomfortable dating someone you live with, move.

Hey, Faggot:

I'm not some drooling troll scamming on every waiter or bartender I meet. I'm a nice, stable, better-than-average-looking guy who is infatuated and clueless how to proceed: There's a guy I encounter in a context where I am a customer of his. For the sake of discussion, say it's a restaurant I go to frequently, but it could be a store where I shop or some other place where there's a degree of interaction but not much opportunity to develop anything further. He's friendly when I see him, but that's how he seems to be with most customers. This guy is very attractive and probably gets hit on by other customers a lot.

So, what's a boy to do? Wait, hoping I'll encounter him in some non-business situation? Seems too passive. Plunge forward with a dinner invitation? Too aggressive, and I'd probably throw up first out of nerves. Any suggestions?

Dateless

Hey, D:

If the guy's really hot and works in a public place frequented by fags, he doubtless gets hit on all the time. So hit on him. If he's into you, you've scored. If he ain't, I'm sure he's gotten very good at politely passing on passes from guys he's not into. Invite him to dinner. Pass him your phone number. Send him flowers. Shit or get off the pot. Don't be one of those pathetic chicken-shit fags so terrified of rejection he never makes a pass at a guy.

Hey, Faggot:

As far as I know, I'm straight. I haven't had anything I could call a crush on a man, but I have had problems in my relationships with women. I usually wind up with women I'm not really attracted to, or develop crushes on lesbians, women who are married or otherwise occupied with other men. Often the more impossible the possibility, the more worked up I get—almost like I want to keep myself occupied wanting rather than having. And sometimes I get hot flashes when I'm sitting next to gay men on the bus and in other close situations.

So what do you think: am I a neurotic whose fear and lack of confidence drives him to wonder if he's gay rather than deal with women, or am I a closet queer, too afraid to make any moves?

Queer?

Hey, Q:

Just because you're an inept heterosexual, it doesn't automatically follow that you're queer. Homosexuality is not a consolation prize. You may have some bisexual impulses, hence your hot flashes on the bus, or maybe you have Multiple Chemical Sensitivity and the gay men you're sitting next to are wearing too much cologne. Who knows? But if your primary sexual interest is women, you're straight no matter how often you strike out with the chicks.

You do sound like you have some, forgive me, "intimacy issues." Pursuing women you can't have is a bad sign, and while crushing out on dykes is understandable—lesbians are so cool—it's kinda pointless. Find a girl you're attracted to and hit on her.

Hey, Faggot:

I'm a 20s breederish kinda woman and I've got a dilemma. I've been having these pretty intense wet dream kinda deals about a friend of mine. I also lust after her during the waking hours, so I know it's not just a passing thing. I have, on a couple of occasions, had sex with women. Pretty recently, in fact. The problem is, on all of these occasions, I was intoxicated. It wasn't that I didn't want to do it, but rather, I was too shy. Alcohol reduces inhibitions, but it also decreases sensitivity. So, what should I do? I'd like for things to get more interesting with her (I believe she's receptive), but don't know how to go about it without the use of chemicals. Any suggestions? I suppose this disqualifies me from the "breeder" category, doesn't it?

Kinda Shy

Hey, Kinda Shy:

You lust after women, have wet dreams about women, and have sex with women. Yeah, I'd say that pretty much disqualifies you from the breeder category.

On to your problem: you're usually sloshed when you have

sex with girls, and it "decreases sensitivity, among other things." So don't get drunk. But when you're not smashed, you don't have the guts to hit on girls. Hm. What to do? Get drunk, hit on girls, but have sex with them later, when you're sober. Get smashed, tell your friend you want to bang her lights out—but not tonight. Tonight you've got to iron dust ruffles. "But here's my phone number, call me tomorrow and we'll fuck." Then go for it clean and sober.

Hey, Faggot:

Women like me as a friend. I'm not good-looking at all, I don't expect to get laid much and I don't even try. I'm not crying poor me, my point is this: All I really want is pussy. But I just want to eat it and nothing else. I don't have to be loved, I don't have to be touched, all I want is to eat some of the women in my life. I like and respect the women that I know and they like and respect me, but I have no interest in fucking or any commitment beyond friendship. I am a good listener and I can take direction when it comes to eating pussy. After all, especially in this area, women know best. My question is, am I twisted? Should I seek psychiatric help because this is all I really like to do sexually? And is this something that any woman in her right mind would be interested in? Would it be a mistake to even approach a woman I know and appreciate with such a proposition?

Dinner Date

Hey, DD:

It's one thing to honestly assess your looks and quite another to disqualify yourself from romance because you think you're too unattractive for anyone to love. So you're not good-looking, so you're ugly, even; there are plenty of ugly women running around out there with pussies that deserve attention.

Take out a personal ad. Tell 'em you're average- to below-average-looking and seeking same; and be explicit—tell 'em what you really want. If you get an answer, exchange photos before you meet face-to-face and then, if she's still interested, you can meet for "dinner."

Hey, Faggot:

Please explain to your male readers—both het and bisexual—that women, at least my friends, go to "gay bars" to avoid being hit on, cruised, or harassed by men. "Gay bars" offer women a place to relax, socialize, or just get drunk without having to worry about the above behaviors.

Let Women Relax

Hey, LWR:

Unfortunately for you, bubaleh, straight boys have caught on to straight girls hanging out in gay bars. As a breeder boy put it to me, "It's easier approaching straight women in gay bars. They're not so defensive. And they're usually drunker than they would be in a straight bar."

Since we can't keep straight boys out of queer bars any more than we can keep straight girls out, resign yourselves to brushing off the occasional sloppy-drunk breeder boy prowling the queer bars.

But, hey: few straight boys are brave enough to venture into dyke bars, so you might try hanging out with the lesbians. You'll be able to kick back and relax without fear of unwanted attention from stray breeder boys. Of course, you still run the risk of being approached, but at least it will be sisters hitting, cruising, and harassing.

Hey, Faggot:

A couple of weeks ago you got a letter from a woman who said that she and her friends go to gay bars to get away from men who hit on them. Why is it that women who complain about men being too aggressive are the same women who go to places that have reps for being "meat markets"?

News flash, ladies! Men go to "meat markets" to get laid. That is the number one priority for 80 percent of the guys who go out on weekends. We don't want to dance with you—note the guys on the dance floor who just go through the motions— and we definitely don't buy you all those drinks just to be nice people. If you go to these types of clubs, we rightfully assume you're looking to get fucked. If this is not your reason for being in the club, then you deserve to be harassed and hit on.

This is what it boils down to. If you're not at a meat market to put out for guys then you have no business being there. And we don't go to meat markets to buy drinks for dick teasers. I would rather be in a club with 200 men and 15 women who want to put out than in a club filled with women who don't put out.

Put Out

Hey, PO:

Sometimes I wonder why women even talk to men. But since my experiences in "breeder meat markets" are limited, I won't comment on your observations. But I'll happily print replies from any "dick teasers" who'd like to respond to Prince Charming's letter.

Hey, Put Out:

Women go out to clubs to have fun, maybe meet some interesting people, maybe dance, maybe fuck. But we are out to have what *we* say is a fun time—"fun" means not getting hit on by immature, maladjusted dick heads who can't take no for an answer. We are in the clubs for our good time. If that jibes with your good time, fine; if it doesn't, get over it.

Hey, Put Out:

I'm a breeder female, and it seems I've concealed my true motives for going to bars—it wasn't that I wanted to drink a beer, dance to groovy tunes, or meet up with my friends. I was really scheming to attract an outstanding specimen of manhood like our buddy Put Out, only to cynically deny him the strings-free sex I had so obviously promised by sitting on a bar stool ignoring him!

"Put Out" isn't getting any because many women can smell a rape-minded sociopath from across the room.

Hey, Put Out:

Women never "deserve" to be harassed or hit on. But I certainly can understand your frustration: I've gone to "meat market" bars—to hang out, meet my friends, listen to music—and met women who flirted with me. Some even initiated the flirt, let me buy them drinks all night and then, at closing time, said "bye bye" and walked right out of the bar. When I asked for their phone numbers, they tell me they're not interested, "have a boyfriend," or worse yet, give me an incorrect number. "Put Out" should be called on his bullshit, but so should women who treat men like walking bar tabs. Disrespect is a two-way street.

Hey, Put Out:

Clubs are places where women and men go to socialize and have fun. If you are frustrated by women who, for some unfathomable reason, won't put out for you rockhead Romeos in exchange for a dance or a drink, why don't you save yourself the time and trouble and go to a whorehouse? Though you may find the women there a bit more expensive than the one-drink fucks you seek at clubs, at least you know your time and trouble will be well spent. At a whorehouse you won't have to worry about running into "dick teasers."

Hey, Put Out:

Why not cut the bullshit games and just walk up to a woman and say, "Hey, wanna fuck me?" If she doesn't, then you won't be out drink money or time wasted. Good luck, sporto, you're going to need it.

Hey, Put Out:

Women buy men drinks all the time; where have you been?

Hey, Put Out:

You definitely sound like a jerk, but I do have to agree with your basic point: There are a lot of women out there who are teases. But as a woman who does put out and isn't a tease, I'd like to point out that you miss the point too: you sound like the kind of jerk who thinks that because a woman is out cruising, she's obligated to immediately spread her legs for anyone who asks. Well, Prince Charming, if you hit on me in some meat rack and I say, "No, thank you," it's not because I don't put out. Maybe it's because you're too ugly, or you have b.o., or I don't like your shoes, or maybe it's just that your macho, straight-boy attitude is a turnoff.

Hey, Put Out:

A woman lets you buy her a drink because you might be someone she'd like. Anywhere along the line she can change her mind, just like you can—after the first drink, or the last dance, or after she takes her clothes off. If she changes her mind, you might understandably be disappointed. But she does not owe you anything. Your dick, your arrogance, and your tiny brain entitle you to exactly nothing. And why would you even want to fuck someone who has decided, for whatever reason, that she's not interested in you?

Hey, Put Out:

No one likes to go out to a club and get pestered, pawed, and annoyed by some alcohol/hormone-intoxicated lout. Even worse is when the lout cannot take a hint, subtle or otherwise—this goes for women as well as men. So I'm going to give you guys (and gals) a few hints:

1. Drunk sex is not great sex. Ninety percent of sex is brain chemistry. Excessive alcohol is chemical castration. And these days, sex is dangerous. Pound several double 'kazes into yourself and your quarry and have drunk sex with someone you barely know? Thanks, but I'd rather play Russian Roulette with an automatic.

2. Ladies, all good bartenders know that if women stop coming to the club, guys won't come, and they won't make money. Bartenders, doormen, and wait staff are your friends! If someone doesn't take the hint and is becoming annoying, *tell them*.
3. Look "please" and "thank you" up in the dictionary. Guys: She wants an animal in the bedroom, not in public.
4. No pressure. A 5- or 10-minute flirt with name-catching and a quick exit will get you much further than hanging around like a vulture, shelling out cash for drinks. It also leaves you free to meet other people.
5. It never hurt to ask for or offer a phone number. If she doesn't want it or give it, no sweat. Either she's involved, there's no real spark, or she just don't wanna. So what? If you do get a number—this is important—*relax*. She may not sleep with you now or ever, but you are a contender.
6. Be honest! If things progress and all you want is sex, tell her! Maybe that's what she wants. If it doesn't mesh, it doesn't. Maybe she has friends who just wanna fuck.

Hey, Faggot:

I am writing you about an honest problem that may sound trite, but feels serious to me.

I'm a het male who wants a real relationship with a good woman, but instead always winds up in short-lived flings. Women pull me into bed quickly and eventually reveal their true insane selves. I blow off many right from the start, because I can tell it will go nowhere. Inevitably, though, loneliness or lust—a seemingly inexorable desire to help a sexy woman climax—delivers me yet another hollow intimacy. It was originally exciting, but after many years I'm tired and want more. How do I break my wanton ways?

A Man Who Loves Women

Hey, AMWLW:

Let me see if I follow: you break up with just about every woman you date before the relationship has a chance to go anywhere because you "know from the start it will go nowhere"? Have you ever heard of "self-fulfilling prophecies"? If you make up your mind in advance that something, anything—a job, an affair, a marriage, a blow job—isn't going to work, it usually doesn't.

For someone who signs letters "The Man Who Loves Women," it doesn't sound as if you like women very much. What you're perceiving as "insanity" is probably a reaction to the resentment you're carrying into every new relationship. You've been burned by women in the past, so what? It happens. We get burnt, we burn others. If you can't give each new girlfriend the benefit of the doubt—if you can't see your way clear to holding her blameless for the actions of your previous girlfriends—you have no business entering into new relationships. Until you change your attitude, no relationship of yours will survive for long.

Hey, Faggot:

I am a friendly, happy guy in my late twenties blessed with classic Hollywood looks. I get a lot of attention from gay men, who are always charming and often flirtatious. I don't mind this at all and find it flattering, but I am as het as they come.

My problem is that I see plenty of lovely women, and sometimes they seem interested, but they nearly always look away quickly, shutting off any possibility of a conversation. I'm not talking about drunken meat markets; I mean in the Laundromats, cafes, and day-to-day places where romance might begin naturally. The closest thing I've seen to anything like that is my casual encounters with gay men! Where is the passion, the spontaneity and the sense of possibility in the breeder community?

Is it that het women are so pissed off, cynical or jaded that they can't open themselves up for romance? I know there is some passion out there, but what prevents them from acting upon it? And I don't buy the dreaded AIDS argument, because gay men have a lot more to worry about and from what I've seen, they have no such problems. In fact, the entire gay community seems more relaxed about sex! Why can't straight women be more like gay men?

Hollywood

Hey, Hollywood:

Sometimes I feel sorry for straight guys. You're socialized or programmed to be sluts, but the objects of straight guy desire—straight women—are either socialized or programmed to not be sluts. Whose brilliant idea was it to wire men and women in such a way as to render them sexually incompatible?

This is just one of the many reasons I'm so glad I'm queer. The objects of my desire—men—are wired just like I am: we're all guys, we gay-boys, and we *understand* each other. So, Hollywood, the reason straight women don't behave like gay men probably has something to do with the fact that straight women aren't men. Gay men are men like straight men, and our willingness to throw ourselves at complete strangers, which you so rightly admire, is in a lot of ways peculiar to our sex—it's something gay men and straight men share.

So why don't women act like men? First, they're not men. Second, for most of human history, heterosexual sex has had much graver consequences for women than for men: children. The man can shoot and walk away, the woman is stuck with a kid for the next fifteen or twenty years. There's also the little issue of what slimy shits so many straight men are. Even without the threat of getting preggers, women have to worry about harassment, physical violence, and rape. Those women who aren't receptive to your pickup lines in the supermarket have probably been hassled (or worse) by guys they've met in similar "innocent" circumstances.

Most women I know prefer to meet men through friends or at work—they want some small assurance that the guy they're thinking about dating isn't a psycho killer, a rapist, a sociopath, a misogynist pig, a frat boy or a Republican. They want references. Sure, women are passionate—all the women I know like sex—but most are afraid that by being "spontaneous," and going with their "sense of possibility," they'll be opening themselves up to the very real "possibility" of being "spontaneously" raped.

And, straight boys, consider this: straight women might be more like gay men if straight sex was more like gay sex. Right now, straight sex means vaginal intercourse. Well, women might be more into casual sex if het sex didn't mean she had to get fucked. To be penetrated is to assume most of the risk, not just of pregnancy and disease, but the psychic risk as well. Letting another person in your body is sometimes as big a mind-fuck as it is a body-fuck, and not something everyone can be casual about. This isn't the way gay sex works. When a guy goes to bed with a guy, penetration is never assumed. It has to be agreed to, and very often, isn't even on the menu. And, unlike most breeder sex, both the participants in gay sex have most likely been penetrated themselves, so both understand why someone might not want to for some reason, and are willing to "settle" for hand jobs or head instead.

Most straight boys are not willing to "settle" for a hand job. So long as women are expected to get fucked every time they go to bed with a straight boy, so long as vaginal intercourse is a given, women will remain less likely to hop in the sack as indiscriminately as men do—gay and straight. If straights could define "sex" to include acts that don't require penetration—frottage, mutual masturbation, non-penetrative oral sex (licking under, over and around)—you'd get laid more.

Hey, Faggot:

Why does gay life suck so much? Irregardless of AIDSphobia, homophobia or whatever, gay men treat each other, mostly, as fantasy sex objects (I too). I've been having sex with men exclusively since I was 17. Although I've always dreamt of romance with Mr. Stud Muffin (kissing me, holding me in his muscular arms, with his wonderful, muscular legs wrapped around me), I have nearly always taken cheap sex in lieu of depression and loneliness, which only leads to more emptiness.

At the ripe old age of 37, I'm ready to call it quits. Maybe two men, no matter how "hot" or "horny" they may be for each other, just aren't meant to be together for more than a few cheap, sexual encounters. I go to the baths, I even worked in one for a month a year or so ago (disgusting: dealing with sheets filled with shit, blood, and who knows what). Yes, hot sex scenes can be fun, but *lonely, lonely, lonely* after you've shot your load, pulled out, wiped off and said, "Thanks, pardner!"

Where is the love? Lasting love? True love? Why must gay life be so lonely, bitter, alcoholic, drug-addicted, backstabbing? Why can't we band together as gay men and promote "relationships" and *love* as the ideal, not just firm butts and large cocks? In between all your anatomical descriptions of the g-spot and eating out butt hole, talk a little about how fucked-up gay life so often is for gay men.

Peter

Hey, Peter:

Let's get the important stuff out of the way first: it's "regardless," not "irregardless."

On to your question: Why does gay life suck? Gee, my gay life doesn't suck. My gay friend Kevin's life is okay. And Dave is having a grand time. Even my boyfriend, li'l Terry, seems content. So the question isn't, "Why does gay life suck?" but rather, "Why does your gay life suck?" Not, "What's wrong with gay men?" but, "What's wrong with you?"

Yes, there are lots of fucked-up gay men in the world. On average, we drink more, smoke more, take more drugs, and fuck more than straight people do. Sometimes for the right reasons: coming out can put us in touch with our desires in a positive, freeing way, resulting in our being more socially and sexually adventurous. But lots of gay men do these things for the wrong reasons: they're out there trying to destroy themselves and others with drugs, booze, sex, cigs, and bad attitudes. Growing up gay in a homophobic world can be a wildly traumatic experience. A gay man rejected by his family, taught to hate himself by his church, abandoned by his friends—he may grow up to act out on that self-hatred, abusing his lovers and his "community." But please note: gay people don't fuck up gay people, straight people do. We are who we are because straight people make us this way. We don't raise ourselves.

But: whatever abuse we may suffer as children, or be forced to endure as adults, is no excuse to treat each other like shit, spread HIV, drink too much, or whatever. Yes, lots of gay men are damaged goods. The trick is to: (a) make sure you're not damaged goods yourself, and if you are, to get some help, and (b) avoid gay men who are damaged goods and aren't getting help.

Now, some practical tips: gay life, like straight life, is a series of what? Of choices, snacktray. You make choices about your priorities, your friends, what "scene" you attach yourself to, etc. If your gay life is a miserable one, it's probably because you're making, what? Bad choices.

From reading your letter, it's pretty clear that you've been looking for love in all the wrong places. You won't meet husband material in a bathhouse. Gay bathhouses are whorehouses, differing from the hetero variety only in that ours are entirely staffed by volunteers. A straight guy looking for a wife in a whorehouse isn't going to have much luck. Not that there aren't any quality women in whorehouses—there are—but they're not there looking for husbands. And you shouldn't be looking for husbands in whorehouses either.

Additionally, you sound like one of those guys who complains he can't find a lover, when the real problem is that you can't find a lover who looks like Brad Pitt or Cougar Cash. Fantasy boyfriends are often just that. Here's where we can borrow a page from the breeder playbook: average-looking straight people usually settle down with other average-looking straight people. If falling in love and settling down is what you want to do, you're going to have to do some settling for. No two people are perfect for each other; long-term relationships are a series of tensely negotiated truces. If you can't hack it, get thee to a bathhouse, go!

But on your way to the tubs, don't call into question the ability of the rest of the gay men in the world to "truly" love each other just because you're sexually and emotionally stunted.

And don't have higher expectations of the gay community than you would of any other community. I get so sick of listening to guys complain about the gay "community" not being a real community because they can't find a lover, or they don't do well at the baths, or they were mistreated by someone or other who happens to be gay. Does everyone in the deaf "community" love each other unreservedly? How about the IV-drug-using "community"? Does the entire Jewish "community" get along? Of course not! The gay "community" is not responsible for making you happy, making you feel welcome, or finding you a boyfriend. That's your job. The gay "community" is an opportunity, a space you can visit or live in. It is not a birthday party being thrown for you by your mother.

Finally, the community cannot collectively decide to "promote relationships and *love* as the ideal, not just firm butts and large cocks." *You* are perfectly free, however, to promote those values in *your* own life. Nor can the community "band together" as a whole: it's too large, we're too diverse. We don't all like or agree or get along with each other. Even if the day comes when gay people are not abused or oppressed, there will still be plenty of fucked-up gay men in the world, just as there are fucked-up people everywhere, gay, straight, whatever. *You* are perfectly free, however, to band together with other individual gay men you do like, form your own nurturing, loving circle of friends, and change your own life for the better.

Hey, Faggot:

I'm a male breeder, 23 years old, and very much "undersized." I'm good-looking (could've "scored" many times) but I don't want to be laughed at. I know I'm small but how big is an average guy anyway?

Cool, Confused & Embarrassed

Hey, CCE:

You've got a small dick—it's not the end of the world, and knowing the average isn't going to make your dick any bigger. Guys with small dicks get laid all the time. If small-dicked guys couldn't get laid, the gene for small dicks would've died out thousands of years ago thanks to natural selection, and there wouldn't be guys with small dicks running around today. So, you will have a sex life. Dick size is important to some people and not so important to others. Find someone who it's not important to. Some girls prefer small dicks—some girls have small pussies. And dick isn't everything. So you have a small dick, how big's your forearm? How big's your tongue?

Hey, Faggot:

Here's the deal: I'm a totally isolated and inhibited 21-year-old that's never had much of a social life in the past and now, as a result, am a total social clod. I feel completely out of touch with people. I mean, I can talk to them, but I never go beyond the chitchat level of conversation. I guess part of the reason why is because it's really hard for me to open up to strangers and act naturally and also because my life is just too boring for words.

So here I am, this friendless, pathetic, sad and lonely misfit in desperate need of a friend to talk to or just hang out with. What should I do? Where are the best places to meet people? (Please, don't tell me to go to a bar or check out newspaper ads.) How do I make friends? How do I get the guts to approach someone?

Solitary Soul Searching 4 Solace

Hey, SSS4S:

I wish I knew some secret for making friends, but I don't. My friends are people I've worked with or met during extracurricular activities. I didn't set out to "make" them my friends, it just happened. We met, worked together, chatted, did small social things together and . . . became friends.

I'm going to channel Ann Landers for you now . . . have you considered joining social or service organizations? How about a political organization? If you're working with people, you have to talk to them. So put yourself in situations where you have no choice but to connect. And don't feel awkward about limiting conversation to chitchat at first—all friendships start with inane chitchat. You can't talk about God, the universe and your own personal spiritual bullshit/mystical journey with some-one you've just met. You'll scare 'em off.

Hey, Faggot:

I'm a sexually active male in my mid-twenties and I have a problem that's been really messing with my mind, and my whole outlook on my sexual future/relationships. Every time I have intercourse with a woman, I can never reach an orgasm. But when I masturbate, I spew streams. Is this some mental dysfunction of mine, or is it that the women I've been with just can't satisfy me? I desperately need to cure this problem, for I do plan to marry and have children. I find myself masturbat-ing every day now, wondering if it's all in "the stroke." What advice/techniques can you give that may cure my ill?

Can't Cum With You

Hey, CCWU:

Four parts performance anxiety, and one part self-fulfilling prophecy: that's the cocktail you're sippin'. You're in your mid-twenties, and you've had some bad experiences, and now you're convinced you'll never reach orgasm during intercourse, so you . . . don't. Why? Cuz you can't? Cuz the women you're sleeping with don't turn you on "enough"? No, because of the pressure you're placing on yourself.

So, take the pressure off. When you have sex, you expect your partner expects you expect you're going to have an orgasm. The anticipation of failure—failure to meet all those expectations—makes you anxious: so alter those expectations, and your anxiety should lessen. Tell the next nice girl you meet and take to bed that you're not interested in intercourse, only outercourse—masturbate together—tell her that you'd like to get to know her better before you start having intercourse. Chicks dig that intimacy stuff.

As your comfort level with your new partner increases, inform her that, although you enjoy intercourse very much, you haven't always been able to achieve orgasm during intercourse. Tell her the truth, but be causal about it—it's not a major malfunction! Tell her, "Intercourse just doesn't rub me the right way, I guess." By this point, of course, she'll be so blown away by your cunnilingus skills, and the loving attention you've paid her during the weeks you've spent exploring non-penetrative sex, that she won't give a shit.

When the time comes to incorporate intercourse into your sex life, think of it as foreplay. Explore different angles, and positions—and then move on to other things—masturbation, blow jobs, cunnilingus, whatever. Maybe you need to be on the bottom for your dick to get the kind of rubbin' it needs, or on your side, or doggie style, or hanging upside down with your hands tied behind your back: through low-stakes explorations you may stumble over some specific position that does the trick, or you'll find that just being relieved of the pressure to come allows you to enjoy the fucking and you . . . come!

Hey, Faggot:

I'm a partially reformed 28-year-old breeder who learned that two males can have as much fun and satisfy one another as well as a male and a female can. This knowledge came as a result of 8 years, 7 months and 18 days as a guest of the Washington State Department of Corrections.

Now for my question/problem. Does it still mean anything if a male wears an earring on just the right, or on both sides?

The reason for the question: I'm chillin' at a bar, dancing and drinking with a couple, male and female. We seem to be clicking, so they invite me back to his apartment for a bong and some more slow dancing. This turns into both of us boys on her breasts and dry humping each other through our pants, and we were both packin' hards. Then another girl shows up at the door, and rags all over the girlfriend over not being at her house by 11 P.M.—they both have to drive to Vancouver at 6 A.M.—so the girl leaves with her friend.

He says it's cool if I still want to crash and says I can have half of his bed since the couch is saggy. We hit the sheets and I figure we're going to pick up where we were interrupted, but when I touch him he blows a fucking fuse and threatens to smash my face, and I find myself out in the cold rain at 2:45 A.M.

He had a single pierced left and a double pierced right ear.

All of this to ask: is there some way to tell by looking if someone is a player or if they're just wanna-bes?

Learned the Hard Way

Hey, LTHW:

Once upon a time, earrings meant something. But nowadays, if you wanna know if someone's a "player," you have to ask. There are straight-identified men out there who groove on a little boy-boy contact, but only so long as a woman is part of the action. Two men and one woman going at it, in your host's mind, was a "straight" three-way. Two men going at it after she took off was "gay" sex.

Hey, Faggot:

I met this girl on a blind date set up by a mutual friend. We seemed to hit it off and enjoyed each other's company. For various reasons, I decided to take things slow, but it seemed like I was getting the green light. Little things, like walking arm in arm, good night kisses, the way she looked at me, etc. I thought there was a real spark. I took her to nice restaurants and every time she came over there was a present of some sort (flowers, etc.) waiting for her. Real old-fashioned dating rituals. Then on our Valentine's celebration—by now our fifth date—she mentioned her boyfriend of five years.

The friend who fixed us up had mentioned a boyfriend, but it was more to the effect that she was breaking up and trying to get rid of him. When I discussed this matter with my date, she said she thought we were just friends from the beginning and there were no romantic feelings from her side. But the presents, etc? She just thought I was a really nice guy.

So, two questions: how could I have fucked up so bad in the interpretation of her signals—do I need to take a class or something? How should I confront the mutual friend?

Crossed Wires

Hey, CW:

You weren't misreading signals, she was misleading you. She let you assume things which weren't true—as good as lying—allowing you to believe she was single, available, and interested, all with complete disregard for your feelings! You don't need "to take a class," she needs to get some. You have a right to be pissed off, and I suggest you exercise that right. And it's her you "need to confront," not your mutual friend.

Friends, even best friends, do not buy us chocolate, send us flowers, walk arm in arm, or celebrate Valentine's Day together. And responsible adults do not do these sorts of things with people they're not interested in romantically. She didn't think you were a "nice guy," she thought you were a sucker, and she played you for one. Get mad.

Hey, Faggot:

I've met and had sex with some of the hottest men in gay bathhouses. I've sexed up some really hot Greek god/model types. But now I'm looking for more than fleeting moments of anonymous sex. How do I get these men's attention outside the bathhouse?

Mark

Hey, M:

How do you get a man's attention *inside* a bathhouse? You approach him. Same goes for outside. Try substituting "Can I buy you a beer?" for "Can I suck your dick?"

Hey, Faggot:

I'm gay, and after four years I am single again. Before becoming involved in another relationship, and while I'm still marginally attractive, I want to sow some wild oats and whore around a bit. So, each weekend I set out to the bars in search of carnal pleasure.

The problem is, once I get there, I try smiling at people, but I fear I just come across as "touched." Last night, I stalked a man for about an hour, but to no avail. He didn't even know I was there. So, I turn to you for help. I would appreciate any input you could give me on cruising techniques and etiquette. Time is running out. I'm almost thirty.

Tramp Wanna Be

Hey, Tramp:

The guy you "stalked" knew you were there—he just didn't care. If after a few minutes of earnest cruising, a guy gives nothing back—not a smile or a hello—pick the damn clue up and go stalk someone else.

Gay or straight, if you're looking for one-night stands in bars, here's a few pointers: don't go out alone. Someone interacting with a group of friends is always more attractive than someone lurking in the corner. Hang with your friends, and every once in a while, go for a stroll through the bar. If you see someone you like, go up and say hello. Don't "lurk." Jeffrey Dahmer "lurked" in bars. People want to see the person they're attracted to playing well with others. Guys will think, "Hey, he has friends. He must be okay. I'll fuck him."

But if oat-sowing sex is all you're after, why bother with bars? Get your ass to a bathhouse. You're much more likely to find what you're looking for, and "lurking" is perfectly acceptable behavior.

Hey, Faggot:

I'm a sixteen-year-old queer boy living in a small town, but I'm very comfortable with my sexuality. I have no guilt about my gayness, I'm "out" to friends, and lead a healthy fantasy life. There is one problem: How do I hook up? I can't find a guy. School is full of fag-hating jocks and mousy computer geeks. I've tried to find groups, clubs, etc. for meeting guys my age, but there aren't any in my area.

This sounds like "My So-called Life," but this isn't about sex: I'll settle for someone to talk to. While I am by no means Brad Pitt or Albert Einstein, I am far from being ugly or stupid. Tell me where to start.

                                                            No Cute Name

Hey, NCN:

I'll betcha some of those "fag-hating jocks" at your high school are as queer or queerer than you are, but it may be years before they scrape up the courage to come out. And that's your problem: Most gay guys your age aren't out yet. There may be older guys interested in "mentoring" you sexually—probably at a nearby truck stop—but they're a bad risk: Many gay men's first sexual experiences are with older men, and while lotsa guys remember these experiences fondly, many do not. Unfortunately, there's no rule of thumb I can give you to help tell the difference between a guy in his 20s or older with your best interests at heart and a guy interested in taking advantage of your youth and inexperience.

So kids your own age are closeted, and older guys are a bad risk: what do you do? You wait. And you masturbate a lot. Get your ass out of high school, go to a big state university somewhere in a city with a large gay community, and you'll be beating the Brad Pitts and Albert Einsteins off with a stick. And if in the meantime one of those horny jocks comes out to you in a moment of drunken abandon, go for it.

Hey, Faggot:

I am a girl and almost 15 years old. I love women; I find myself very attracted to them, and I live openly as a dyke. I have come out to my parents. My mother is still in denial. She says this is a "phase."

My problem is that sometimes I find myself looking at a cute guy and I doubt myself. It's like I think I know what I am, but maybe I don't. I have kissed both a guy and a girl. I enjoyed kissing the girl more because the guy got an erection. Penises totally turn me off. Am I truly a lesbian? I can't put myself back in the closet after almost a year of coming out and all the bullshit that goes with it. I'd like to be positive of what I am. If I'm going to identify as a full-fledged dyke, I'd like to know that I can truly bear that label.

Am I a Dyke?

Hey, AIAD:

Honey, you're only 15 years old. Go a bit easier on yourself. Are you a true lesbian? I don't know—you could be, but what's your rush? I'm not telling you to go back in the closet, perish the thought. Just give it time, listen to your body, listen to your pussy. If you're a dyke, your pussy will let you know. You might be—horrors!—a lesbo-leaning bisexual, or maybe just one of those true lesbians who occasionally finds a boy attractive. It happens. It's nothing to stress yourself out about, and you won't be any less the dyke for it.

P.S. Your mother will get over it. Mine did. Yours will. It just takes time.

Hey, Faggot:

Generally speaking, the following five attitudes exist in the heterosexual male community regarding fat women:

Perverts: Those who think fucking fat women is just deliciously perverse.

Bigots: Those who believe fat women are ugly, undisciplined, etc., etc., are unwilling to acknowledge evidence to the contrary, and who rely on trashing fat women to furnish most of their Minimum Daily Pseudo-He-Man Macho Confidence Requirement.

Automatons: Those who—while not overtly abusive—have nevertheless accepted the temporarily prevailing myths regarding fat women.

Fetishers: Those obsessed with big tits/butts/thighs, but who have little or no interest in a woman's heart/mind/soul/well-being/sense of humor, etc. These may actually be decent guys and okay for a quickie, but what if one wants an honest-to-gosh relationship?

Sentient: Those straight men who are attracted to women for a variety of personal reasons that may include nuances of appearance, but which have nothing to do with bigoted cultural standards; understand the marketing of hatred of fat women is up there with corsets, foot binding and other such weirdness; want encounters with women that are supportive, romantic and fun as well as sexual.

I've only met men who fit into the first four categories. Do straight men who are "sentient" really exist, or was the Universe created by sadists?

> Healthy, Disciplined, Sexual, Sensual, Smart, Strong, Non-Overeating, Active, Pretty, Single Fat Chick

Hey, Fat Chick:

I'm not sure if the Universe was created by sadists, but they certainly seem to have been left in charge for the last several thousand years. When food was scarce and women were thin, fat was beautiful. Now food is plentiful and women aren't so skinny, rail-thin is beautiful. I'm sure some "sentient" straight men exist. Perhaps they'll write in. Guys?

Hey, Faggot:

I do not know if my situation is unique, but I love fat women—over 300 pounds. Most of the ladies I have dated or tried to date think I am hard up for sex, or all I want is sex and nothing more. No matter how much I tell a woman, or show a woman, that I want to have a relationship, and really care for and truly love her, she does not seem to believe me.

I have tried flowers, candy, romantic getaways, etc., to show that I am not just after sex. I want a girlfriend/wife/significant other that is a large lady. If all I wanted was sex I would go to a prostitute. How can I convince these bigger ladies that there are men like myself that would rather be with them than with no-meat-on-their-bones model types?

Fat Lover

Hey, FL:

While some fat women are happy being heavy, many are not. Being approached by a guy who's into you for being fat, a guy attracted to the very thing you've been made to feel unattractive about, can be traumatic. Fat people suffer for being fat, are ridiculed, made to feel grotesque and unlovable. Then you come along, FL, panting after flab. Can you understand how that would make an insecure fat chick uncomfortable?

Your biggest problem, judging from your letter, is your approach. It sounds like you're constantly reassuring the women you ask out that you like their bodies. Bringing up your date's size, even if to reassure her, will probably give her the not-all-that-inaccurate impression that you're only interested in her for her body. Women for the most part don't like guys who are only interested in their bodies. We all assume that people who ask us out are physically attracted to us on some level, and the fat women you ask out are quite capable of making that same assumption. Refrain from reassuring them so much, stop drawing attention to your "fetish," and you might have better luck.

Hey, Faggot:

I'm a big girl sending you a warm, smoochy thanks for your excellent response to "Fat Lover." Bravo to you, first, for your statement that some fat women like their bodies, and for the well-phrased, "Fat people suffer for being fat, are ridiculed, made to feel grotesque and unlovable." Well-phrased because nowhere did you say, as so many small-minded, lookist assholes do, that we deserve that hatred or bring it upon ourselves (due to our lack of self-control, inability to lose weight, slovenly habits, poor self-image, etc.). Thank you for noting the crime without blaming the victim.

"Fat Lover" is what we in the large-sized community call a "fat admirer" (FA), and many of us have very mixed feelings about these guys. You summed it up when you stated that nobody wants to be pursued solely for their physical appearance. No woman wants to be reduced to a chunk of meat.

Because large-sized women who seek relationships often meet with disappointment, rejection, and even disgust from those who cannot find it in themselves to accept and embrace a body that happens to look like a real, individual human female instead of a *Cosmo* fashion layout, many of us end up feeling like FAs are our only option. "Nobody out there loves me. Everyone's turned off by my body. Well, except Mr. Fat Lover. Hmmmm."

The answer? I'd like to encourage FAs to move beyond their fetish and toward loving women as people rather than bodies. I'd like to encourage big girls to never settle for a partner solely because he (or she) is willing to accept one's size. And I'd like to encourage everyone to start broadening their fuckin' twisted definitions of what is beautiful, what is desirable and what is lovable. The real world has a lot more to offer than the pages of *Cosmo* do.

Fat in Seattle

Hey, FIS:

If my response to Fat Lover didn't offend you, it was an over-sight, I guess, because I hold some of the beliefs you credit to "small-minded, lookist assholes." While I don't believe fat peo-ple "deserve" abuse, and I recognize that some obese people have medical problems, the vast majority of fat people are responsible for their weight problems. Most fat people do "bring it [fat, not ridicule] on themselves."

If a person is comfortable being fat, it's nobody's fucking business. But that doesn't mean the rest of us have to pretend fat people aren't responsible for being fat in order to make fat peo-ple feel better about . . . being fat. And while I think the bodies marketed in *Cosmo* and *YM*, and, incidentally, *International Male* and *Out* magazine, are unrealistic, I don't think ordering people to "broaden" their tastes is going to get you anywhere.

Having been all over the world, I can tell you that there aren't nearly as many 300-pounders "over there" as there are "over here," so the "genes" argument doesn't hold up. The fact of the matter is that we North Americans eat too much and move too little, resulting in—surprise—lots of us being fat. Fat is something we do to ourselves, and we need to take responsi-bility for it. And if that's blaming the victim, well, then I'm blam-ing the victim.

Hey, Faggot:

You just couldn't leave well enough alone, could you?

Your response to "Fat Lover" was good, and I was in agree-ment with the subsequent letter written by "Fat in Seattle," which thanked you for not dumping all over fat people in your reply to "Fat Lover." But you really blew it in your response to her letter, when you launched into your "you bring this all on yourselves" diatribe.

Just to set the record straight: I personally am not asking you, or anyone else, to "pretend that fat people aren't responsible for being fat people in order to make fat people feel better about being fat people." A lot of us are responsible, a lot of us are not. Like everything else in life, it is rarely that simple. *So what?* The point is, it's none of your damn business how or why I got fat.

Keep your goddamned unasked-for opinions to yourself.

A Former Fan

Hey, AFF:

Uh, gee, in most advice columns, the columnist responds to the letters he or she receives. So my goddamned opinion on the fat issue was asked for.

As you point out, problems are rarely simple. But, as a reasonable, non-fat-phobic person (really, I am), I find the "fat is complex, it just happens, nothin' can be done, ain't nobody's fault" arguments troubling. For instance: According to a 1996 Harris poll, three out of four adults in the United States are overweight (using the Metropolitan Life insurance tables as a reference)—not to be confused with obese—compared to one in five 20 years ago (per the USDA). How exactly did this happen? Did the explosion of desk jobs, fast-food franchises, videocassette recorders, and gourmet ice cream have anything to do with this development, or did it happen by . . . accident? And does thinking about why we, as a society, got so suddenly and collectively fat make one a bigot?

Hey, Faggot:

I once thought your attitude toward fat women as being sexually authentic was a breath of fresh air, given the otherwise abysmally ignorant and usually cruel cultural stereotypes on this subject. Imagine my disappointment when I saw you blatting out the same old mindless saws about "the vast majority" of fat people being "responsible for their weight problems."

Precisely what am I supposed to be taking responsibility for? For being unhealthy? I'm not. Ironically, one of the few places I can get credit for behaving in a healthy fashion is at my doctor's office. For being a lazy, gluttonous slob? I'm not. I seriously doubt that I could have spent four years working full-time, commuting two hours a day, maintaining a regular, moderate exercise program, and writing a book in my spare time, if I spent all my time lying around and eating. Now if you want to say that people should take responsibility for lousy health habits, fine, but understand that you'll have to include many millions of thin people in that category, as well as leave out a lot of fat people who are doing the best they can with the cards they've been dealt.

Any responsible scientist will tell you that it is considerably more complex than a matter of calories in vs. calories out, and that science is nowhere near understanding precisely why some people can stuff their faces all day, never exercise, and remain thin, while others gain weight very easily and remain fat no matter what they do. So, with all due respect, may I suggest that you stick to your area of expertise and refrain from making blanket statements that suggest that the "vast majority" of fat people are one and the same person, with identical habits.

And you're making a large mistake if you think that only people who weigh 300 pounds and up are labeled as fat these days. As I've been out promoting my book, I hear constantly from women of all sizes about the emotional and psychological abuse they are exposed to just because they don't weigh what they did when they were 14 years old.

In weight prejudice, the abuse begins with the assumption that all, or most, fat people are alike, and are all pigs. In homophobia, it begins with the assumption that all, or most, gay people are alike, and are all perverts. But I doubt you appreciate it when homophobes suggest that they'll accept you as a homosexual if you promise never to act on your sexuality, or that the kind of sex you have is cheap and meaningless because it's not the "right" kind of sex. Similarly, I don't appreciate it when weight bigots tell me I'm not entitled to eat certain kinds of foods, or enjoy life in general, or that I should make myself miserable, sick, or obsessed so that I can look like them. Whether or not I am comfortable being fat, what I do or put in my mouth is still "nobody's fucking business" but my own, just as it's nobody's business what you choose to put in any orifice of your body.

W. Charisse Goodman
Author
The Invisible Woman:
Confronting Weight Prejudice in America

Hey, Faggot:

I am a young-at-heart bisexual female and my problem is that I'm in love with a man who has become a very good friend. We slept together once and I just can't stop thinking about him. I "pet the bunny" (the female equivalent of "spank the monkey") at least three times a week about this man. When we're together, which we are a lot, I feel like I'm on fire inside. I've never met anyone who turned me on so much and I want to sleep with him again.

The problem? We're good friends now and he's said he doesn't want to ruin that. Also he's been burnt by women before and he's gun-shy. I listen to him talk about women he's attracted to—I'm his friend, right?—and I feel jealous, though I try to hide it. I don't want to lose a good friend but I can barely keep my hands off his hot body! I don't want to overstep his boundaries, as I have boundary issues of my own and understand how that works. But I can't stop thinking about that one glorious night we spent. Dan, this man is one of the best lovers I've ever had and seeing him, being next to him, is making me absolutely crazy. What to do?

Carrying a Torch

Hey, CT:

What to do? *Take the fucking hint!* The inability of people to take the hint, judging from my mail, has reached epidemic proportions. Forgive me in advance for the both-barrels blasting I'm about to give you, but I'm hoping others can learn from your mistakes.

1. "We're such good friends; I don't want to ruin that" is the oldest brush-off line still in circulation. It's the living dinosaur of brush-off lines, older than Ann Landers, Abigail Van Buren and Isadora Alman *combined*! Take the hint! He was trying to be nice—he doesn't want to be your lover, not for fear of losing your friendship but because he isn't, for whatever reason, attracted to you anymore. Learn to read between the lines, divine those hidden meanings.

2. Fill in the Blank: "I've been burned by (Pick one: Men, Women, Theater Critics, Sheep, Waiters, Advice Columnists, Crazed Subway Bombers, Presidential Candidates, All of the Above) before, so I'm a little gun-shy." What is that, class? *That is the second oldest brush-off line in the world.* Woo! Woo! Here comes the clue train! All aboard!

3. He talks to you about other women? Hasn't he been "burnt by women before"? Hello?

4. Mixed signals? Oh, please: he isn't sending you mixed signals, you're just reading them into his actions. It's called "wishful thinking."

5. Just because he's one of the greatest lays you've ever had doesn't mean you're the greatest lay he's ever had.

6. Boundaries are wonderful things, and your willingness to confront your own boundary issues is commendable. While we're on the subject, I respectfully suggest you expand your "boundaries" so that the ability to take a hint falls somewhere within them.

7. Do yourself the favor of staying away from him until his hold on you is broken. Masturbate about someone or something else, and hang out with friends you don't want to fuck.

Hey, Faggot:

I am a 30-year-old male. For the past year I've been experimenting with the two-girl ménage à trois. After having "broken up" with my girlfriend three years ago—after five years of living together (I didn't want to have kids)—and after becoming sick of the single bars, etc., I decided to "order in."

I ordered a couple of Asian babes and loved life for an hour. I've done this several times and now feel like I've had my share of empty, loveless fun. And . . . I've finally met someone. When the subject of past lovers came up, I froze. She knew something was up, and I'm pretty sure she's going to ask again. Should I tell her of my "fantasy fulfillment" or keep my recent past to myself? She could be the one.

Feeling Sorry I Slutted

Hey, FSIS:

Tell her, "I had a kinda slutty period after breaking up with my last long-term girlfriend." If she wants to hear more, tell her you had a few one-night stands, and a couple of three-ways. You don't have to go into how you met these girls, and if you don't act like there was anything out of the slut-ordinary about these experiences, she won't ask. Commit the sin of omission, and get tested for every bug under the sun.

Hey, Faggot:

Here's a question I've never seen addressed in any advice column. I'm a reasonably healthy and functional heterosexual woman who prefers fags to straight men. This isn't a recent thing, or a reaction to some tortured relationship. Even when I was a kid, the other kids I played with were all boys that liked to play with dolls, and grew up to be flight attendants. Now, I find that all the guys I find attractive are gay, and openly so. I even think gay porn is hot.

I really can't explain this. I'm not afraid of straight men, or afraid of sex: I've had plenty of boyfriends, and some long-term relationships, but nothing seems to turn me on as much as a guy who's very much in touch with his feminine side. Given a crowd of attractive men, I always manage to pick out the fruity ones. It's become a joke among my friends.

Is this evidence of some bizarre psychological problem on my part? Does this doom me to a life of sexlessness and misery? What should I do?

Help

Hey, H:

If being attracted to men unconvinced that flatulence = high comedy qualifies as a "psychological problem," then you and I should start a support group. You are not alone in being attracted to men in touch with what has been mislabeled as their "femininity." I say "mislabeled" because thus labeling good table manners, reasonable personal hygiene, the having of feelings, and the willpower not to let big ol' farts rip whenever nature calls has created a tremendous disincentive for insecure straight boys to acquire these social graces. If all those things are "feminine," then being "masculine" requires one to eat like a pig, smell bad, feel nothing, and fart lots.

But I think you've got hold of the wrong end of the stick: you've convinced yourself that you're attracted to "gay men," when what you're attracted to are effeminate men. Not all effeminate men are gay, and, I should mention, not all gay men are effeminate. You just need to get out there and find yourself a gay-acting/gay-appearing straight boy. They exist, and here's the proof:

Hey, Faggot:

People think I'm gay. As a heterosexual male, I've never had problems with homosexuals in the least, but being a rather shy, somewhat insecure fella, I really don't need another hurdle to jump over when trying to meet women. It's mostly heterosexuals who are confused: I've only been hit on a couple of times by men. I don't know if it's because I can match colors, or I don't do enough macho posturing. Without becoming a homophobe, what can I do to send out the correct signals to potential partners?

Help

Hey, H:

You could fart more.

If you're swishy, then women will assume you're queer. So if you want to get laid, you're going to have to get less shy about approaching women—for potential partners to get the correct signals, you're going to have to be a little more proactive about sending them. Call it the curse of the heterosexual hairdresser/florist/waiter/senior presidential adviser: if you don't tell people you're straight, everyone naturally assumes you're gay.

Asking women out, wining, dining, and fucking them is a pretty convincing way of demonstrating you're straight. I hear from women all the time who are in love with a particular gay man, or attracted to gay men in general, or sick of macho posturing. Your swishiness is a point in your favor with scores of women. Go find one.

Hey, Faggot:

I am a 32-year-old white male, divorced for over two years now, and I can't seem to get past the 3rd or 4th date with a woman. When I got married—at the tender age of 23—I was very much looking forward to having a family and living the American Dream. But after the first year of marriage, my wife was not pregnant.

As it turns out, I have a very low sperm count. Bluntly put: I am shooting blanks. We tried several expensive treatments, none of which worked. This led to a lot of guilt, shame, heartbreak, and blame, and, ultimately, to divorce.

Now, whenever I get close to a woman, I can't bring myself to tell her that I can't have children. If I do tell a woman, she disappears. Every woman my age wants to get married and have children. But what is a guy like me to do?

S.I.

Hey, S.I.:

Don't blame your failed marriage—or your inability to date successfully—on your low sperm count. If not being able to make babies ended your marriage, your marriage wasn't built on a very solid foundation; sooner or later, probably sooner, it would've ended regardless of how many puppies you two pumped out. When a couple wants to have children, one partner's sterility can be a big, fat bummer—but it is not an insurmountable obstacle, especially when the one with the "problem" is the male: are there no spunk banks in your part of the country?

Your recent dating troubles, I'm guessing, have little to do with your sterility. There are plenty of single women in this world who, like you, can't have children, and Lord knows there are women out there who don't want children, or who already have children—women who would regard sterility as a point in your favor. Find one. Marry her if she'll have you. Still want kids? Adopt. Foster-parent. Help her raise her kids.

But until you meet that special someone, don't point at your balls every time you're dumped and say, "It's all your fault." You may have other social maladaptations that drive the chicks away. Take a good hard look at yourself and ask, "Is it really my sperm count? Or is it something else? My breath? The way I treat women? My posture? My party affiliation?" Ask female friends for their honest opinions—if you don't have any female friends, that's a pretty good sign something's wrong—and work on improving your social skills.

Hey, Faggot:

I am a single 22-year-old black college student. I've always been attracted to white females for the simple fact that they have sexy bodies and they know how to treat their men. So I wanted to know what it takes for a hot one to notice me. I can offer a lot, including pussy-eating and romantic evenings.

So tell me what I should do so that I may have the women of my dreams.

Loves White Women

Hey, LWW:

White women, like other women, can be had two ways: You can rent them, or you can ask them out. Either way, just mumble in your best bass-baritone, "Hey, baby, you've got a sexy body. I bet you know how to treat your men." White chicks dig that kinda hepcat talk.

Hey, Faggot:

I saw that letter from the black guy who prefers white women and had a rollicking good laugh.

This poor slob really believes the way to a white woman's heart is "pussy-eating and romantic evenings"? My advice: Stop reading *Hustler* magazine, honey. I've polled white women, and practically none of them listed "Potential Pussy-Eating Capability" as an initial indicator of a good date, spouse, slave, etc.

A person's choice of whom they happen to be attracted to is very subjective. Although it's fine to privately consider race, it's ridiculous to think that race determines whether a woman "knows how to treat her men." If he doesn't believe me, he need only ask all the guys who have filed for divorce from white women. Good women come in all sorts of packages, and if he's attracted to a particular type of woman, it is *just because.*

One of the Good Ones

Hey, OOTGO:

Couldn't agree with you more. When LWW said he was attracted to white chicks because they "have sexy bodies and know how to treat their men," he as good as said black women don't have sexy bodies or know how to treat their men. Finding fault with people you're not attracted to is a lazy way to justify your feelings about the people you are attracted to. LWW is like those godawful gay men who dump all over women's bodies when they try and explain why they're attracted to men. It's an asshole thing to do, regardless of who you're dumping on, and it makes people really angry. Read on.

Hey, Faggot:

When I read the letter from "Loves White Chicks," I couldn't wait to read the tongue-lashing you'd give him in response. While I detected sarcasm, alas, I was unfulfilled. Then I thought: Why should you take issue with a self-hating, breeder, quasi-black man? So I will:

Dear Mister Loves-Whitey-Because-You-Can't-Stand-Yourself: The only fact to be gleaned from your "all white women have sexy bodies/know how to treat their men" letter is that a dolt wrote it. That you need assistance in getting a white chick further proves your vapidity. The kind of white chicks you want to date probably want you simply because you're a dumb black buck with a big dick. Being a delicious black chick who knows how to treat any man, I have no problem with trying everything on the dating buffet—black, white, whatever. But if you want a broad just because she's white and presumably won't give you any lip, don't pull an O.J. when she dumps your trifling ass for a bigger, blacker, more-money-makin' dick than yours—pussy-eating skills notwithstanding.

Tanya in SF

Hey, Faggot:

I read with interest the letter from the black college student interested in white women because they have "sexy bodies" and know how to "treat their men." I am a white male married to a black woman, and my wife treats me better than any white woman ever did.

I prefer the sisters because they are strong emotionally, know who they are, and are the best-looking women in the world, not to mention incredible lovers. A lot of men shy away from black women because of the intelligence, inner strength, and resolve these women possess.

I am certainly not dumping on white women, nor would I ever criticize another person's choice of sexual partners. I just feel it is time we start giving black women the recognition they so richly deserve. Cindy Crawford who? Give me Tyra Banks any day!

Loves Black Women

Hey, LBW:

You certainly are "dumping on white women," LBW. Saying you prefer black women because they're "strong emotionally" implies that white women are weak; stating that black women are the best-looking women in the world implies that women of other races are not as good-looking. Claiming black women "know who they are" implies white women don't know who they are.

There's an easy way out of the hole Loves Black Women and Loves White Women seem so intent on digging for themselves: "I" statements. It's psychobabble, I know, but in this case it really works! Picture this: LBW, LWW, and I are all sitting in a bar talking about what makes our dicks hard. "I'm more attracted to black women than white women," says Loves Black Women; "in fact, it is my personal opinion that black women are the most beautiful women in the world." "Well, I find white women to be sexier than black women, and I am therefore more attracted to white chicks," says Loves White Women. "Women are nice," I offer, "but I find good-lookin' men—black or white—infinitely sexier than women."

Ta-da! By using "I" statements we've avoided putting down people we don't find attractive! But even if someone fails to use an "I" statement when talking about what turns them on, we can increase the peace by hearing that important "I" even when some dummy leaves it out. If someone says, "White women leave the sexiest skid marks," hear "I think white women leave the sexiest skid marks"—because that is, after all, what they mean.

Hey, Faggot:

I'm a single straight woman in my late 20s, and I'd like to be in a relationship. Oh, yeah: I'm also a virgin. From my teenage years through early adulthood, abstaining from sex wasn't a big deal for me. I wasn't ready for it, and I wanted to wait until I was in love, or at least in "deep like."

Well, I've *been* ready for the last few years! I'm extremely cognizant of my sexual needs and desires. Masturbation isn't enough, because I crave physical intimacy with another person. The men I find sexually attractive either (a) are not interested in me or (b) turn out to be complete boneheads.

Frankly, I'm tired of waiting for a "deep, meaningful relationship" to come along. So much so that I'm seriously considering taking the one-night-stand route (which has never been appealing to me). Furthermore, sexual/emotional/intellectual compatibility are intertwined assets which I have a difficult time separating. The result is that I find myself jealous of those people who can fuck first and ask questions later.

Should I hold out for "Mr. Right," or go for "Mr. Right Now"?
Last of the Red Hot Virgins

Hey, LOTRHV:

Sometimes Mr. Right Now turns out to be Mr. Right. You'd be surprised how many cheap and meaningless flings blossom, in time, into deep and meaningful relationships. A one-night stand becomes a two-nighter, then three, four, and five. Before you know it, that stranger is your boyfriend, and you're having to tell your family the most appalling lies about how you met.

So the next time you're attracted to some guy—and he's attracted to you—fuck him! He might be the one! Then again, he might not. He might be another of those complete boneheads—but if you fuck him right away, you won't know that until after you've lost your virginity.

Hey, Faggot:

I'm a 21-year-old male college student and still a virgin. I like women, and am open to anything from a one-night fling to a lasting relationship. I'm nice, and fairly smart, but not very attractive or interesting. I read how you advised a virgin near age 40 to go to a "professional." I would like to try that, but don't have a clue as to how to go about it. Obviously you can't be very specific (with the stupid illegality of it and all), but any way you could point me in the right direction would be appreciated.

Can't Wait Anymore

Hey, CWA:

Just between us fellas, those "escort" ads at the back of finer weekly publications, well, very few of those escorts actually are in the bidness of "escorting" people around museums or art galleries. "Escort" is a euphemism, like "powder room," or "donor maintenance." If you'd like to employ an "escort," call and make an appointment. Don't ask how much a blow job will run you; she'll assume you're a cop and hang up. Just ask what her hourly rate is—so far as the law is concerned, you're purchasing companionship, which is not illegal. Make an appointment to meet in a safe, mutually agreeable location—like a hotel room—and don't act like a creep. She'll know what you want, and she'll know what to do. Be respectful, let her lead, use condoms, and tip the lady.

Hey, Faggot:

Little bit of advice for the 21-year-old virgin: Don't visit an escort for your first time! This advice comes from a 23-year-old virgin. Yeah, it's tough at times—especially with most of society telling you that all couples are fulfilled and happy, and all singles are sad and incomplete. But in the future, when you think back to your first time, would you like to remember something special with someone you cared about, or a sexually unsafe encounter that left you with a considerably lighter wallet?

You described yourself as "not very attractive or interesting." Sounds like your problem's with your self-image, not your virginity! There are groups and organizations for people interested in both mainstream and incredibly obscure hobbies. Maybe you can find someone there, and the first time can actually mean something. If not, hang tight, and . . . enjoy yourself, if you know what I mean. It's bound to come along—almost no one gets to be 40 years old and still a virgin.

Me, I know why I'm still a virgin: a 257-pound man is not exactly that attractive to the opposite sex! But I know why I'm unattractive, and I'm doing something about it, getting my load lightened and my head screwed on tighter. Don't be passive, waiting for the girl to come to you. Ask women out even if you're dead sure they'll turn you down, get involved in hobbies and activities, or even take out a personal ad, for Pete's sake! Even if at first you're not successful, you'll at least feel in control, like you're doing something about your love life and maybe opening up some romantic possibilities. I'm not faulting you, Dan. He asked for advice on how to use an escort, and you answered. I just feel strongly about this subject.

Waiting in Chicago

Hey, WIC:

You're content waiting, and I think that's grand. Really. And I admire your commitment, though I should warn you, there are plenty of 40-year-old virgins: I get letters from them all the time. In general, I think your advice to Can't Wait Anymore is good—but there are two bones I'd like to pick with you. First, an experience with an escort can be something special. And plenty of first-time experiences with no escort present are less than special—ask anyone who's actually lost their virginity.

Secondly, you imply that an experience with an escort is inherently "unsafe." Most people get STDs doing "something special" with someone they care about, and not from escorts. All the escorts I know insist on condoms.

Hey, Faggot:

I am an attractive GWM, 28 years old, 5'2", 130 pounds and very boyish looking. Because of my looks, most men who are attracted to me end up being the kind of men who fantasize about young boys—the underage type—that I still resemble. I feel this is wrong, even in fantasy. In the beginning I just thought it was bad luck that I kept meeting sex offenders; then I came to realize that the "young boy" fantasy is pervasive in the gay community. I am a 28-year-old man, so good-looking people stare, yet I am so repulsed by the fantasies or realities surrounding this whole little-boy thing that I am practically a recluse.

What's a man trapped in an underage boy's body supposed to do?! I want a normal, non–sex offender as a partner, not a father/daddy/master. I want a friend.

Lonely and Over 18

Hey, LO18:

If you can't learn to make a distinction between guys attracted to boyish-looking men and guys attracted to actual boys you're going to remain a miserable recluse, kiddo. If you're cute and boyish, you're gonna attract the occasional card-carrying NAMBLA member, and so what? Tell the sex offenders to fuck off. But there are men out there attracted to boyish men who are not sex offenders.

Forgive the psychobabble—I use it ever so sparingly—but you're projecting: not entirely comfortable with your looks, you assume the worst about anyone and everyone who's attracted to you. "That guy over there is cruising me. He must be another one of those creepy boy-fuckers. Guess I'll go home and pout."

The "young boy" thing is no more "pervasive" among gay men than the Lolita thing is among straight men (though straight men with Lolita obsessions, to their credit, don't form "civil rights" organizations). It may seem to you as if all gay men are into boys, but that's because your sample is skewed: NAMBLA guys hit on you, because you look like a boy. NAMBLA types don't hit on me: I don't look like a boy. You saying, "All gay men are into little boys," because a lot of the men who hit on you are into boys, makes about as much sense as me saying, "No gay men are into boys," because none of the men who hit on me are into little boys.

There are worse things than being boyish and beautiful. Stop mopin'.

Hey, Faggot:

I'm a newly single man becoming sexually active again after 18 months of masturbation. With two women I recently have had the problem—in about half of our encounters—of being hard through foreplay but only barely hard enough when the time came for penetration. Since I always begin masturbating by touching my nipples—they're very sensitive—I fear that I have retrained myself to respond mostly to this stimulus.

Unfortunately, with these women, nipple stimulation does not have the same effect. Initially it makes me hard, but it fails to do much after a short while. If this is only a case of learning bad habits by having solo sex, how can I retrain my body, especially when I still enjoy jerking off and it's most fun if I touch my nipples? The women thought it was about how they looked, and I'm starting to get frustrated, because I never had this problem before.

Help

Hey, H:

Your half-the-time problem probably has more to do with concentration and focus than with deep-seated psychological problems or masturbatory "training." You could spend hundreds of dollars on a sex therapist, or you can spend 10 bucks on a trip to a sex-toy store. Pick yourself up a cock ring. They fit snugly at the base of your cock, and once you're excited, the blood gets in, but it don't get out—not until you're finished with it. Get an adjustable one with a buckle or snap, and you won't risk a trip to the emergency room to have a too-snug cock ring sawn off.

And, hey: if you think your lady friends are at all hip to advanced sex toys, you might want to pick up some tit clamps. They look scarier than they feel, but if you love tit stimulation, you'll love tit clamps.

Hey, Faggot:

Here's the deal: I'm this 28-year-old wild Sagittarian hetero guy stuck in this healthy but weakened aging 58-year-old body. I've got talents and qualities coming out the kazoo. I'm a man of power, accomplishment, compassion, funny, intelligent, and spiritual. And I can keep it up all night and know tantric-type moves and erotic practices that keep a partner sliding off the sheets. And I love being with women!

The problem is I don't want the Serious Relationship most single women seem to want. Yet the more adventurous and wild sex-positive women, young or old, married or not, seem to want the younger boy-type studs for their adventures. I've tried a few pickups in bars or on the ski slopes, and I've answered a few personal ads, but most potential partners seem unwilling to even try the preliminaries with a guy my age. Any suggestions?

"Sean Connery"

Hey, Sean:

Most women want commitment—and many men do too. If, at your age, you want regular sex and you don't want to pay for it (some of those artists, poets, and musicians might not be averse to having a patron, if you follow my drift), you're going to have to find a nice woman around your own age and settle down, gramps.

Hey, Faggot:

Sometimes I feel all alone in the world. I am an androgynous spirit. Sex to me means spirituality, tenderness, kindness, loving another human being as myself, passionate kisses, emotional merging, having the self-respect to look another human being in the eyes when you fuck them. Enjoying another person's thoughts and memories. Love is blind. Call me a freak, but that's my libido.

LM

Hey, LM:

Your "libido" sounds really evolved. You, on the other hand, sound like a drip—which might have more to do with your loneliness than your androgyny. Sex can be all the wonderful things you claim it always is for you (never fuck for fuck's sake?), but if there's one thing I know for sure about sex it's this: Having sex, even tender, loving, passionate, look-'em-in-the-eyes (never been blindfolded?), merge-with-me sex with someone who won't shut up about how they're feeling so tender, so passionate, so completely merged, so blah, blah, blah—destroys whatever spiritual vibe you get going. It's hard to feel tender and passionate about someone you wanna choke to death.

Hey, Faggot:

Last summer I met "Lucy," an amazing woman. To my delight, we soon started dating. We were physically intimate, though we never had sexual intercourse. I very quickly fell in love with her, and I felt she loved me too. Unfortunately, I was wrong. Lucy suddenly and unexpectedly broke up with me when things were going very well. She said she'd like to remain friends, but that a relationship was not what she needed.

Months passed and we hardly talked, even though we were still "friends." I cried a lot. I had seen her at social functions a few times after our breakup. Tears came to my eyes when I saw her. I could only think of not being with her.

A few months later Lucy moved into the apartment complex where I reside. Now, all I do is find myself creating silly excuses to go see her. I still love her and I'd take her back in an instant. As a 25-year-old male, I think I have my life pretty well in order.

But I have never obsessed over any woman and I can't figure out why I care. I don't want to move out of my apartment building.

I don't want to seek professional help, mainly because I can't afford it. Also, I met her boyfriend (new one) and I'm stunned that after going out with a guy like me she's now dating a rather ho-hum gent with no fashion sense and bad hair. Not that I'm jealous—yeah, sure! What should I do? Not do? Help!

Without a Clue

Hey, WAC:

Maybe Lucy dumped you because you're a conceited crybaby.

I'm not being fair: you're certainly not the first person to take comfort in finding fault with an ex's new lover; and the fact that you're in touch with feelings—lonely nights at home bawling—indicates that you're well in touch. And that's charming.

But while this relationship may have been "going very well" as far as you were concerned, good ol' Lucy obviously didn't feel the same way—otherwise she wouldn't have dumped your well-groomed, well-dressed, sensitive ass, would she? Maybe she thought you were a jerk, maybe she thought you were a lousy lay, maybe she honestly prefers ill-dressed men with bad hair to well-turned-out Fabios such as yourself. Maybe, maybe, maybe.

You probably should have gotten yourself some answers when she dumped you. "Let's be friends" and "I'm not interested in a relationship right now" are polite face-saving code. These phrases spare the breaker-upper from having to lay out exactly why he or she doesn't want to see the breaker-uppee anymore, and conversely spares the breaker-uppee from having to listen to the break-upper tick off his or her faults.

Hey, Faggot:

For the past three months, I've been dating someone who has serious health problems. He claims he is HIV-negative, and since he is not in a high-risk group (he is a monogamous heterosexual male, no drugs) I have not asked him to get tested. His health problems started off as minor—allergies, colds, injuries from working out—but have become progressively worse. As a result, most of my free time is spent taking care of him. Most of what I do is pretty mundane: shopping, cooking, cleaning, laundry and providing emotional support (plus the occasional blow job when he's up to it). He is growing increasingly demanding, and I'm starting to resent it. I understand he is in pain, but his constant criticisms and insults are wearing me out. I don't want to spend the rest of my summer taking care of a very mean-spirited baby, but I feel that leaving him now would be cruel considering his health. I tell myself we aren't married, and we have only been dating for a few months, during which time I have tried very hard to be supportive. If the situation were reversed, I seriously doubt he would do the same for me. He claims to have a large social circle but no one has volunteered to help him. Friends tell me I should leave and get on with my life. What do you think?

Compassion Fatigued in San Francisco

Hey, CFISF:

I'm hoping by now you've had the good sense to leave him, or he's had the courtesy to die. If he hasn't dropped dead and you're still with him, you are one world-class chump. If he's too sick to get up off the couch and do his own laundry or get his own chow, let him get a nurse. Don't be a doormat.

Hey, Faggot:

I have been seeing a guy for two months. We both work in the same company, but in different departments—it's totally safe. His situation: He's separated, divorce papers are in process, it might be ugly. He works a billion hours a week and has to move in December. All of this is creating a bit of stress on his part, I'm sure. I am over at his place a minimum of three nights a week, hang out with his friends; we have a wonderful time together, have amazing sex together, but he doesn't consider me his girlfriend since, as he put it, "it's too heavy a label" for him right now. I know it's only been a couple of months, but I've fallen for him, and even though I don't want to rush things, I feel the title of "girlfriend" is not a heavy label, and at this point is an earned one. Is this a lack of commitment on his part—even though it was his idea to have a monogamous relationship—or am I just being weird and old-fashioned?

Boyfriendless

Hey, B:

As he's in the middle of a divorce, maybe you could be the grown-up and cut him a little semantic slack. For all practical purposes, you are his girlfriend—sleeping over, hanging out, having sex—and if you don't make an enormo deal of it, he'll come round eventually. But for the time being, "girlfriend"—not a heavy label as far as you're concerned—is a heavy label so far as he's concerned. Let it go.

But if it's all that friggin' important to you to be called "girlfriend," important enough that you're willing to force the issue and perhaps lose this guy, you do have some leverage. Tell him you don't make monogamous commitments to guys with whom you don't have—at the very least—a boyfriend/girlfriend relationship. And limit your sleep-overs to once a week. If a casual arrangement is what he wants, then that's all you should give him. If he wants more, he needs to give more.

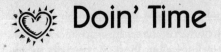

Doin' Time

Long-term Relationships

Before I get to questions from folks trapped in long-term relationships, there are a few things I'd like to get off my chest.

Frequently, when I sit down to read my mail, there'll be a letter from one of my many critics. Their chief complaint is that I'm too mean to the fragile souls who write in asking for advice. Well, it's true, I am mean—just mean enough to be entertaining, not mean enough to harm anyone. No one I've ever advised has jumped from the top of a tall building clutching a tearstained copy of the *Village Voice*; whereas Howard Stern, the immensely wealthy, world-famous shock jock my critics frequently compare me to (which I do not see), could be accused of having driven the estranged wife of a rival DJ to commit suicide by convincing her, and everyone else in Boston, that her husband was a jerk. I can't understand why my asshole critics accuse me of being the gay Howard Stern—including an asshole rival columnist.

My response to this misplaced concern for my readers is this: folks who send me letters have read my column. If I'm mean, they're aware of it, and have made a free and informed choice to send me a letter. Folks who haven't read my column don't know I exist and couldn't possibly send me a letter. The brave souls who do write me don't need the protection of busy-body do-gooders. They're grown-ups, already. And let's not forget that this is advice, not binding arbitration. According to my dictionary, advice is "an opinion about what could or should be done," so folks are free to disregard my advice, seek out second opinions, write to other advice columnists, or see a shrink. I'm not tying people up and making them write me letters any more than I'm holding a gun to their heads and forcing them to act on my "bad" advice.

My critics also accuse me of not being enough of a romantic to have a job in the romance field. You'll see here in "Doin' Time," that I will sometimes advise people to leave a husband, or cheat on a girlfriend, or lie to someone they love. This upsets my critics. "You don't know what love is," they write, "because if you did, you wouldn't give the advice that you do." Invariably, they go on to call me a whore, one of those promiscuous homos that couldn't pick five of his ex-boyfriends out of a five-man lineup of five of his ex-boyfriends. While being a whore may mean I know an awful lot about butt plugs and blow jobs, it doesn't mean I know anything about love—LUV—so I should shut my trap about it.

In response, I'd like to point out to my critics that accusing someone of never having been in love is a *mean* thing to do, you pack of hypocrites. And in my case, it's not only mean, it's also a lie. I have experienced romantic love, for periods of hours, days, weeks—even years! Not that anyone needs to have been in a long-term relationship in order to give advice about long-term relationships. Most of the problems confronting folks in long-term relationships are pretty similar to those faced by folks in brand-new relationships, only of greater duration. And, hey: don't Catholic priests counsel married couples all the time? Where's the outrage when it comes to those altar-boy-raping celibates giving advice?

I'm currently in a long-termish relationship, one not without problems, but that's showing signs of inertia-induced permanence. He's lovely, and we're in love, and while we have "issues" that ten years ago I would have considered deal breakers, I'm older, wiser, and lazier now, and so I'm willing to hang in there. While I have not yet reached the true-love finish line—being with someone until death do us part, a dark and perverse standard by which to judge the "success" of a relationship—I have too been "in love," and therefore feel qualified to offer an expert opinion to the brave men and women in long-term relationships who send me questions.

Also, as I'm fond of telling my critics: Don't like my advice? Don't ask for it. Don't like my column? Don't read it. Got better advice? Get your own fucking advice column.

There, I feel better!

Hey, Faggot:

What is so wonderful about intercourse? I recently married a man I met when we were freshmen in college. We were virgins on our wedding day; however, from the moment we knew we would get married, we were sexually active in every other way. We would sleep together in the nude at least two to three times per week, and could both climax two to three times each time we engaged in sex. Indeed, we became quite creative in finding new ways to achieve orgasm without intercourse.

However, since our wedding day, things have gone downhill. At first my husband had trouble penetrating—he would prematurely ejaculate, when I had yet to reach orgasm. Even when we try outercourse, our experiences with intercourse have been so bad that we just can't recapture the magic that existed before.

What is wrong with us? What can we do to salvage our sex life?

                    Desperately Seeking Orgasm

Hey, DSO:

Stop feeling like—now that you're married grown-ups—you gotta have intercourse. Return to the sex that was working for you before you were married and try not to think of "outercourse" as make-do until you can work back up to intercourse, but as your preferred mode of sexual pleasure/getting yer rocks off, at least for now.

When you do decide to take another stab at intercourse, don't get hung up on simultaneous orgasms. They're nice, but they aren't the definition of a "successful" sex act. Whether you're fucking or sucking or jerking off on the phone, you haven't done anything "wrong" if one person comes first. Coming together is likelier to happen in daytime TV and porno videos than in real life. So he came first—so he prematurely ejaculated, even—he's got fingers, he's got toes, he's got a tongue: he can still get you off.

Talk to your husband: he may be feeling like a failure for "coming too quickly." This might be the reason he's reluctant, or unable, to mess around these days. When he tried to "do" intercourse with you, he couldn't. Now he fears if he tries to "do" it again and can't, he'll feel like an even bigger failure. So take the pressure off by taking intercourse off the menu for a while.

Incidentally, "saving it" is where you went wrong. Because of the buildup you guys gave penetration you were, quite naturally, disappointed when it didn't go like gangbusters the first few times. But any kind of sex takes practice before you get good at it. Who gives the world's best blow job the first time they have a dick in their mouth? Blow jobs take practice! Cunnilingus takes practice! Kissing takes practice! Anything worth doing takes practice—and that includes intercourse.

Hey, Faggot:

I'm a 26-year-old woman. My 28-year-old boyfriend and I have great sex, but the actual intercourse part of it never lasts more than a few minutes (premature ejaculation). Is there anything you or your readers can suggest he/I/we can do to prolong our encounters? Low-maintenance, please. We don't wanna have to work during sex.

Wait!

Hey, W:

A sex therapist might be able help, but they're very "high-maintenance." So here's a low-maintenance suggestion that worked for a long-ago, faraway boyfriend of mine. Like your boyfriend, he came too quickly. But if we kept on messing around after his first orgasm, he got hard again in about 15 minutes. That second blessed bone would last and last. Give it a try: bring your boyfriend to a little preliminary orgasm, without much buildup, and keep on rolling around till he's ready for more.

Hey, Faggot:

I'm a 29-year-old gay male. My boyfriend of one year dumped (I hate that word) me in February. He was the person I thought I would spend the rest of my life with. The split was amicable, but painful. His reasons for leaving were that he thought we got involved too soon (his previous relationship of five years ended just a few months before we became involved) and said he needed space and time to be single.

At first, I hoped he would experiment with being single, then realize it wasn't what he wanted, and then come running back to me. I have started to accept that after five months, that's probably not going to happen.

I hoped we would be able to be friends, but the last couple of times I saw him were painful for both of us. I want to be friends with him, but it hurts too much. I think the same is true for him. Maybe it's just too soon.

I am trying to get on with my life. I went to a gay support group for a few weeks, talked to a therapist, have been journalling, volunteering, working out daily, trying to spend time with friends and trying not to keep my feelings inside. My friends will vouch for me: I have been talking about my feelings a lot. I've been doing all the right things to try and heal, but it's not happening. I'm getting impatient and worn down. I'm not used to being such a mess.

I still cry nearly every day. I think about him all the time. I lose a lot of sleep. I have been trying to let go, but I don't know what else to do. I've been rejected before, but never by someone who meant so much to me. I've never been through this kind of pain before and I hate it.

Any suggestions?

Sleepless in Saint Paul, Minnesota

Hey, SISPM:

You live in the Midwest, I'm from the Midwest; can't you scrape together some of that middle-American tight-lipped dysfunctionality? For the last twenty years, we've been told that when we're in pain, we need to work through it, let it out, open up. That works for some people. But there's a lot to be said for shutting your mouth, putting it out of your head, and moving on. Support groups, "journalling," therapists, boring our friends to death—often these "grieving" techniques keep us focused on what's making us miserable and prolong our agony. They don't help us heal faster, they keep the wounds open—and open wounds are not attractive.

Give up on this guy. He dumped you—stop wallowing. Make up your mind not to think about him or if you must, dwell on his faults and physical flaws. Fuck him! The last five months of your life have been hell, and it's his fault—get mad!

Hey, Faggot:

I've been thinking about writing "Savage Love" for a while, but my concerns seem too basic, traditional and altogether too het.

I was in a three-year relationship with a breeder girlfriend in Seattle; for two of the three years we lived across the country from each other. We had a bitter split recently.

A fundamental question or two for you—can lies ever be told out of sensitivity and protection for your partner and their feelings? What is the best way to overcome inconsistent monogamous focus and unfaithfulness coupled with deceit? These are very boring and breederish, but you have a straightforward insightful touch, so I thought I'd ask. We are not communicating now, at her request, despite my previous attempts at apology and a commitment to real change in behavior and a real desire at reconciliation.

Andrew

Hey, Andrew:

Once upon a time, I was in the habit of lying to my lovers until one day, examining the most recent boot print on my ass, I finally figured it the fuck out: lying had to be getting me in more trouble than the truth could. Not that I knew for sure—the truth wasn't a habit with me—but I had an inkling. So I stopped telling my lovers lies—what-I-thought-they-wanted-to-hear lies, omission lies, face-saving lies, lie lies—and whadayaknow? I had fewer boot prints on my ass.

You hid an affair from your long-distance lover. She found out about it, and now she won't speak to you. Had you called her and said, "The long-distance thing isn't working for me, I'd like to see other people," maybe things would've worked out differently. She may not have been thrilled, but you might have had the option, down the road, of getting back together, an option that isn't open to you now.

Finally, what's so "het" about your concerns? Queers tell fibs to our partners—if we don't lie to our lovers, who will? And we're famous for "inconsistent monogamous focus."

Hey, Faggot:

My girlfriend is a very sexual person by nature, in a very healthy way. I'm in my mid-20s, fairly inexperienced sexually, and fairly well-endowed. Okay, extremely well-endowed . . . and therein lies the problem. My girlfriend is a petite woman, scarcely five feet tall. Everything else is proportional. Put bluntly, I do not fit. There is an extremely painful ripping of her vagina when we have intercourse, which as a consequence has not been often.

Despite our best, most heavily lubricated efforts, we seem to be making little progress.

Sex is awesome, but it's not necessarily about penetration. Despite my attachment to intercourse, I would be willing to forgo it to stay with this woman. Unfortunately, she may not be willing to do the same to stay with me.

I want this to work more than anything I've ever wanted, and I think she feels the same. However, I will not settle for satisfying 90 percent of her needs, and coming up short on the other 10 percent. I'm afraid I'm falling in love with someone I may have to walk away from for both our sakes. Any advice would be graciously appreciated.

Too Much of a Good Thing

Hey, TMOAGT:

I got in touch with two experts on your behalf: Marcy Bloom of the Aradia Women's Health Center in Seattle, and Nancy Jordyce, an OB-GYN in private practice in the lovely state of New Mexico.

Marcy had this to say: "It could be a physical concern or a counseling concern." If it's a counseling concern, the rap goes like this: "How vigorous is their sexual activity, are they using a gradual buildup with appropriate amounts of lubrication? His letter makes it sound like they are communicating, but are they taking their time, putting the penis in slowly and gradually?"

If it's a physical problem: "There are surgical procedures, but they're drastic. Any surgical procedure should be viewed as a last resort," says Marcy. Regardless, Marcy recommends that, as a first step toward solving the problem, your girlfriend go in for a gynecological assessment, which is where our next guest expert comes in.

Dr. Jordyce told me your girlfriend's problem might be that her vaginal opening is too small, possibly because her hymen is still partially intact. If that's the case, "a relatively simple hymenectomy would clear the problem right up."

"But," the doctor continued, "if this woman was born with a vagina that is small due to a birth defect (cervix too low, etc.)

then reconstructive surgery may be needed, based, of course, on the defect. She should go see a gynecologist."

When I asked Marcy Bloom if the problem could simply be that you have a big penis and your girlfriend has a small vagina, she said: "When people talk about small vaginas and big penises, what does that mean? That she's five feet tall is irrelevant. Ten- and 12-pound babies come out of vaginas! It's extra-rare that men don't fit into women's vaginas. They're just in need of further advice from skilled health care providers— including mental health providers." Go get some.

Hey, Faggot:

I was wondering if you could clue me in on your opinion as to the whole sex versus emotional love thing? For the past seven years, I've had this amazingly close relationship with another man. The sex has almost always been good, yet I still have occasional tricks on the side. We've talked about it and he's cool with the idea, yet my guilt keeps me from divulging the reality. Can you have a tight relationship and indulge in other sexual encounters?

Having My Cake

Hey, Marie Antoinette:

The seven years you've been in this amazingly close relationship, you've been fucking around behind this guy's back, he just doesn't know about it. So, clueless, aren't you already having a tight relationship while indulging in other sexual encounters?

You have two options. Tell him you're going to start having sex on the side and you wanted him to know so everything would be out in the open, giving him the impression you haven't been cheating on him up to now. From then on, you'll no longer have to hide your outside activities and you'll feel less guilt. The trouble with this approach is he's going to wonder, after what he supposes were seven happily monogamous years together, why you would want to step out on him now. He might think you're losing interest, and start shopping around for a new lover himself.

Your other option is to come clean: Confess your sins of omission—"Remember when we talked about whether it would be okay if we tricked with other people . . . well, it wasn't hypothetical for me." Impress upon him that all the years you've been "amazingly close" none of these other guys ever tempted you away from him.

One last thought: your lover's probably aware of what's been going on. Don't assume he's so stupid, or you're so clever, that you successfully hid seven years' worth of cheating, especially if you are so "amazingly close."

Hey, Faggot:

I'm a breeder chick who has been in a monogamous relationship for nine years. I'm very into my solid marriage, I'm having fun, satisfied and content. And yet I've met this guy who can with a few words or a touch light a fire below my navel, igniting erotic feelings and thoughts that fill my every moment. I love my husband (he's my companion for life) and I care for this friend of mine and I want them both. I'm thinking of bringing them together to tell them each how I feel. Any advice?

Mmmm Baby

Hey, MB:

If your only reason for arranging this three-way is to get in the other guy's pants, don't do it. Three-ways only work when all three people want to have sex with each other; everybody has to be equally into it. A three-way with lopsided desire—you really want the other guy, your husband wants to please you, the other guy wants you—leads to heartache. Your husband will watch you bang this guy's brains out and feel like the only reason he was invited was so you could cheat on him without cheating on him. If you're going to cheat, cheat honest. Inviting the person you're cheating on to watch you cheat adds insult to injury.

But if you must, here's a plan: with your husband, broach the subject of a three-way with another guy. Don't tell him you have anyone in mind. See how he feels about it. If it's a go, see how the other guy feels. If he's into it, tell your husband you found somebody you'd like to have a three-way with. Bring them together, get 'em smashed and bang their brains out. Don't forget to pay attention to your husband.

Hey, Faggot:

A woman friend and I are interested in having a three-way with another gyrl. Trouble is, we're not sure of the ethics for such an evening. Once we've found a third party, whom likely one of us will know, what is the best way to proceed? Do we go out and have a few drinks together to get to know one another better, giving us a chance to abort it if we don't all mesh, or should we plan an evening from start to finish at the house and just assume all will go as planned? I've heard most three-ways don't turn out as well as most want them to. What is your advice to get us going with some direction so we can bypass the "Now that we're here, what do we do next?" scenario.

Aiming to Please

Hey, ATP:

Don't assume. Go out for a few drinks. Meet on neutral ground—a bar or a restaurant—somewhere you're all on equal footing, where no one has home-court advantage. Meeting at your place is too high-pressure—your third may feel she has to go through with it. If you do decide to go through with it, all three of you should give each other permission to call it off at any time for any reason. If she becomes uncomfortable—or you do, or your partner does—take a time-out or call it off.

To avoid any "Now we're here . . ." awkwardness, you and your lover should work out in advance just how you intend to get things rolling—make a game plan. Remember, you're hosting this party and she's your guest; she'll expect you two to take the lead.

Hey, Faggot:

I am a 16-year-old bi girl. And I have never had a girl-on-girl relationship. Recently I have found that I have feelings other than the strictly platonic for a new friend I met at school. Okay, let's call it a crush. My boyfriend is cool with it. I have reason to believe she is not straight and perhaps she likes me also, or maybe my logic is clouded by infatuation. So, other than "Wanna go fuck?" how do I tell her I am interested without her thinking it's the only reason why I want her as my friend . . . what the fuck do I do?

Mary Queen of Scots

Hey, Mary:

This probably isn't what you should do, it's bad, it involves substance abuse, not to mention being a manipulative and dysfunctional little tramp; but, I did it in high school and it worked for me. Invite her to a party with you and your boyfriend, get her completely smashed, get yourselves completely smashed, and somehow wind up in a room alone. If there isn't anywhere to be alone at the party, throw a six-pack in the back of your boyfriend's car and drive as fast and as recklessly as you can to some secluded spot. When you're alone, start making out with your boyfriend in front of her, then look up like "Oh, my gosh, I'm like so embarrassed you're like watching us so totally do this . . ." Then give her a smile, lean over and plant one on her. This is your boyfriend's signal to pass out or excuse himself to go throw up, leaving you two alone. And you bang her brains out. The next day, if she's embarrassed and uncomfortable about what happened, you can chalk it up to alcohol and pretend it never happened. If she's fine, repeat the whole experience, minus boyfriend and booze.

Hey, Faggot:

I am a gay woman who is heavily involved with another woman. We have been together for two years, and we have decided to invite a third person in to add a little excitement. We found a willing woman, and after a little small talk, we hit the sack. My partner and I decided that this woman was a "tongue of pleasure."

I know this doesn't sound like a problem, but this has now been going on for three months, and I am starting to regret the whole situation. I never get to be alone with my lover anymore, and when we are alone all she talks about is how the third person pleases her so much. However, I've noticed that the third has a nasty stench, and she no longer turns me on. I may just sound jealous, but how am I supposed to feel, and what should I tell my partner?

Please Help

Hey, PH:

Sometimes a three-way is just a three-way, and sometimes a three-way is a sign. In your case, it's a bad sign. When a three-way works, it augments the passion the two primary partners have for one another. When a three-way doesn't work, it supplants that passion. And that's what's up with your girlfriend— she's over you, she's into that other woman. Are you going to wait for your girlfriend to dump you, or are you going to dump her first?

Hey, Faggot:

I am a young, happily married woman. My husband and I have never looked for someone to bring into our relationship, but we have always had an understanding that we would discuss opening our relationship if the right person/people came along.

Well, the right person did come along, and he is sincere, considerate, loving, and sexy! The sex is incredible, but our relationship is rich in many other ways.

I know people in long-term relationships who are free to have separate sexual encounters, but I have never seen another relationship in which a couple opens their relationship to include another person. I wish I could talk about this with someone who understands or has been in a similar situation. What is your experience with group sex? In particular, have you any experience with ongoing, committed relationships involving three or more people?

PMM

Hey, PMM:

My experience with group sex is limited: the occasional three-way, and one out-of-hand 30th birthday party. As all of my "ongoing, committed relationships" have been one-at-a-time affairs, I don't have any blazing, personal insights to share with you on this subject. Besides, what you and the boys are up to, PMM, isn't really "group sex," but *polyfidelity*—a loving, sexual, committed relationship involving three or more people.

Dr. Deborah M. Anapol is the author of *Love Without Limits*, a self-helpish book which makes the case for polyfidelity, and "responsible non-monogamy." Here's what she had to say about your situation:

"She is not alone," said the doc, when I read her your letter. "Contrary to popular opinion, many people are having long-term, committed, multi-partner relationships. To do so successfully, I recommend getting in touch with others who are exploring this territory. From her attitude about it, it sounds like she's on the right track." While many people, including me, would describe your relationship as a polyfidelity, Deborah prefers the term *polyamory*, "which means many loves, and includes polyfidelity as well as open marriages and intimate networks."

What's the difference between polyamory and swinging? In swinging, people are usually interested in having sex first and maybe becoming friends later. "In polyamory, it's more likely that people want to become friends first and become lovers later. The emphasis is on the relationship, not on sex."

Hey, Faggot:

My girlfriend often gives me head, but she won't let me return the favor. I've tried repeatedly to go down on her, but she always cringes and turns her vittles away from me. When I ask why, she just answers, "Why would any man want to put his mouth where I pee?" I don't want to find another woman for this, but sometimes I can't even enjoy sex with her because I know my lips will never go below her navel. For me, there is nothing quite like the aroma and taste of real pussy juice. Is there anything I can do to gradually make her succumb to me?

Thirsty

Hey, Thirsty:

You pee with the dick she puts in her mouth, right? Confront her about this bizarre double standard. "Honey, I wanna put my mouth where you pee, for the exact same reasons you wanna put your mouth where I pee. S'fun."

I'm guessing—hoping!—she already knows men pee with their dicks, and she's simply blurting out, "Why would any man want to put his mouth where I pee?" because what's really going on in her head is more complicated and harder to articulate. It probably goes like this: "I was taught by (a) my mother (b) nuns (c) feminine hygiene product commercials that women's genitals are dirty and unattractive, and that they should be scrubbed with Brillo pads, flushed with noxious chemicals, and stuffed with sterile paper products. Since I believe my twat is filthy and putrid, how can I allow you, the man I love, to push your face into it?"

It's a hang-up. Your mission is to undo the damage done to your girlfriend in her formative years. You must convince her to love her twat in all its flowering, flushed, flowing beauty. Talk to her about eating pussy, why you love it, and what you love about her pussy in particular. Lick your sticky fingers and wax eloquent about how delicious her juices are and how sublime it would be to enjoy them right from the source. Hang-ups of this sort can be overcome by a determined partner. Good lick.

Hey, Faggot:

I'm a married woman who has been having a fling with a married man for three years now. I have a modern husband who doesn't mind if I have recreational sex. My lover's wife, however, would have a total coronary and divorce him pronto if she found out. Here's the problem: I blow him when we're together, and he gets me off manually. I can't get him to go any further. There's always some reason why we can't go to a hotel for fun and games, mostly time issues and the wife expecting him home. Why can't I get more out of him? I've never heard of a guy who only wants one thing, they usually want two or three. What gives?

LD

Hey, LD:

What gives? You do—blow jobs on demand. Since I can't question him, and your mouth is full when you two get together, we can only speculate as to his major malfunction. My guess goes like this: maybe he's only interested in blow jobs because oral sex is the only thing he's not getting at home—the wife doesn't give head—so he gets it from you. Or maybe your lover doesn't consider oral sex "real" sex. Since he "only" gets blow jobs from you, he isn't "really" cheating on the wife. Or maybe oral sex in parked cars is the only thing he's interested in—plenty of guys do only want one thing. The next time you rendezvous, ask him what's up. If he won't tell you, don't blow him—you do have some leverage here. Good luck, slut.

Hey, Faggot:

I'm a 26-year-old mostly het female. My boyfriend and I have been together for almost four years and lived together for most of that. Although we are very different from each other, we are definitely in love, and we have a sweet, caring relationship.

When we met, we were both extremely inexperienced sexually—he because he's quite shy, and me because I'm quite unattractive and few men were ever interested in me physically. Our sexual relationship started out fine—we both learned a lot together, and we were comfortable with each other. However, over the years his curiosity, drive and passion have decreased and mine have blossomed. We are now having serious problems.

I want to have a lot more sex. I want to try many, many things that we haven't tried—position, techniques, anal sex, a threesome, fantasies . . . I am finally, after way too many years of repression and low self-esteem, ready to let myself go sexually. My boyfriend absolutely is not into this. He isn't interested in trying anything. He doesn't even initiate sex anymore—it's all up to me. He has never performed oral sex on me, and I feel like a reject if I beg him to. He has no explanation for why he is uncomfortable and unwilling to expand our sexual relationship; he says he loves me, but he can't make himself change.

I am left feeling so hopeless and rejected. I am a full-grown adult now, finally at a stage where I can do what I want to sexually, and now I feel denied the pleasures that I could be experiencing. I don't want to leave my boyfriend, but I feel like I'm doing something bad and wrong when he doesn't share my desire. I feel like I must absolutely turn him off. I am trying so hard to get over my self-hatred, but I'm filled with it in this situation—I'm feeling so insecure. I've thought about calling the personal ads, but I'm afraid that due to my unattractiveness I'd be rejected there too, and more rejection would just be too much. I don't know where to go with this anymore.

Trying to Get What I Need

Hey, TTGWIN:

Because you are—by your own admission—physically unattractive, you probably fear losing this boyfriend. How would you find another? But wouldn't you feel better, more in control, trying to find someone else—someone with whom you might have a more satisfying sexual relationship—even if it meant being single for a while?

You say your relationship is loving, but he must be aware of how miserable his reluctance to experiment and his refusal to initiate sex are making you. His indifference to your pain doesn't sound "sweet" or "caring" to me. He's making you miserable and making the relationship intolerably painful for you. And why? Because he's shy? Or maybe because he wants out and doesn't have the guts to end it himself. So he's just going to keep making your life hell until you end it. So end it.

Try the personals. Take out an ad and be up-front about your looks, your desires and your strengths. Hopefully, a guy with similar desires and strengths will answer your ad, maybe a guy who also feels unattractive physically and, like you, fears rejection because of his looks. And feel free to shop around before you break it off with your current boyfriend. If your lover cuts you off sexually, you have every right to look for it elsewhere. If you're really afraid of being alone, don't dump him until you've found someone else.

Hey, Faggot:

My husband was a segregationist: there was plenty of affection during sex, but when it came to sleeping, there was his side of the bed and my side of the bed and never the twain shall meet. I wanted to cuddle as we drifted off to sleep and as we woke up—he wanted to be left alone. Why share a bed with someone if they have that attitude?

Well, I solved the problem, and I would like to use your column to advise others who have the same problem. One night, I went to bed naked. Without saying anything, he cuddled up to me. It has worked like a charm ever since.

Content Barbara

Hey, CB:

Excuse me, but did you mail this letter to me accidentally? Are you sure you didn't mean to send this to Ann Landers? Or her sister? It reads like the soft-core sex tips that pass for "naughty" in Ann and Abby's very fine advice columns.

But in case you did mean to send it to me—me! butt-fucking, SM, watersports, rimming, fisting, me!—here's my take: Your "solution," while cute and cozy, won't necessarily work for all couples with the same problem. Take me and my boyfriend: he likes to cuddle, and I can't sleep with him pressed up against me. He's one of those people who heat up like a furnace when he's asleep, yet he complains he's "cold," wants the windows shut, and the heat cranked up, and sleeps under two—count 'em, two—down comforters. I like to sleep under a sheet. If he "snuggles" me, bringing his comforters and his surface-temperature-of-the-sun self over to my side of the bed, I can't sleep. Now, Barbara, your solution—my boyfriend crawling into bed naked and tempting me over to his side of the bed—isn't going to do him any good, as he'd still be a furnace, and I won't get any sleep.

And anyway, we already sleep naked. But thanks for sharing.

Hey, Faggot:

I have a boyfriend of several years and I love him more than anything. But aside from one or two fumbling attempts in early youth, he's been my only sexual partner in my twenty-something years. The sex isn't bad, and the relationship is wonderful, but I don't want to have any regrets or doubts down the road. How can I tell a hypersensitive, insecure man that I'd like to put a perfect relationship on hiatus so I can fuck other guys?

Penny

Hey, P:

Don't tell him—lie to him. Break up with him, but don't tell him the real reason. Make something up; fear of intimacy, early-onset midlife crisis, alien abduction, whatever. While you're "single," get out there and fuck other guys. Hopefully, he'll be too wrecked from having been dumped for no good reason to date anyone else. When you're ready to get back together—after you've had your fill—hopefully he'll still be unattached. Tell him how much you've missed him, how foolish you were for throwing away what you two had, and beg him to take you back. Of course, he may not want you back at that point, but that's the risk "I need to get out and sow my wild oats" types run: not everyone, not even "wonderful" guys, are willing to wait.

Hey, Faggot:

My boyfriend and I—he's 33, I'm 41—have been in a steady open relationship for two years. We have spoken about sharing partners; only once we did. Also, we spoke about doing our own thing—him seeing other women, me seeing other men or women (I'm bi). Until recently, nothing had transpired on either side.

Last week, he answered a personal ad and seemed to hit it off with "her." Keep in mind, this is the man that takes me to fine restaurants, buys me clothes and gifts, helps me financially, amongst other things. He told me about her, but won't tell her about me. Do you think he's living up to the meaning of "open relationship"?

Unsigned

Hey, U:

If he's failed to mention your existence to the girl he's seeing on the side, your boyfriend is not "living up to the meaning of open relationships." Open relationships require honesty—with all the involved parties. Without honesty, open relationships are just so much fucking around. In your case, he's not cheating on you, he's cheating on his new "girlfriend." She may find out about you, and it could get ugly. Or . . . have you considered the possibility that he might be shopping around? Maybe he's reluctant to tell the other woman about you because you're not going to be in the picture much longer. In the meantime, enjoy the chow, chachka, and chump change.

Hey, Faggot:

Is beating off while watching naked women dancing a normal expression of sexuality? I recently found out my boyfriend is an occasional/regular customer at one of those women-behind-glass strip places. I am anxiety-ridden. Am I just naive, or should I be concerned?

Panicky

Hey, P:

Nearly all men masturbate—as do most women—and most of us require a little visual stimulation when we masturbate: videos, dirty magazines, dancers in peep shows. If his visits to the peep clubs aren't disrupting his life, distracting him from your relationship, or depleting your joint checking account, then there isn't anything to be concerned about. If it creeps you out, if you can't stand the idea of him going to peep shows, you can go ballistic, demand he stop, and threaten to break up with him if he doesn't. He'll promise to stop; but he won't stop—he'll just do a better job of hiding it from you.

No one person can be all things sexually to another person; pretending we can be, or should be, places unnecessary strain on our relationships. Our lovers have fantasies that do not involve us, have had experiences that did not involve us, and may from time to time have experiences that do not involve us. What we should seek in a committed erotic relationship is primacy in another person's erotic life, not exclusivity ("don't look at anybody else, don't think about anybody else, don't touch anybody else"). Complete and total exclusivity is unrealistic: the body can be monogamous, but the mind cannot. When we try to restrain our lovers' imaginations—when we attempt to police their fantasies—we become an obstacle, something that stands between them and their inner erotic life. An obstacle is resented, and nothing kills sexual passion faster than resentment. Give him permission, within reason, to have his fun, and he'll love you for it. Withhold permission and he'll resent you.

Hey, Faggot:

I am a former slut, currently involved in a monogamous relationship. But one can't burn the candle at both ends forever. Besides, I was curious to find out what the "joys and rewards" of monogamy were all about. So I found myself a beautiful new lover, with whom I have common interests in and out of bed.

My problems, however, are the "shards of past relations splintering my skin." I just can't seem to get the sights, sounds, or smells out of my head! Sometimes I just go with it and enjoy my memories, but my new lover can sense when something else has been on my mind. I have no fear of cheating during my current relationship, I know I can survive. My question to you and your readers is, how do you cope with the memories? And when you do have one of those jaunts down memory lane and your lover catches you with a look in your eye, are you obliged to tell them the truth, or do you make up some story about the fantastic lunch you had earlier in the day?

Bursting at the Seams

Hey, BATS:

With the exception of Moonies and Mormons, very few of us marry blank slates—everyone has a past, and memories can't be wiped away. But no one wants to listen to a current squeeze go on about the kissing/blow job/cunnilingus/knot-tying skills of an ex. Honesty is not always the best policy; sometimes a little deceit is the courteous thing to do. Make up something about lunch.

Hey, Faggot:

I have been living with my boyfriend now for two years, we have known each other for seven years, but since we started living together things have escalated from serious to very serious. I love him, this is for sure. He is wonderful, honest, kind, and all that. This guy does not have a mean bone in his body. I even had an affair recently, told him, and he forgave me.

The problem? I must be one of those people who has a constant wandering eye, and right now I think I am in love/lust with another man. It's occurred to me recently that if it isn't one love interest on the side, it's another. I don't want to lose my lover, but I know being honest would finish us off this time around, so what am I to do about this other guy? I guess there is a simple solution—confess and move on, but all I want is just to have sex with this other guy. Besides lying or telling the truth or talking about opening our bedroom, which my boyfriend has already objected to, what should I do?

On Fire

Hey, OF:

My mother was visiting when your letter came, so I showed it to her. "I think you should be monogamous," said Mom. "I think everyone should be monogamous." Why? "I just don't think we were meant to be promiscuous." Why? "I don't know. You should find someone you like and settle down with that person." Why? "Because that's what mothers want their kids to do, that's why. It brings order to the world. Stability. So, in my opinion, you shouldn't act on your feelings for this man who is not your boyfriend. Not all decisions should be based on how you feel."

As for your lover, Mom said, "He sounds too forgiving. Forgiveness is important, I'm a forgiveness fan, but it sounds like he's being a doormat. If monogamy is important to him, and you can't control yourself, maybe you two aren't a match."

Hey Faggot,

I'm a breeder chick newlywed and I am very happy with my marriage. So here's my problem: for the last five years I have had a crush on a guy at work (and I mean big-time-wanna-fuck-his-brains-out crush!). I never pursued it because I knew he was married, though I knew he knew I liked him.

Now, since he found out I got married, he has started pursuing me! This is a huge mind-fuck. I know what I should do and I know what I want to do and they are not the same thing. There is nothing lacking in my marriage, but this baggage of lust is consuming me. Help!

No Name

Hey, NN:

While you were single, he didn't want to fuck around with you for fear of messing up his marriage. Now that you're married, he's thinking it's safe to mess around—you'd both be coming from the same place, you both have partners and would, hopefully, go into the affair fully cognizant of its limitations.

So, what to do? Be direct: ask him why he's suddenly so flirtatious. If he proposes a wild affair, look deep inside and ask yourself this question: "When I'm 80, will I look back and wish I'd banged this guy's brains out?" If the answer is "yes," go fer it.

Hey, Faggot:

I'm here today to chastise you for your hasty advice to the breeder female newlywed with the redhots for a married guy in her office.

Over the course of 17 years with one guy, I have faced Newlywed's Dilemma several excruciating times. Here are my words of wisdom: There is nothing in the world that approximates the voyage of discovery that is a long-term, committed relationship. The story you write together is an ongoing act of creation that will give back to you many times what you put into it. In my experience, an outside love puts a serious monkey wrench into this process. In my heart, anyway, there simply isn't room for both committed marriage and that other guy I just gotta have.

The question is not will she kick herself when she's eighty for not having fucked this guy's brains out (she may), but will she kick herself harder for having blown the chance at the slow miracle that True Love offers.

Been There, Here's Better

Hey, BTHB:

Huh? Oh, excuse me. I must have dozed off for a minute. Could you repeat the question?

Hey, Faggot:

I'm sorry you dozed off during Been There, Here's Better's letter. She made some good points: marriage takes commitment and it can be worth it.

I'm sure you're way too hip to appreciate these sentiments, but let's examine what marriage is about. People expect monogamy and honesty when they marry. If someone wants to screw around and it's fine with their partner, then great. But how often does that happen? Isn't it much more likely that affairs will either have to be hidden (honesty suffers) or brought into the marriage, where they're usually about as welcome as a live grenade?

Marriage isn't easy, and it's probably not for everyone. But it can be great, and shouldn't be yawned off.

Seeing It Differently Now

Hey, SIDN:

When it comes to straight people waxing poetic about marriage, my pain threshold is pretty low. When two straight people get married, they not only "commit" to each other, society commits to them. Fuck "the sanctity of marriage," what you're really getting is a heap of social and financial benefits—tax breaks, health insurance, inheritance rights, social security, rights of survivorship, the right to make decisions about your partner's estate and other legal stuff, all of which is denied queer couples.

Marriage is about rights, not about monogamy. Thousands and thousands of couples, straight and queer, prove every day you don't have to be monogamous to be married or married to be monogamous. But whenever the subject of queer marriage rights comes up, even on-our-side straights head for the hills. Why are so many straights threatened by the idea of allowing queers to marry? Why is recognizing gay and lesbian relationships for what they are—the moral equivalent of heterosexual relationships—such a stumbling block for so many straight people?

Hey, Faggot:

Why! Why! Why! "Why are so many straights threatened by the idea of allowing queers to marry?" "Why is recognizing gay and lesbian relationships for what they are . . ." I could almost hear the deeply-nasal-toned whining "why" as if you didn't have the slightest clue why the world will never accept male homosexuality, ever. You can march, walk, parade, and get as "in your face" as you want and it will never be accepted.

Here's why: The world cannot put that stamp of approval on your choice because of the anal intercourse thing. There is just something so absolutely disgusting about putting one's penis up an area where there are bacterial feces, and I don't care how much you guys scrub and clean back there. This is absolutely unhealthy, whether you are the recipient—the anal canal was not built or meant to be pummeled, thrusted into—or whether you are the one inserting. Even if there were no such thing as HIV, it would be unhealthy. Even if you use condoms, it is still unhealthy for the recipient, whose anal passage is bruised and mauled.

Now if every homosexual stood up and said "We no longer condone or practice anal intercourse . . ." then that would be another matter. Then the world would have very little to say regarding matters of two men loving and perhaps even marrying one another. If people knew that homosexual men had given up the anal thing completely, then I do believe people would come round and accept that choice.

But let's face it. That is just not going to happen. The male human needs to feel the sensation of penetration. Without that, men just wouldn't be fully men. So, "queers" are in a real double bind here, one I'm afraid they will never be able to extricate themselves from, unless of course they as a group publicly and privately renounced anal intercourse. Love between men and sexual love between men is not wrong. Anal intercourse is.

Now that this letter has given you a serious reality-check, I dare you to publish it. You can't, you won't.

P.R.

Hey, P.R.

Look, you bigot motherfucker, I don't know where you've done your butt-fucking research, but the last 10,000 or so times I've had anal sex, no one went away "bruised and mauled." Properly done—plenty of lube, condoms, and consideration—anal sex, whether homo or hetero, is as good for you as any other kind of sex. Conduct a little research on the subject—go fuck yourself—and then we'll talk.

As for your novel suggestion that gay men renounce anal sex, suppose every fag in the United States promised to give up anal sex tomorrow. Then will we be deserving of the same rights and privileges as straight people? Or will there suddenly be something else we have to swear off—drag, cock rings, men's choruses, camp—because it makes insecure straight people uncomfortable? And if we were to swear off anal sex, wouldn't verifying our compliance be a bother? What are you going to do, stuff motion-sensor alarms up all our butts? And what about dykes—what's your justification for discriminating against lesbians? Women's Music? Cats? Ellen? And what about straight people who have anal sex?

If two men want to fuck each other in the butt, armpits, mouth, or eye sockets, it's nobody's business but theirs. Your disgust with what you imagine gay men to be doing in bed— not all gay men have anal sex, you know—is poor cover for your small-minded bigotry. Anal sex isn't what stands between queers and full civil rights, people like you do.

Hey, Faggot:

I am a 23-year-old gay male. Recently, I broke up with my boyfriend because it was obvious he didn't want to be monogamous. We were both attractive, intelligent, and very much in love, but fidelity issues and mistrust drove us apart. Even when he agreed to be monogamous, he was collecting phone numbers, flirting in bars, and driving me crazy with suspicion. I became psychologically abusive and cold out of sheer frustration.

After we parted my world fell apart. The time I had spent with him has become painfully torturous alone. Every object reminds me of him, and I cry daily over the one person whom I loved, trusted, and lost.

Am I unrealistic to expect monogamy? Should I have compromised a little? Books I have read on male couples purport that roughly 5 percent stay monogamous. Was I expecting too much? How can I get over this paralyzing depression and the love I still feel for him? Is there a support group out there? I would like to hear from men who have experienced this and/or believe in monogamy.

Struggling to Mend a Broken Heart

Hey, Struggling:

You two weren't a match. Your slightly unrealistic need for absolute fidelity and his need for lotsa sex partners—or, if he wasn't cheating on you, his need to leave a bar with a dozen phone numbers in his pocket—doomed this relationship from the get-go. It doesn't sound like you were getting much out of this relationship, besides an ulcer, so it needed to end—not because he "failed" monogamy, but because you two weren't meant for each other.

Were you being unrealistic by expecting monogamy? Yeah, I'd say so. Gay men excel at all sorts of things, but monogamy ain't one of them. On the other hand, expecting consideration and respect from your partner is not unrealistic. If he agreed to be true to you and only you, and kept collecting phone numbers and behaving as if he were single, then you had every right to be upset. Your anger, your frustration, and your suspiciousness were born of his deceit, not his inability to be monogamous.

Hey, Faggot:

I am in some serious trouble here! I have a really wonderful girlfriend and I'm very much in love with her. We're also best friends and get along great. The only problem is sex. I know, who doesn't have problems with sex? But mine is a sad, sad case. She has a most elevated sex drive and mine plummets into reverse. I find her very attractive, and get turned on just thinking about her, but every time she wants to make love to me, I'm either too tired from work, or just not in the mood.

We've talked about it before, and she never gets mad or frustrated with me. I don't know what to do. I want to make her happy and satisfy her—I really just want to fuck. My mind says, "Yes, yes, yes!" but my body tells me to go to hell. I desperately need some advice or hints to get my drive in gear!

Hangin' in Neutral

Hey, HIN:

Every time she wants to fuck, you're too tired or not in the mood? *Every time?* And she never gets mad or frustrated. Hm. Well, she's either cheating on you, has a great relationship with her vibrator, or is some sort of latter-day saint.

But you know what I really think is up? She may not be communicating any frustration with your lack-o-libido, but she's frustrated. Why isn't she letting on? Who knows? Maybe, stupidly, she wants to spare your feelings, hoping this dry spell will end sooner or later; or maybe she's hoping you'll lose that high-pressure job, leaving you with more time and energy.

But you need to see to those needs now, and get your ass (and cock, and tongue, and fingers, and brain) in gear. If she's bottling it up—as I suspect she is—she's not going to say anything until her "frustrations" are balls-out, relationship-busting "resentments." The first you hear of her dissatisfaction may be the day she announces she's found someone who can attend to her needs.

Too tired? Fuck in the morning. Work less. Not in the mood? Play along for a few minutes and you'll find yourself getting into the mood. If there's some other reason you're "not interested"— you don't find her sexually attractive, you're a fag, you're secretly into fat chicks and she weighs 95 pounds—don't be cruel and drag this out. Do her a favor and dump her.

Hey, Faggot:

I am a 24-year-old female and my husband is a 37-year-old male. I have a very serious problem when it comes to our sex life. My husband doesn't give me any foreplay or oral sex no matter how much I ask for it. I put it to him very nicely—how much I would like for him to do it—but it just don't get done: his knees always hurt, or he has a backache. Backache or not, he likes for me to do him. Lately I've been thinking of seeking comfort from someone a little younger.

Could you give me some clever rude advice on how to ask him in a shitty-ass way to give me some head?

Backed Up

P.S. I haven't had an orgasm in three years.

Hey, BU:

Here's a snappy, smart-ass line that might do the trick: "Eat my pussy or I'll break your legs." If that doesn't work, try this one: "Honey, you're going to eat my pussy or I'm going to divorce your sorry ass." Or the next time he wants some head, say: "Does my baby-lamb want a blow job? Well fuck off, you selfish bastard. Do you know it's been three fucking years since I had an orgasm?! Suck your own god-damned dick, you self-centered motherfucker!"

As for steppin' out on him: sure thing, go for it. Your husband sounds like the type who'd rather be cheated on than pestered for sex. Find yourself a hot number around your own age with a tongue that won't quit. Then take out a large life insurance policy on the box of rocks you married, encourage him to take up drinking and driving, and keep your fingers crossed.

Hey, Faggot:

My husband of almost six years digs gay and lesbian bondage porn. The problems that I'm having are (a) he thinks it's his secret, (b) he's lousy at hiding the material, (c) I'm feeling neglected.

We have a young child, which means you can't leave this type of material lying around. And I'm more than a little miffed that he uses his limited sexual energy on himself when I'm here expressing my desire and willingness to add some kink to our life. We have a box of toys that we employ once in a while, and only when I bring it up; but he has his own toys that he thinks are hidden (in his clothes, but guess who puts away his shirts?).

He refuses to discuss the matter, which makes me wonder if this is just embarrassment, or if he thinks this makes him gay (does it?). I'm trying to give the guy the benefit of the doubt, but I'd like him to be more careful with this stuff (toddler curiosity knows no bounds), and maybe think of me to satisfy his kinkier desires once in a while. I feel like the kid who doesn't get asked to be on the team.

Confused

Hey, C:

If your husband were gay, he wouldn't be looking at lesbian bondage porn. It's just as likely that he's a straight guy who happens to be turned on by queer bondage porn—it happens. I know a few kinky straight men who prefer gay bondage porn to straight bondage porn, because the actual bondage—the "rope work," the equipment—is better in gay bondage porn.

He has to discuss this with you. Insist, and if he resists, make his life hell until he gives in: throw away his mags, hide his toys. If you want to drag him off to a shrink for some couples counseling, go to one who works with sexuality issues from a kink-positive perspective: it's not his kink that's the problem, it's that he's being such a freak about it.

Here's what I think you're likely to discover if and when he opens up: while he enjoys sex with you, his bondage fantasies involve strangers. A lot of bondage fans find playing with someone they have a love/marriage relationship with much less exciting than playing with someone they can relate to on a strictly fantasy level. If that's his major malfunction, you'll either have to accept that he has a fantasy life that you are only marginally a part of, and find a place in your home for him to safely store his mags and toys; or you can involve yourself in his fantasy life by having no-intercourse three-ways with bondage freaks he meets through SM clubs or personal ads. Then you'll be on the team.

Hey, Faggot:

Last year my husband had an affair with a 20-year-old bisexual who knew he was married. Everyone knew—friends and family—and no one told me. I feel betrayed on so many levels, it's hard to describe. And in the end, I most hate that bitch. She did the worst, by sleeping with a married man. I want vengeance. Should I deny myself?

A

Hey, A:

No person, not even a bisexual person, can sleep with a married man who won't cheat on his wife. Lady, it is not up to the rest of the world to refrain from having sex with your husband; it's up to your husband to refrain from having sex with the rest of the world, especially if his partner—you—values monogamy, commitment, exclusivity, and the rest of those relationship-exploding land mines. Your anger is misplaced. He cheated on you, she didn't. Avenge yourself on him, not her.

Hey, Faggot:

My boyfriend hit me and I don't know what to do about it.

We've been together three and a half years, and he never hit me before.

We were arguing, I was standing behind him—yelling—and he spun on his heel and slapped me. Until that moment I never believed he was capable of hitting me. After the slap, I just sort of stood there, speechless. He hit me *hard*—the inside of my cheek ripped on my teeth.

We hadn't been drinking; the argument was fierce, but no more than arguments we've had in the past. He apologized for hours, and seems genuinely contrite and as upset about the whole situation as I am.

Should I break up with him? I drive around town with a "You Can't Beat a Woman" bumper sticker on my car, I take self-defense classes, and—how's this for ironic?—both of my sisters work in battered women's shelters. I don't want to break up with him, but I feel like I ought to—every time I look at my car I feel like a world-class hypocrite—which is making me feel guilty. I know about patterns and cycles of abuse, and "abuser" profiles—and nothing about him or our relationship falls into those categories. As far as he knows, we're "on hold" while I sort this out. What do I do?

LH

Hey, LH:

My first impulse is to tell you to leave him. If women dumped men who hit the first time it happened, think of the lives that would be saved. So the answer seems obvious: Leave him. But, you know, I've never been hit, and have never had to make the decision you're facing. Choices that look black-and-white from the outside are often a lot grayer when you're on the inside.

You don't give me much information about him, the way he fights, or what he's like when he's angry. You say he doesn't fit "the profile of an abuser," whatever that means (he didn't win the Heisman Trophy?), and that his conduct was "out of character." But if he's the type who can't be reasoned with when angry, engages in emotional blackmail, or becomes "a different person" when he's upset, he will hit you again. If he's these things, leave him.

You need to talk to somebody about this; letters to sex advice columns are not strong enough medicine. If you can't bring yourself to tell your sisters about it, tell a friend—hell, tell them all. Abusers, should your boyfriend turn out to be one, depend on their victim's isolation and dependence, so be neither isolated nor dependent. If he's embarrassed that you didn't keep his secret, well, good.

If after discussing this with your friends, you decide to take him back, exact a price: counseling, therapy—he may not fit the profile of an "abuser," but he did abuse you. Make him understand that there will be no third chance. If he ever hits you again, you will turn on your heel, walk out the door, and never see him or speak to him again. And you will go straight to the police and file assault charges.

Hey, Faggot:

I think you missed a beat (no pun intended) in your advice to LH, who was smacked by her boyfriend. She says that she was standing behind her boyfriend, yelling at him, when he turned around and hit her. She doesn't say what she was yelling.

What the fuck does the out-of-control bitch expect? That she can scream and not expect repercussions? Any man screaming at another man would expect a violent reaction. What makes her think that she should be treated differently?

You should have told her to learn how to control her rage. Otherwise she can expect to keep getting socked in the face by men and women alike.

BI

Hey, BI:

Excuse me, but a little screaming and yelling, like crying, is healthy and good for a relationship—get it out, and like that. But "socking" your partner is never healthy, never good, never kosher. Physical abuse is not an appropriate response to verbal abuse, and in no way is a sock in the jaw the moral equivalent of a raised voice.

What would an appropriate response have been? Her boyfriend could've screamed right back at her; he could have stormed out; slammed a door in her face; stayed out all night and had sex with some floozy. But hit her? No.

Hey, Faggot:

I appreciate your measured approach to advising LH regarding her assault by a boyfriend, but I want to encourage LH to split the scene ASAP.

As an attorney working in divorce and anti-harassment protection, I see violence from an odd perspective. I am usually involved in protecting a client's rights after the violence has worn a path through the relationship. I am writing to offer this bottom-line perspective: LH will be assaulted again by her boyfriend. It's just a matter of time.

I know that sounds jaded and hopeless, but the contrary is true. I have hope that victims of violence will find a relationship with a boyfriend/girlfriend who is not violent. Get out of a relationship where you have been treated violently. *No matter what.*

I am not saying your measured approach was bad advice. I am saying that your first impulse to tell LH to "leave his sorry ass" was better advice.

BW

Hey, Faggot:

I am a 21-year-old inexperienced female. I am presently in love and in a relationship—very serious—with a man from the Mideast. He's asked me to marry him. I haven't had much experience with men, but he has committed to me in heart, mind, and soul. In fact so much that I think he's obsessive.

He calls me at work five times a day, every day and on the weekends even more. We don't live together, and he says he calls so much because he misses me. But he's done some scary things: he threatened to kill me if I leave him. I tried to leave him once, and he made a huge scene and exploded, grabbing me and forcing me into his car and back to his home, where he forced me to have sex. He says it's my destiny to be with him: Allah says so. I told one friend what was going on, and she said that's just how Middle Eastern men are with their women.

I'm afraid he'll try to kill me if we do ever break up. He says he couldn't stand to see me with someone else. I don't have anyone I can talk to about this, so I thought I'd write. What do you think about this situation?

NEF

Hey, NEF:

My opinion: You're not in a serious relationship, you're in serious trouble. If you stay with this guy, you are going to get hurt. Your boyfriend's behavior has nothing to do with love, the Mideast, or what Allah thinks your destiny might be; it has everything to do with his being an abusive, violent, controlling asshole.

For a second opinion, I shared your letter with Lois Loontjens, the Executive Director of New Beginnings, a crisis shelter for women in the Pacific Northwest. "I think that she is in great danger, and is correct to think he may try to kill her if she leaves him," Loontjens said. "If you look at murders in general, the number of women murdered by their intimate partners is simply staggering."

Let's have a gander at those numbers, shall we? According to the U.S. Department of Justice's Violence Against Women Office, 30 percent of all female homicide victims are murdered by their husbands, ex-husbands, or boyfriends (only 3 percent of male homicide victims are murdered by their wives, ex-wives, or girlfriends); 26 percent of all rapes and sexual assaults directed against women are committed by men they're married to or dating; and husbands, exes, and boyfriends commit more than a million violent acts directed against women they're involved with every year.

So, should you, um, like—duh—leave this guy? "I would not give someone that kind of direct advice," Loontjens said. "She's only asking what we think about this situation. I would say this situation scares me." Okay, the situation scares me too. So if you do decide to get out of this scary situation, what's the best way to do it? "She will need to commit to leaving whole-heartedly. If she tries to leave and fails, she will get hurt. So it's not okay to try, you have to accomplish it. When she leaves, the danger will escalate—he is not going to be happy about losing control of her.

"When she leaves him, she will need to become invisible in an instant kind of way. If he has access to her at her workplace, she is going to need to get the 100 percent support of her employer. But she [might] have to give up her job. She's certainly going to need to give up her apartment, or wherever it is that she lives, since he has access to her there." He's the jerk, why should you have to give up your job and home? "The reality here is that he has already assaulted her, kidnapped her, raped her, and threatened to kill her, and none of that is fair either. What's fair isn't the issue, getting out of this situation alive and safe and healthy is the issue."

If you're unwilling to give up your job and leave your home, you can go to the police, get a restraining order, hire a body-guard, or purchase a shiny new AK-47. But you gotta leave: if you stay with this guy, you are going to get hurt, things will escalate. He might try and harm you if you leave him, but he will definitely harm you if you stay. So go. Once you're out, how can you avoid getting into the same situation again? "Women can learn to recognize the signs early on," Loontjens told me. "He tries to keep you from your friends. When some-one doesn't seem to have a life, other than you, that's a sign. When someone calls you constantly, or keeps calling after he's been rebuffed, that's a sign. Not a sign that there's some-thing wonderful and irresistible about you, but that there's something seriously wrong with him."

Finally, as for this guy being from the Mideast, Loontjens said, "Your boyfriend's behavior has nothing to do with where he's from." In case you—or the idiot who told you that abusive is "just how Middle Eastern men are"—doubt Loontjens on this point, I gave my sister, Laura, a call.

Laura's been dating a wonderful Arab guy for two years now. Has Samir ever abused her and blamed it on Allah? "Oh, my God, no! He treats me like a queen, but not in an obsessive way, he respects me and treats me like an equal." (Which would make him a queen too, I guess.) Has she noticed any cul-tural differences dating an Arab guy? "You do hear, 'Oh, Arab men like to control their women.' Some of them are like that, but some of every kind of men are like that. It's insulting for her friend to say this guy behaves this way because he's an 'Arab': an insult to my boyfriend who's an Arab and doesn't act this way. It's like saying all Irish guys are lazy drunken bums."

Hey, Faggot:

I've been in love with the same lady for five years. We fell in love the moment we met. We've always had great sex, never had any problems. We fit together like gloves. Everybody remarks on what a great couple we make. She is now reaching her 30s, and I am reaching my mid-30s.

The problem? I want to get married, but she still wants to "chase the dream." Recently she moved out west as a "temporary" career move. She told me she was "thinking" about marriage but still wanted to live the "jet set" life for a little while longer—I burnt out on that scene long ago. However, I'm not a stick-in-the-mud. I can still rock. We talk on the phone every other day or so, and she sounds like she misses me. Am I fooling myself? Should I be looking for someone who has found what she wants from life and is happy with it, or should I wait this one out? I was burnt once before in a similar situation. I don't want to be burnt again.

Don't Wanna Be Nobody's Fool

Hey, DWBNF:

She's hedging her bets. She's keeping you on hold while she sorts out whether marriage, and everything that comes along with it—like you—is what she wants. Call her and tell her you support her explorations, and you honestly believe she should chase that dream, jet those sets, blah, blah, blah, so that when she decides to settle down, she'll feel good about the decision and won't spend the rest of her life with you wondering what might have been.

Then tell her that while she's out there chasing down dreams you need to break it off. Say, "We can stay in touch, but someone might come along who wants the things I want, and wants them now. But if I'm still in a committed-but-on-hiatus relationship when that someone comes along, my dream might pass me by." Then add, "If I'm still free when you decide to settle down, I'm all yours."

Are you pressuring her? Yeah, a bit. But so what? She can't have it completely her way. If she doesn't want what you want—if she doesn't want you—she needs to cut you loose.

Hey, Faggot:

My boyfriend and I have been dating for five and a half years. The whole time it's been long-distance. He will finally be graduating from college this year, and at last we have the chance to be together. However, he wants to move to L.A. to pursue his dream of being an actor. I hate L.A., and I don't want to move there. Besides, I moved to Chicago six months ago, and I like it. Should I be offended that he doesn't want to move to Chicago and be with me? I mean, he certainly could pursue an acting career here. Or should I move to L.A.? Maybe I should forget the whole thing and put a personal ad in the *Reader.* Please give me some advice I can live with. ·

Distantly in Love

Hey, DIL:

There's no winning this one. His position is, "If you really loved me, you'd move to L.A." And your position is, "If you really loved me, you'd move to Chicago." Under most circumstances, I would declare this one a draw and order you two to break up.

But in your case, I'm going to advise you to move to L.A. First of all, you've only been in Chicago for six months. It's not like he's asking you to pull up deep roots and move to some frozen wasteland and marry him there. And, come on: if he really wants to make a living as an actor, he does need to move to L.A. Acting in Chicago has its rewards, none of them financial.

And here's another good reason to move to L.A.: odds are good that once you get to L.A. this relationship will fall apart pretty quickly, as so many long-term, long-distance relationships do once the partners finally "have the chance to be together." When it does fall apart, you can move back to Chicago, take out personal ads, and find yourself a man with a real career. If you go with him and things do work out, once he gets rich and famous, he'll dump you regardless, become a Scientologist, and marry some piece of supermodel trash. Then you can take him for half of what he's worth (provided the Scientologists haven't beaten you to it), move back to sweet home Chicago, and buy yourself all the boyfriends you want.

Hey, Faggot:

Is frigidity reversible? I used to love sex and recently can't get into it unless high (on H) and then I love it. Unfortunately, my man can't get it up while high (we've been together for two and a half years and I really love him and his lovemaking styles). Please don't preach about drugs. I know they are bad for me. I've been working in peep shows for three years for the money. I really don't like dancing; the men repulse me and most of the women do too. I feel bad for my lover. He is very patient and loving and tries to understand. I want to fuck, but these flitting images of fat masturbating men or some chance murmur of love I've heard that day (under less than loving circumstances) leave me dry and withdrawn.

Any advice? Don't be glib. I'm truly . . .

Hurting

Hey, Hurting:

Problem: He can't get it up on H and you can't do it if you're not on H. Solution: Don't get high at the same time. You shoot up and he stays straight, and then you'll be able to fuck.

But listen, girlfriend, getting high at different times may fix your sex life, but you have larger problems. Frigidity doesn't sound like the problem; your job does. If the dancing is making you miserable, ruining your sex life, and driving you to drugs, give it up! The money may be good, but is it worth the misery? There are good reasons to do drugs and bad reasons to do drugs, just like there are good and bad reasons to drink, eat, and screw. If you're doing drugs because you have to and not because you want to, then something is wrong. Ask yourself: "Am I taking this (or drinking this, or eating this, or screwing this) for fun or because if I don't I'll go nuts?" If you're doing it for fun, okay, do it. Otherwise, make some changes.

Hey, Faggot:

Although my girlfriend and myself are not married, we are perpetual live-ins and have a very close relationship. But we're not having sex very often. For me, it's just not exciting, kinky, or adventurous enough. She is into sex, but she is more conservative and "inexperienced." We have discussed this to the point of exhaustion. I had a heavy sexual relationship with a sexual dynamo and nympho a few years back who was very comfortable with nudity and had a high sex drive. We did it all, everywhere, anytime, all the time. It was pure, raw, and aggressive. I can't get it out of my mind.

My girlfriend doesn't know that I compare and has told me to "teach" her things. I've tried, but it's got to come from the inside. The sex drive has to be a natural, innate desire. When my ex and I were together, we *never* talked about it, we just did it and it clicked. It never required thought or planning or discussion. Is this relationship doomed? Is it normal to compare girlfriends?

Kink Aficionado

Hey, KA:

It's perfectly normal to compare present loves to past loves—it's impossible not to. But whether or not it's true, it's good policy to tell your current lover that they're the best sex you've ever had. If it's true, ain't life grand. If it's not, after telling them they're the best sex you've ever had, get to work on making them the best you've ever had.

This relationship is not doomed—so long as you're willing to work on making your present girlfriend the slut your ex-girlfriend was. And the exact wrong way to accomplish this is by discussing her sexual inadequacies "to the point of exhaustion." Shut up and fuck. She's expressed an interest in being taught things—so teach. Drives may be innate, but tastes can definitely be acquired.

Hey, Faggot:

When my husband and I met we were promiscuous, drug-ingesting, late-nite fiends. Then we decided to get married, move across the country and start fresh. We are much happier living this saner lifestyle, except for one thing: my husband doesn't find me at all sexually appealing anymore. He says he loves me, thinks I'm good-looking and a great fuck, but he just can't get it up for me anymore.

When I was a tramp and we were fucked-up all the time, it was great. Now I'm suddenly the Virgin Mary, and my patience is running out. Personally, I believe sex is a very important element of a relationship. And it doesn't have to be all sweetness and cuddles—I love to get handcuffed to the bed or fucked up the ass. And, yes, he knows all of this, we've talked and talked about it.

So, what is it? Buy a yacht for some shrink? Any advice you can cram into your column would be better than the avoidance method we're practicing now.

Getting Nun

Hey, GN:

What brought you two together was your shared drug habit. Nothing wrong with that: shared interests and hobbies are important, especially in the early stages of a relationship. Trouble comes when drug abuse—which is not to be confused with controlled, responsible drug use—is all you share. When one or the other or both kick the habit, it may become apparent that not only don't you have anything in common, but that you aren't even that attracted to each other.

So, you and your young man had drugs in common. Now you ain't got nothin' in common. You could start abusing drugs again and see if that doesn't bring the spark back; or admit that this marriage was built on a lousy foundation, get a friendly divorce, and look for new partners.

Hey, Faggot:

I met a guy last year that really turned my world around. I'd never been with a man that made me feel quite so connected. But he would sometimes become moody and verbally abusive. It turns out he was abusing drugs behind my back while we were seeing each other. We "made some space," and he encouraged the creation of more space by staying on the drugs and avoiding me. I was hurt, and disappointed.

Well, we had a reunion late this year after he checked himself into a rehab clinic. It was absolutely the most incredible lovemaking I've ever known. His visit left me feeling euphoric and very confused. I feel passionately attracted to this man, but I am scared to believe it's love.

I have learned from a mutual friend of some sexual encounters he had during the time we were apart. He was high most of the time. Should I let the things he did when we were apart affect me? How should I proceed with a recovering addict? I feel like I love this guy intensely, but I'm not sure where to channel that energy.

FN

Hey, FN:

Love will not redeem this guy. His recovery has to be something he does himself, for himself. If you allow him to identify you as the reason he's kicking his various bad habits, you're asking for trouble: he may come to resent you for standing between him and his drugs; for fear of losing you, he may not be able to admit he's had a relapse, which may prevent him from getting help when he needs it down the road, which would then lead to more lies and deceit.

But, by all means, if he turns you on, go for it. Be realistic about the fact that he's damaged goods, and be on the lookout for any signs of relapse. Has he suddenly emptied your checking account? Hocked your VCR? Bad signs. Addicts can be charming and delightful and sexy and passionate, and they can also be lying deceitful fucks. But so can people who've never touched drugs, so what does that prove?

As for his tramping around on that last big bender, let him know you're aware of what a slut he was before he went into rehab. See how well he deals with that issue: How honest is he? Do you get the sense he's lying to you? How he handles telling you about his recent sexual escapades is a pretty good indication of whether you'll be able to trust him alone with your VCR.

Hey, Faggot:

I'm a 28-year-old BGF who is in love with a woman that I just adore. This woman I'm in love with had a lover. We were together for one year while she was still with her lover of four years. They aren't together anymore, but at the same time she broke up with her lover, she also stopped seeing me.

Our times together were nothing but beautiful. We shared everything together, even saying we were going to run away together, and never hurt each other. I just don't understand what went wrong. One minute we were like peas and carrots and the next thing I know she's claiming she wants to cool out, which I could understand.

But now she is dating someone else, and she doesn't hardly ever call me or see me anymore. Once upon a time, I was all good on the side, but now she doesn't want to be bothered. She says she still loves me, and misses being with me, but she never follows through when I try to make time to spend with her. I'm just an emotional wreck. I love her with all my heart, and there is nothing I wouldn't do for her. Please give me some good advice. I'm hurting.

JC

Hey, JC:

The best advice I can give you is to know when you've been dumped, and you've been dumped, girlfriend. She either didn't mean the things she said to you, or her feelings changed. Either way, she's moved on, and you should too. And you know what? Not spending time with you, not calling, behaving as if she can't be "bothered," those are the nicest things she could possibly do for you. Indulging you would only prolong your agony.

Hey, Faggot:

I am a very attractive, intelligent woman. I model and have my own business. For the past three years, I have been living with my fiancé. My problem is that my fiancé masturbates day and night, despite the fact that we have a good sex life. He does this when he thinks I'm not looking. I catch him doing it flipping through the Victoria's Secret catalog; at the computer downloading sex pages on the Net; even watching TV ("Babewatch," certain MTV videos, and those ridiculous USA movies).

When I catch him, he immediately turns his back or covers himself. I just give him "the look" and walk away. I also catch him "eyeing" attractive girls in the mall, on the street, basically wherever we go. I have begun to get a complex. Am I not pretty enough? Should I get implants (even though I've modeled for bra ads)? Does he want a blonde? What is he looking for when he has me? Most men would kill for a date with me!

I consulted my girlfriend, and she thinks he's a freak. I even asked my gynecologist if it was normal for a man to masturbate when he is in a satisfying relationship and, if so, how often and why. After my cave doctor got over the embarrassment of the question, he told me that some men prefer their own hand no matter how experienced or skilled the woman. Should I confront my fiancé, or would that make matters worse?

Second Best

Hey, SB:

There are really two problems here: his compulsive masturbation, and your unrealistic expectations.

First, his prob: he needs to see a therapist or someone who

can help him get a grip on just when and where he gets a grip on. Grown-ups don't drop trou and start pulling away whenever the mood strikes 'em (with the possible exception of the 43rd President of the United States). Jerk off in the bedroom, not the living room; under the covers, not in front of the TV (unless you live alone); bathroom doors have locks on them for all sorts of reasons—maybe he was home beating off when this info was covered in his human sexuality class in the fifth grade.

Likewise, most grown-ups know it's inconsiderate to leer at hypothetical sex partners in front of your actual sex partner(s). If you must check others out, do so subtly, whether your lover is present or not. It sounds like your intended is having a hard time distinguishing between these appropriate and inappropriate behaviors, between where he ends and you (and your feelings) begin. A shrink might be able to help him make those distinctions.

You can help him understand the seriousness of the problem, and motivate him to get his ass to a shrink, if you confront him with more than "the look" the next time you catch him beating off to *Baywatch*. You might want to try using your words. If getting caught gives him a thrill, you're going to have to figure out together how to channel his catch-me kicks into less abusive and more inclusive sexual activities.

Buy yourself a stun gun. Or some pepper spray. Whenever you catch your fiancé beating off in front of the computer or TV, blast him. It's called "aversion therapy." Even if it doesn't solve the problem, it will make "getting caught" more exciting for both of you.

On to your problem: unrealistic expectations. It is unrealistic to expect that your man, having unlimited access to your fine self, shouldn't masturbate, or notice other women. In the three years you've been with your fiancé, have you never looked at another man? Everybody masturbates, especially boys; and everybody looks, especially boys—even boys engaged to bra models.

Hey, Faggot:

I couldn't believe your response to "Second Best." What the hell is wrong with masturbating while in a relationship? What the hell is wrong with masturbating a lot while in a relationship? How does that qualify SB's fiancé for therapy? She said they have a good sex life. He never jacked off in public, or when her parents were visiting: Where's the harm? So what if he wants to wank to the Victoria's Secret catalog and *Baywatch*?! If there's a problem here, I think it is her lack of self-esteem. ("Should I get implants? Does he want a blonde?") Being in a relationship doesn't mean you own the other person's genitalia!

Sticking Up for Jack

Hey, SUFJ:

SB's boyfriend's problem was not masturbation, but consideration—his lack of any. She sounds insecure, but who isn't? And who wouldn't be under her circumstances? Yes, everybody masturbates. I do, but not where or when my boyfriend can find me. Not because I'm ashamed, but because I'm polite. Just because something isn't wrong doesn't mean it's appropriate under any and all circumstances. And just because there's nothing wrong with masturbation doesn't mean that a person's masturbatory habits can't cause problems in their relationship. Take this poor woman's situation:

"My boyfriend . . . would rather masturbate than have sex. He masturbates four or five times a day, and at night he says he's 'too tired' for sex, and just rolls over. But then as soon as he thinks I've fallen asleep he starts masturbating. This is starting to disgust me and make me think there's something wrong with him, me, or both of us. Maybe I don't turn him on, maybe he's too lazy to have sex, maybe he's gay? Please help."

This poor woman's boyfriend might be gay, or she might not turn him on, or perhaps he's suddenly taken a compulsive interest in something odd—boots, bowel movements, Boy Scouts—

that he's too ashamed to share with her, but can't get a boner without concentrating on. Or maybe he's a freak. But this much we do know: he has a private little sex life going on in his head, a sex life that does not involve his girlfriend at all. If my boyfriend had a sex life that didn't involve me at all, I would dump him, and I recommend she do the same.

Hey, Faggot:

I'm married, and my wife and I have the most beautiful, passionate sex. But sometimes I can't hold back to come with her. When I come early, I usually go soft in her. She doesn't mind, because I always make sure she gets hers either orally or with my hand, but I hate it. Do you have any advice on techniques for either holding orgasms back or keeping it up after you come? I just love making love to my wife, and don't want it to stop. But sometimes my penis just won't keep going.

Cum and Gone

Hey, C&G:

Breeders, especially boys, attach way too much importance to simultaneous orgasms. Orgasms are distinct, separate events, not a single shared moment of bliss. Because men usually take less time to come than women, obsessing about "coming together" places pressure on a woman to fake an appropriately timed orgasm so as not to bruise her little man's spun-glass ego.

You do have options. Bring the little lady to an orgasm or two *before* you fuck her. Once she's up and running, her orgasms should come closer together, and you won't have to hold out. You can also raise your oh-my-god-I'm-gonna-come threshold by getting to know your body better. When do you pass the point of no return? Try working up to that point, and pulling back, working up, pulling back. Practice together, while you're fucking: get close, rest inside her, repeat. Practice by yourself when you masturbate. And a cock ring might be a good short-term solution. Go to ye olde neighborhood sex shoppe and buy an adjustable cock ring, go home, fit it snugly around the base of your cock behind your balls, and fuck. The cock ring restricts the blood flow out of your penis, and will keep you hard after you come, stud.

Hey, Faggot:

I am a 27-year-old female, and I need some advice on something that has been bothering me. I met my boyfriend while visiting Atlanta on vacation. Our sex life is healthy with the exception of him getting a limp dick every now and again—I know that's normal, Dan.

One day my boyfriend brought up the fact that he decided to ask a guy out he knew was gay. My boyfriend is very open and into experimenting, so this type of thing wasn't totally out of character. He said all they did was meet for beers, and they talked about the fact that he was just experimenting. He assured me all they did was hold hands and the guy gave him a kiss goodnight. I think it's pretty cool of him to experiment, but for some reason I can't get over the fact that he may be repressing some homosexual feelings. I mean, is he gay? He is Catholic and says that not only is he not into the idea of being with a man, he thinks it is morally wrong. A lot of gay men come on to him; in fact a good friend of his expressed interest in a sexual relationship.

Do you see a pattern? I feel like I should drop it, but I feel my female sixth sense taking over. My biggest fear is that down the line he will decide to experiment again, and this time he'll like it. Help! I'm thinking about marrying this guy!

Concerned

P.S. I hope I don't come across as a homophobe. Some of my best pals are gay. I just want to marry a nice straight boy who wants oodles and oodles of kids and can't keep his hands off *me*.

Hey, C:

Listen to that sixth sense of yours, girlfriend, it's giving you the shit. Men are not straight cuz they think being gay is "morally wrong," they're straight cuz they wanna, gotta, fuck women.

What your boyfriend, as a Catholic, was taught to believe about homosexuality (no, no!) is in conflict with what his dick is telling him about homosexuality (yes, yes!) Hence the half-assed rationalizations around his "experimentations." I mean, come on: If homosexuality is wrong, what on earth does he think same-sex dates, same-sex hand-holding, and same-sex kissing are? At what point does same-sex romance shift from innocent experimentation to moral "wrong"? Everything you've described is cliché closet-case stuff. Little rationalizations like, "Okay, if I promise not to suck dick, I can go out on a date with a guy," are quickly followed by larger ones like, "Okay, I can suck dick, but only if I don't know the guy's name and I'm never going to see him again." Should you marry this guy? Absolutely not.

Hey, Faggot:

Guess you've heard it all, so maybe this won't sound too weird: I've been married for a long, long time, and my husband and I have accumulated our share of unsolved problems. Sex was pleasant at best, and I faked orgasms more often than I care to remember, even though he was willing to do what it took.

Last year I had a lover, and he turned me on like my husband never has. Not that he did anything different, really—he even had a smaller prick—but I could feel him in every cell of my body, and I found myself initiating things my husband could never talk me into. I had completely forgotten how much fun sex could be. My question is: Does sexual attraction hit you like a thunderbolt, or can you make it happen? Could you have a satisfying relationship without it, or does this mean my marriage is doomed?

                                                    Not Sixteen Anymore

Hey, NSA:

I just finished reading *Sex for Christians: The Limits and Liberties of Sexual Living* by Lewis B. Smeades, which is not as skinny a book as one would think (or feel compelled to joke about), but that's probably because it was written in the early '70s, before the ascendancy of the sexphobic Religious Right. As Susan Faludi points out in *Backlash: The Undeclared War Against Women*, Christian sex manuals were once surprisingly progressive, even coming out in support of sex-fer-pleasure and a woman's right to the odd orgasm. Anyway, here's a little Jesus-freak wisdom about marriage from *Sex for Christians:*

"Once it was considered all right to marry for security, comfort, and responsible parenthood. Now we are considered unromantic and calculating if we marry for anything less than erotic desire. We are expected to cultivate, celebrate, and voluptuously enjoy sexual life together for our own sakes."

Insightful, huh? I won't print the stuff about what a rotten hell-bound sack o' shit you are for having committed adultery, just as I spared myself the chapter on "Distorted Sexuality." But I think ol' Lewis is on to something here: maybe your marriage isn't about sex. Sexual attraction either hits you like a thunder-bolt or creeps up on you as you get to know someone better, but you can't force it. From the sound of your letter, there were never thunderbolts with your husband, and if sexual attraction was going to creep up on you, it probably would have crept by now.

So, you can kill yourself, get a divorce, or accept that maybe your marriage is about something other than erotic desire—security, comfort, kids, money, social position—things that you may find great satisfaction in, just not sexual satisfaction. Nowhere is it written that a marriage is a failure if the sex isn't good. And there are no guarantees: just because you feel someone in every cell of your body today doesn't mean he'll have the same effect on you next week, next year, or 20 years from now. Had you run off with your lover, you might have found yourself facing the exact same problem you have now with your husband in a few short years. So, take the pressure off: stop thinking of your marriage as a failure just because your husband is a lousy lay, and credit the relationship for what works. And take the odd lover now and again for kicks.

Almost Everything Breeder Boys Need to Know About Women's Genitals

When I started writing "Savage Love" seven years ago, I was pretty clueless about issues concerning the genitals of women. Consequently, in the early days, I made some major blunders out of ignorance—not malice. One of these blunders is included at the beginning of this chapter, for your amusement and edification. My ignorance can be excused—have I mentioned that I'm a *fag*, ladies and gentlemen; what for do I need to know from women's genitals? What cannot be excused, however, is the complete and total ignorance of women's genitals and sexual response demonstrated by the straight boys who send me questions week after week. Letters arrive every day from men who've been sleeping with women for years and yet don't know the most basic vagi-facts—where the clit is, what the clit is for, for crying out loud! You'd think desire—to say nothing of a good-faith effort to be a halfway decent lay—would prompt straight boys to get these questions answered before they have sex, not after!

Now, boys, I'm being hard on you because that's one of the perks of being "Hey, Faggot." But I will cut you this small bit of slack: it's not all your fault. Many women contribute to and perpetuate straight male ignorance of female genitals and sexual response. As you will see in this chapter, straight women bed down with boys, are frequently left unsatisfied, but do not say anything to the boys, so the boys don't know they need to improve. A lot of boys are bad in bed because the women they've been sleeping with allow them to get away with it.

Well, I won't let you get away with it. While this chapter is all about women's genitals, orgasms, and sexual pleasure—with questions from men and women, straight, bi, and gay—this chapter is really for you, boys. Originally when we started pulling this book together, my editor suggested I do a chapter on women's stuff for women. But after lo these many years reading your letters, boys, I knew that you were the ones who needed a chapter on women's stuff, not the girls. Here you'll find just about everything you need to know about women, pussy, clits, labia—the whole ball of flesh—all the info you need to transform yourselves from inept goofballs who never get invited back for seconds into good providers of women's orgasms.

Before we spelunk in, there are two other issues I'd like to address. My "Savage Love" readers frequently write in to ask if I've ever had sex with a woman. Recently, a rival advice columnist—who shall remain nameless, but whose initials are ISADORA ALMAN—told her readers that they shouldn't listen to anything I had to say about the subject, since I'd never even seen a vagina, so what would I know?

Well, for the record, I have had sex with a woman, Ms. Alman. With a *few* women, as a matter of fact. Sadly, it wasn't out of any genuinely felt desire, or a sense of sexual adventurousness, but desperation. When I was teenager, I didn't think I would ever have the courage to come out. If I was going to be straight—or fake being straight—I was going to have to have sex with women. I felt exactly nothing when I was doing it, and nothing when I was done—other than damp. My body may have been in the room, but by necessity my mind was someplace else. When people ask how I actually did the breeder deed, I demonstrate: I close my eyes, mutter, "It's a guy, it's a guy, it's a guy . . . ," and move my hips. I pretended the woman under me was a guy with his head turned around 180 degrees, and two very large, dislocated shoulder blades. With nipples.

This wasn't fair to the women I had sex with, of course. But the social pressure I was under wasn't fair either. Now that I no longer am trying to feign straightness, I behave toward women in the most respectful manner at all times. And through my column, I do all I can to ensure that women are getting their props—orgasms and respect—from the straight boys they sleep with.

Now, it is true that I once compared women's genitals to canned hams dropped from great heights. This comment may seem disrespectful on the surface. But it isn't—remember, *I am a fag*. I never had to get over my feelings of "otherness" about women's bodies. Boys and girls all start out feeling vaguely or actively disgusted by the bodies, and specifically the genitals, of the opposite sex. "Gross" was the word we used when I was a kid. But desire eventually kicks in, and straight girls get over feeling that dicks are stinky and gross, and straight boys get over feeling that pussy is stinky and gross—what other choice do they have? And thus is the earth repopulated.

But me? Once again, *I am a fag*. Little gay boys and little lezzie girls are not compelled, as little straight boys and little straight girls are, to get over those stinky and gross feelings; we never have to confront the genitals of the other, and when we do, we're often pretending that we're not. Our desires do not require us to get over it—and so many of us don't. So I feel perfectly justified in saying that I find women's genitals to be . . . "other," or gross. Of course, this is my problem, and a personal and subjective observation, and in no way an accurate reflection of women's genitals, which we all know are just wonderful—if you like that sort of thing.

Hey, Faggot:

I'm frustrated 'cuz I don't have orgasms when my boyfriend and I bang. At first I figured it was a temp deal, and—I hate to admit this—I faked 'em. I reasoned he'd get discouraged and quit trying. Now I'm stuck. He pretty much does what I ask, but I still ain't comin' (and he doesn't know). This hasn't been a problem with past guys, or by myself. What should I do?

O-Free

Hey, O-Free:

Lying is a sin. A faked orgasm is a lie. Faked orgasms are a sin. And you're trapped. He's probably thinking he's quite the stud, "I just look at my girlfriend funny and she cums, dude!"

You could sit him down and tell him the truth—but you'd be running the risk of his never getting an erection again in his shock-shortened life. No straight man can hear, "Honey, all those times you thought you made me come, well . . . it was performance art," without feeling a little smaller. Here's what to do: stop pretending. Let him think, for some mysterious reason, you've suddenly gone non-orgasmic. Getting you going again will be a challenge for him, and most boys love a challenge. Within this deceitful framework, be as honest as you can. Tell him what to do—what did your past boyfriends do that he isn't doing? What do you do by yourself that he isn't doing? Masturbate in front of him, on top of him, next to him. Think of your vagina as a very complicated musical instrument you have to teach him to play, like a mouth harp. But sin no more—the sooner you stop faking 'em, the sooner you'll be having 'em again.

Hey, Faggot:

I am a healthy 19-year-old female and I have been with my present boyfriend for about six months. I lost my virginity to him three months ago, and have remained sexually active since. The problem? My dear, sweet, beautiful boy has no clue that I have yet to experience an orgasm with him.

I have been masturbating since early adolescence and can make myself come in minutes. I have fallen into the "faking" rut—I know that this is cruel, but he would be crushed if he knew the truth. It's not like I don't get any pleasure from the deed, because I do honestly enjoy it. Lately, though, after he orgasms, I have no desire to continue. I pretty much figure this is due to my not wanting to continue the acting bit any further. We have sex frequently, and have tried various positions, but still no climax for me.

T

Hey, T:

Each of your faked orgasms has necessitated the faking of another, because if what he's doing tonight made you come this morning, and the night before that, and the afternoon before that, and the morning before that (oh, to be 19), then he's expecting it will make you come tonight. You, aware of his expectations—expectations you created—feel compelled to oblige him with yet another command-performance climax. And to make matters worse, the lie you're telling, ostensibly to spare his feelings, is resulting in orgasmless sex for you, which is killing your desire, making your sex life a guilt-ridden, tedious chore! *Stop the insanity!!!* Tell him you've been faking, or you too can tell your boyfriend that lesser lie: suddenly and mysteriously, go all non-orgasmic. Make him earn your orgasms!

Hey, Faggot:

A couple of months ago, I made contact with a lesbian girl. She said she was curious and had been fantasizing about having sex with guys (I'm a male . . .). We met on neutral ground and had a drink and talked for a while. I guess she approved of me, because she took me home and we had sex. I tried to strike up a friendship with her afterwards, but I guess it was just a fling. I knew that might happen, but now I can't ask her about two things. She told me something I've never heard before. She said she gets two different kinds of orgasms: Clitoral and vaginal. Do you know anything about this distinction?

Also, while we were exploring, she shed a few tears, saying she was breaking through a lot of emotional barriers. I see people struggling through emotional barriers society has built against queers. But what sort of social pressures would lead to this defense against a majority-condoned sexual behavior?

I'm Still Learning

Hey, ISL:

Women have vaginas. They also have clits, little fleshy nubs, outside of their vaginas, usually pretty close to the vaginal opening. Women can have two types of orgasm, a vaginal orgasm from stimulation inside the vaginal canal or a clitoral orgasm from stimulation of the clitoris. But most women need clitoral stimulation to achieve orgasm. The clit is in a spot that during average het sex doesn't get much stimulation. You have to go out of your breeder-boy-let-me-get-this-thing-in-you way to stimulate a woman's clitoris. Get on it with your fingers, mouth, whatever.

"Most women don't come from just being fucked. It's important to say most, because some women insist they have orgasms from just getting fucked with no clitoral stimulation at all," says a dyke pal o' mine. In her vast experience with la femme lesbos, my pal has never been with a woman who came from vaginal stimulation alone.

On top of the vaginal/clitoral fracas, now let's wade into the G-spot controversy. "The G-spot is on the upper wall of the vaginal canal, a little rigged spot; it requires direct, focused attention that a penis can't provide. Or reach. Fingers are better, especially fingers attached to other women." My dyke pal can achieve orgasm from G-spot stimulation, but it's a different sort of orgasm than her neighbor-awakening clitoral orgasm.

My pal felt your lesbian lover might have "shed some tears" because she's queer! "Get a clue!" Whether it's a majority-condoned behavior is irrelevant—het sex is not her normal behavior. If I came to your house and screwed your brains out you'd probably shed a few tears too. C'mon, think!

Hey, Faggot:

You recently wrote in your column the following: "Some women are able to have two types of orgasm, a vaginal orgasm from stimulation inside the vaginal canal . . . or a clitoral orgasm from stimulation of the clitoris." This is not true.

Janet Sibley Hyde, in *Understanding Human Sexuality*, writes: "All female orgasms are physiologically the same, regardless of the locus of stimulation. That is, an orgasm always consists of contractions of the orgasmic platform and the muscles around the vagina. . . . Masters and Johnson found that clitoral stimulation is almost always involved in producing orgasm. Because of the way in which the inner lips connect with the clitoral hood, the movement of the penis in and out of the vagina creates traction on the inner lips, which in turn pull the clitoral hood so that it comes back and forth, stimulating the clitoris. Thus even purely 'vaginal' orgasm results from . . . clitoral stimulation."

The vaginal/clitoral orgasm theory originated with Sigmund Freud, who asserted that little girls attain orgasm through masturbation by stimulating the clitoris. He believed women begin having vaginal orgasms as they grow older, through heterosexual intercourse. This theory persisted until very recently, and was very popular during the seventies. Freud's concept of the clitoral orgasm as childish or immature, and the idea of the vaginal orgasm as "better" has caused women much anxiety. Hyde writes: "Freud's formulation . . . has had an impact on the lives of many women. Many have undergone psychoanalysis and spent countless hours agonizing over why they were not able to achieve the elusive vaginal orgasm and why they enjoyed the 'immature' clitoral one so much." This is not only not a minor point, but can actually be harmful to women.

It is disappointing to see this false idea continue to be advocated, especially by your usually informative column!

US

Hey, US:

What I don't know about vaginas could fill, well, several thousand vaginas probably. Until I got this job, I was one of those gynophobic cocksuckers who went all woozy at the sight of a woman's genitals. They look like something dropped from a great height. A canned ham dropped from the 23rd floor of the Empire State Building, I don't know. So, in desperation, I turn to my crack vaginal-issues advisory squad whenever matters vaginal arise. They knew vaginal orgasms were the result of peripheral clitoral stimulation. When they talked about vaginal orgasms they meant "clitoral orgasms resulting from vaginal stimulation." I thought they meant some women could come from fucking with no clitoral stimulation, and others from clitoral stimulation. They assumed—wrongly—that I knew about the whole Freud immature/mature orgasm thing. They further assumed—wrongly—that I knew the debate was settled and that all orgasms were clitoral, but the stimulation leading to them could be vaginal or clitoral. From now on they're going to assume I'm a big dumb dope.

For the record: physiologically speaking, there's only one type of female orgasm—clitoral. But there are different routes to achieving it. You can dive right on the clit and give her the clitoral orgasm she deserves. Or you can do the penis thing, sneak up on the clitoris by yanking all those lips back and forth and give her an accidental orgasm. Only a small number of women can have those accidental orgasms. Not that women can't come fucking, they can, but the majority need some extra help—a hand, a vibrator—in addition to the fucking.

Hey, Faggot:

One night last week I was having sex with my girlfriend, when something happened, and neither one of us has any idea exactly what occurred. She was lying on the corner end of my bed on her stomach and her feet were planted firmly on the hardwood floor. Supporting myself with my arms on the bed and my feet on the floor, I was in a standing position, thrusting deeper than I had ever penetrated inside her vagina. Near the height of this act, a sudden stream of odorless, clear liquid projected from her, soaking a one-square-foot area of the bed and also wetting my underwear and pants, which were around my ankles. Afterward, I asked her what that was, and she didn't even realize it had happened!

Is this an intense orgasm she experienced which caused her to ejaculate fluid? When I go down on her, she has multiple orgasms, but nothing ever squirts out. We tried the same position later but didn't get the same results. We were both hoping you could explain this most unusual occurrence.

Water Bearer

Hey, WB:

There's a gland in your girlfriend's pussy called the paraurethral gland, which is itself surrounded by some squishy tissue called the urethral sponge. For some women, direct stimulation of the paraurethral gland can result in the ejaculation of a clear, usually odorless fluid that is not—*not*—piss or pussy juice. It's ejaculate. The same clump of cells that become the prostate gland in boy babies—the gland that produces male ejaculate—becomes the paraurethral gland in girl babies. Some women, not all, respond to direct and prolonged paraurethral stimulation by producing their own girlie ejaculate.

It wasn't the intensity of your girlfriend's orgasm that resulted in the squirts (though intensity never hurts), but out-of-the-ordinary pressure placed on your girlfriend's p-gland (aka "the G-spot") due to, perhaps, the position you were in coupled with the vigor of your thrusting, stud. Why you've been unable to repeat may have something to do with where the gland is: inside and up, not in a place easily reached by regular ol' vaginal intercourse—you may have been lucky that one time. Combine your orgasm-inducing cunnilingus skills with a little finger action (in and up), and you may drown.

Hey, Faggot:

What is the biological (i.e., survival) significance of female orgasm? Male orgasm, as the pleasurable end result of intercourse, is clearly an incentive to procreate—Darwinism, survival of the fittest, etc. But female orgasm, being the somewhat elusive, often unreliable thing that it is, doesn't seem to fit into the equation as neatly. What's the deal?

Albert

Hey, Albert:

Men's orgasms are an "incentive" to reproduce, and women's orgasms serve no purpose?! Think, doofus: women's orgasms are Mother Nature's way of conning heterosexual women into bedding down with men, thereby risking disease, pregnancy, and conversations about pro sports. They're "incentive" too. Women's orgasms fit very neatly into the equation, but not when a selfish boor is doing the math.

If your female partner's orgasms are "elusive" or "unreliable," perhaps it's because she's screwing a man who views her orgasm as a Darwinist doggie-treat for him and her orgasm as an evolutionary quirk, like webbed toes—interesting but unnecessary, and certainly not worth any extra effort.

Hey, Faggot:

Last week you bashed a fellow named Albert for observing that women's orgasms are sometimes "elusive" or "unreliable." Your opinions on women's orgasms may be slightly more valid than the Pope's opinions on birth control, but as someone with real-world experience in this area, I would like to point a few things out to you.

1. Women have a wide range of orgasmic patterns. They

use a variety of positions, techniques, toys, and fantasies
to achieve orgasm, and the exact mix is individual.

2. Men should not be bashed for not hitting the right spot the
right way the first time. Women should feel free to give
men directions in satisfying them, and they should not
trash men for asking for feedback. Men do well, of course,
to pay attention to what their partners are asking for.

3. There is a logical Darwinian explanation for why, on the
average, it takes women longer to achieve orgasm than
men. To understand this, just ask the question, "What
would be the result if women were bigger and stronger
than men and reached orgasm more easily (sooner)?" The
answer is "no children," since women would come, roll
off the man, and fall asleep without getting impregnated.
Such traits would have a hard time winning at natural
selection.

Evolutionarily Yours,
Dr. Z

Hey, Doc:

1. Right you are.
2. Far too many men—and a few women—view men's orgasms as the culmination of the sex act, and women's
orgasms as a greased pig not worth the time and trouble of
chasing down. If my vast network of heterosexual female
friends, relatives, and co-workers are to be believed, the attitude that "her" orgasm is secondary—not having the pride
of place his does—is something of an epidemic among
straight males. And that attitude deserves bashing.
3. Sounds reasonable. Read on for more theories.

Hey, Faggot:

I am angered by your response to the question asked by
Albert. This is a classic example of what happens when the
trendy ideals of Political Correctness serve to stifle the quest for

an intellectual discussion. Your unwarranted attack on Albert illustrates that people can no longer speak about issues of race, gender, and sexuality without first phrasing their questions in a pastel, inoffensive manner.

The answer to Albert's question is that female orgasm and simple female lubrication makes her vaginal canal less acidic so the sperm can live longer, increasing the chance for procreative success. The spasm of the pelvic floor muscle also assists sperm in moving further toward the ovum. This makes unwanted and/or unexciting mates less likely to impregnate the female than wanted mates. Modern fertility research suggests that female orgasm also increases the chance of producing male offspring because the faster, yet weaker, Y (male) sperm are more susceptible to acidic conditions.

Of course, orgasms are not only used for procreative purposes, they are also used to bond people emotionally, and simply to have a hip-tightening "doggie-treat" with anybody or anything we choose.

Jason S.

Hey, JS:

I am not often accused of being "politically correct," so it's kind of refreshing to be so labeled. But I feel compelled to point out that accusing others of being "politically correct" is the first refuge of lazy bullshitters who can't be bothered to mount a decent argument.

My response to Albert was not an "attack," but rather a rough-and-tumble exchange on the subject of sexuality—the kind of exchange you accuse "political correctness" of stifling. My answer, like Albert's question, was not phrased "in a pastel or inoffensive manner," was it? We both risked offending, didn't we? And that's what you claim to want, isn't it?

Or perhaps the freedom to risk offending by asking "politically incorrect" questions only applies when the questions are reactionary, sexist, racist, or homophobic.

It seems that when one is defending a progressive position, one has to be ever-so-careful of the easily bruised feelings and delicate sensibilities of closed-minded straight white guys and their dupes, lest one be accused of "political correctness." Well, Jason, eat my shit: I'm all for direct questions and open debate— so long as those who claim to want it so badly don't invoke the "politically correct" bogeyman every goddamned time you lose a round.

As for your theory: if female arousal can be correlated with successful impregnation and/or the likelihood of male offspring, wouldn't it follow that, after thousands and thousands of years of breeding, natural selection would've wiped out the "lousy lay" gene? And how was it that boy babies were born before 1973?

Hey, Faggot:

In response to Albert: In 1988, when I took "Primate Behavior" at Humboldt State University, there were several theories in the anthropological world concerning the evolutionary significance of female orgasm.

One explanation states that for hundreds of thousands of years our ancestors lived in "promiscuous" groups, much as our nearest relatives, the pygmy chimpanzees, do today. The majority of individuals in the group interacted with each other sexually, and for this reason the males and females of the group were equally motivated to have as much sexual intercourse as possible with as many different individuals as possible, for the following reasons: males were motivated to distribute the maximum amount of their genes throughout the gene pool, while females were motivated to maximize the amount of male investment in the group's collective offspring. Since the males did not know which offspring were their progeny, they were equally invested in caring for and protecting all the offspring.

Some anthropologists believe that in the situation illustrated above, because males were engaging in intercourse much more frequently than they do today, these "promiscuous" males took much longer to achieve orgasm. It has been further suggested that it was actually (steady yourself for this one!) the contractions during the female's orgasm which triggered the orgasm of the male. Therefore, we can postulate two things: (1) female orgasm was directly related to a more frequent rate of male orgasm, and thus a higher conception rate, i.e., "evolutionary significant," and (2) by ancient standards, "modern males" are largely premature ejaculators. So much for the "elusive" and "unreliable" nature of the female orgasm. It would appear that modern males, from an evolutionary point of view, are the ones who should lay claim to these titles.

Monkey Girl

Hey, Faggot:

I am not too sexually experienced and would like to know if it's possible to reach orgasm by touching your breasts in a certain way. The first time I let my boyfriend fondle my breasts, I had strong sensations similar to masturbation. When I let him rub his penis between my breasts, the same thing happened.

It seems we found a safe way for both of us to satisfy ourselves sexually without having intercourse. How could what I am experiencing be possible?

Jane R

Hey, JR:

Some people, men and women, have sensitive boobs. Rub, lick, nibble, bite, or clamp "wired" tits, and the person attached to them will follow you around begging for more.

You two haven't accidentally stumbled across any supersecret, tantric woo-woo—or "certain ways" to touch breasts—that drives women wild. There is no "B-spot." You're just blessed with a pair of super-sensititties. Having your breasts fondled is a big enough turn-on for you—physically, psychologically, or both—that you can reach orgasm, or something very like orgasm, from tit-play alone. Lucky you.

Hey, Faggot:

Okay, there are all these women out there who can only reach orgasm from oral sex (clitoral stimulation), and complain about men who don't know the technique. Well, I must admit, I'm one of those men. I would love it if you could enlighten me with the *details* on this ever so pleasing act so I can have the pleasure of treating my partners to such wonderful and fulfilling orgasms.

Clueless

Hey, Clueless:

The other night I was out for a late-night snack with a friend I'd always thought was a red-blooded, god-fearin', buttfuckin' All-American fag, and he up and tells me he isn't gay at all, but a bisexual who identifies as gay. "You should be more careful about how you label people, Dan," he said.

Then he told me he had slept with a mutual friend, a woman I thought was a dyke. Curiouser and curiouser!

When our food arrived I asked him if he'd gone down on her, hoping he hadn't—only a real "bi" would. If he hadn't, I could've said, "You're not bi, you're just bi-curious!" But, he had done the deed.

"What's it like?" I asked, wide-eyed. He pointed to my plate of pancakes, smothered in syrup—I'd sort of eaten my way through them, creating a little fjord—and he said, "Push your face into your pancakes and eat them from the bottom up. That's what it's like."

What's the lesson in all of this for you? Don't ask rabbis for pork chop recipes.

Hey, Faggot:

This is in response to Clueless, the guy who wanted to know how to give good head to a chick. Well, I'm a chick who just couldn't resist responding. First of all, Clueless, you are on the right track. You openly admit you are clueless. I commend you for your lack of macho ego. I had a boyfriend who resented my needing to instruct him. So I gritted my teeth while he sucked me off the way another woman (namely: his ex), not myself, would want it.

Every woman is very different in the way she needs a good clit job. I, for instance, actually prefer a good hand job to a mouth job any day. I guess I just fancy what 10 fingers can do, versus one tongue. In short, you need to, with all the openness and humbleness you had in your letter, ask your female lover what it is she wants.

A Woman

Hey, AW:

Your advice is pretty sound—it never hurts to ask—but some people have a hard time talking about sex, and are too embarrassed to answer even a simple question like "What feels good?" He's likelier to get a shrug and an unhelpful "It all feels good" than a detailed set of instructions. In addition to a willingness to ask questions, Clueless is going to need a few tricks up his sleeve, a game plan of his own. Clueless, read on.

Hey, Faggot:

As a breeder who thinks cunnilingus is good squishy fun, and a really neat way to get girls to like you, I feel the need to reach out to my low-watt breeder brother Clueless, who wanted some twat tonguing tips.

Short of getting yourself a girlfriend who is willing to give you instruction, the best thing you can do to educate yourself is go on down to your local porn emporium and rent yourself a video.

Well, the better smut shops have subject sections. If it's a particularly big shop, you might find an entire section devoted to cunnilingus. If that's not the case, start in the "All Sex/Just

Sex" section, where you'll find videos of anywhere from a half an hour to six hours of just the good parts: nonstop hard-core explicit XXX action (saves wear and tear on your VCR's fast-forward function).

Another section you might want to peruse is the "All Girl/Girl-Girl/Lesbian Love" section. Having watched a couple dozen porn flicks over the years, it is my considered opinion that the women have more subtle and sophisticated techniques than the guys.

Yet a third option to consider is one of these newfangled, delicate, and sensitive "couples" videos being cranked out by the likes of Candida Royale, Annie Sprinkle, and Nina Hartley. Since these are aimed at couples (i.e., straight women) they have a lot of foreplay, and strive for a realistic tone. Since you're trying to learn what women like, this would probably be a good place to pick up a few useful tips.

And, finally, you could check out one of the many explicit sex education videos now on the market. I should warn you that I saw one of these, and it was one of the most boring videos of any kind that I had ever seen. It actually made sex dull.

Pussybreath

Hey, P:

The gay porn I've seen bears about as much resemblance to real-life gay sex as—I'm thinking—straight porn does to straight sex. So, while Clueless may pick up a few pointers from porn, he shouldn't rely on it solely for his instruction. I don't recommend he rely on his VCR exclusively. Clueless, read on.

Hey, Faggot:

The things males do in porn films—orally or otherwise—will *not* produce an orgasm in their female partner! The guys in those films (and, tragically, their emulators) ram away, thighs a-slappin', like they were trying to churn butter. You'd hardly get any clitoral stimulation with aerobics like that! And if they try to get their partner off manually, they rub the tender vaginal area like a belt sander! In reality, those exquisite motions that produce the elusive female orgasm are fairly subtle. The squealing, chatty orgasms women have in porn are bought and paid for, guys: faux, faux, faux. The sex in porn is laughable, and not a good example for the lover-in-training.

NOB

Hey, NOB:

Good points. Remember, straight boys: women who appear in porn videos aren't called actresses for nothin'. Clueless, keep reading!

Hey, Faggot:

Here are my Rules of Cunnilingus. I hope these help Clueless and the thousands of other guys just like him all over the world.

1. Is there much (not involving teeth) that a woman can do with her mouth on your dick that *doesn't* feel good? Well, it goes both ways.
2. The clitoris is important. Pay attention to it. If you don't know where it is or what it looks like, be a man and ask her!
3. Don't ignore the rest of it. The clitoris gets sore easily, and there's so much else to explore. Try to stimulate the clitoris indirectly.
4. This is so important: Try something, ask, "Does that feel good?" Try something else. Repeat. Another good question is, "What feels good?" She may be shy at first, but I promise she'll get over it.
5. The female orgasm can take a long time. Thirty seconds is just not going to cut it. Ten minutes is a good *minimum*. My personal guideline? Don't stop until she's an exhausted, sweaty heap.
6. No two women like it exactly the same. Repeat step four

with every woman you try this with. You are always an initiate, never a master.

7. This is the most important rule: If you are sincerely trying to make her feel good, you can't go wrong. Get into it, lose control. I promise you the first time a woman looks down between her legs at you, quivering and shaking, and says, "You are the King of Oral Sex!" it will all be worth it.

DDT

Hey, Faggot:

I'm a hetero woman who thinks her vaginal juices taste a bit bitter. I don't currently have a lover to consult on this; nor do I taste other women so . . . is this normal? What do most women taste like and how does this vary based on time of month, or diet or genetics? Am I normal? Should I be embarrassed the next time someone goes down on me?

Sweet Wannabe

Hey, SW:

"Vaginal secretions, like perspiration, urine, feces, and saliva, are formed from the food and fluids we ingest," said my friend Emily the Doc. "The recipe for sweet breath, nonodorous stool, clear urine, pleasantly salty sweat and yummy juices is a diet high in whole grains, with plenty of lightly steamed veggies, raw fruit, modest amounts of non-farm-raised meats, and lots of fresh water. Processed sugar (pastries, ice cream, cookies), pizza, packaged foods, drugs (including coffee and cigarettes), and alcohol tend to render our bodily fluids foul."

As for what "most women taste like," I'm guessing flavors vary from woman to woman in much the same way they vary from man to man. It's a fascinating subject, though, isn't it, class? So let's open it up for discussion. Boys and girls: what do your sex partner's various juices taste like? And did anyone you were in the habit of tasting successfully alter their flavor by, say, changing their diet?

Hey, Faggot:

As a globe-trotting dyke who considers going down on a woman just about the closest I'll ever get to heaven, I'd like to confirm the variability of women's tastes. For the pussy-juice connoisseur, though, nothing beats the rare and intense flavor of a strong, smoky, dare I say Lapsang souchong–scented pussy. I've come across exactly two women in my life who had this incomparable flavor. One was a sweet socialist veggie who followed the doc's recommended diet. The other survived on a diet of Pizza Hut take-aways and fast-food burgers. Guess some lucky girls are just born with it.

Carellia

Hey, Faggot:

I've been with my current beau for two years, and he tasted slightly salty when we first met. Two suggestions: (1) Have your boyfriend brush his teeth first if he smokes and/or drinks coffee. (2) Have more sex. I found the longer the period between sex, the more bitter he is.

Been There

Hey, Faggot:

You neglected to raise the possibility of an infection or a bacterial imbalance which can occur in the vagina without any noticeable symptoms such as itchiness. This can definitely affect your smell and, presumably, taste. Something called *bacterial vaginosis* can occur when the vagina is out of balance, either on its own or from douching. I recommend any woman concerned about her taste get her wall scraped and checked under a microscope at Planned Parenthood or something.

Also, in your list of politically correct foods affecting taste, you might have also included strong, pungent foods—like garlic—that really do impact people's juice.

Honey Ham

Hey, Everybody:

Just for the record—and to save the sex police the burst blood vessels—that lapping up grrl/boy juices does carry some risk. Though HIV transmission via oral sex appears to be rare, if your partner is HIV+ you could get infected through unprotected oral sex.

Hey, Faggot:

My former lover used to say that he wouldn't eat a pussy he just came in. Last night, my current lover of six months ejaculated inside my yoni before I orgasmed, and I asked him to go down on me. He refused, saying it didn't appeal to him.

I think of my yoni as a sanctuary of creative feminine powers, cupid's cave, and a lotus of her wisdom. If men find their own liquids disgusting and dirty, they shouldn't come inside me to begin with. My yoni is not a trash can for their pollution.

Do a lot of men find oral sex after intercourse "unappealing"? Are they too straight? Too paranoid? *Do* I need a new lover who shares my sexual desires?

Yoni

Hey, Yoni:

I'm turning your question over to Savage Lab's straight boys. Overall, the boys freely admitted to having done the deed, though none seemed particularly enthusiastic about it. Here's what they had to say:

"I found it rather foul. All the cum and pussy juice and sweat combine into one big funk—but if a woman can manage to choke down a wad of come just to make me feel good, I don't mind making the sacrifice for her pleasure. But let's make no mistake: it is one big funky mess." "Maybe he should go down first, get her off at least once, then fuck. She might even have two orgasms or more. Is that enough?" "If they used a condom—not that I'm recommending them—he'd only have to deal with the faintly unpleasant taste of latex."

"I can't imagine that many guys haven't done the 'Hmm, wonder what *that* tastes like?' thing as a teenager. You'd think that would be enough to get you over it. That doesn't make me queer or nothin', does it?" "Yes, I would go down on her, but not in the ol' 69 position on bottom. I don't mind licking a little sperm, but I don't like it dribbling in my eye or, even worse, up my nose."

"It's less fun to lick pussy after intercourse than before it. A post-sex pooky is loosey-goosey and messy, a before-sex one is like a bud waiting to be opened, taut and delicious. Which is why you should always go down on a girl for ages before having intercourse—it makes it more likely she'll come first, and obviates the need for this debate."

Dan here: The straight boys I work with are a pretty homophobia-free bunch of guys, so this sample may not be representative of the average pussy-chompin', faggot-stompin' American male—others may be more paranoid about turning gay from tasting a smidge of their own semen. Finally, you might have better luck getting the boyfriends to eat you out if you refrain from using insipid, silly words like "yoni," and if you stopped with the sanctuary/cupid's cave/lotus-of-her-wisdom nonsense. That kinda "sacred sex" talk is enough to put any man off his lunch, let alone a "sacred vessel" overflowing with his own spunk. Eesh.

Hey, Faggot:

A fun bar, a congenial crowd, the babe was gorgeous. One thing led to another, and, following our second date, we went to bed together at her place. For me, the sex was great—torrid vanilla, writhing missionary. Unfortunately, however, the gorgeous babe did not achieve orgasm, and toward the end she asked me, please, to perform oral sex.

Big problem. Oral sex does not appeal to me, never has. Quite to the contrary. Desperate, stalling for time, I asked her, please, to douche first. For some reason, she took great offense. The atmosphere became chilly. She ordered me to leave "right now, this very instant." Which, pulling on my clothes, I did. I have tried to call her several times since. Each time, upon hearing my voice, she hangs up, kabang.

Since we got along so well before the expulsion, I wonder who was at fault. As far as I am concerned, she had nothing at which to take offense. In my opinion, by kicking me out without a chance for discourse, she greatly overreacted. Do you agree? Or would you say that by seeming to be self-centered and inconsiderate, I was to blame?

The Expellee

Hey, TE:

Not wanting to eat a pussy you've just fucked, that I can understand. Well, actually, not wanting to eat pussy, period, I can understand—but only if you're not into women. But you're straight, you like pussy—and she had the proof: you'd just fucked her pussy, right? Which might have led her to believe you were a pussy-lovin' man. Well, in the last 20 years or so, women have come to expect oral sex from pussy-lovin' men as a matter of course, much as men have come to expect oral sex from cock-lovin' women. So her request—that you finish her off orally—was not all that outrageous, to her mind. Nor is it to mine.

Now, you could have successfully demurred that night by claiming you were a bit squeamish about tasting your own come, or if you'd used a condom, the lube. She might have settled for a little finger action had you said something else. But while a different excuse might have saved the evening, it would only have put off the reckoning: you don't like to eat pussy, come or no come, and instead of telling her the truth, you lied. And the particular lie you told was not, with the infinite number of options available to you, a very good one. Telling her to go douche was as good as telling her she had a skanky pussy, implying that the problem was hers (skank) and not yours (hang-up). Stupid move.

And what if she had douched? Would you have spent your stalled-for 10 minutes while she was in the john gearing up, or would you have thought up some other lame excuse to get out of doing your duty? Maybe you were planning on creating a diversion—setting fire to the kitchen? Phoning in a bomb threat? Wiring your jaw shut?

I wish I could see a videotape of you telling her to douche. Specifically, I'd like to see the look on your face: was disgust evident? Did you look like a man who'd just had a plate of dog-crap ravioli set down in front of him? I suspect you did, and one look at your sour puss told her everything she needed to know about you and her oral-sex future with you—there wasn't going to be one. If oral sex is important to her, and she was insulted by your douche-that-skanky-pussy attitude, why shouldn't she kick your ass out of her apartment? Why should she waste another second on your disrespectful ass? You weren't "seeming to be self-centered and inconsiderate," Expellee, you were self-centered and inconsiderate. So who's to blame? You are.

Hey, Faggot:

I've been sexually active for a year now, and I still haven't had an orgasm. The men I've had sex with have gone out of their way to satisfy me and are very sensitive to my needs, but it's no good. I enjoy sex, but I still feel like I'm missing the best part. Is there something wrong with me or what? Please help.

Halfway There

Hey, HT:

Do you have orgasms when you masturbate? Do you masturbate? If you don't, start. Once you can get yourself off, masturbate with your partner. At first just let him watch. Masturbate as if you were alone, using whatever you usually use: hands, vibrators, fruit and veg. If you feel embarrassed, have him masturbate at the same time. (Or wear a blindfold so you don't have to watch him watching you. Or blindfold him so he can't watch you . . . spice it up and it won't feel like homework.) After you can have regular orgasms with him watching, try using his hands as if they were your own; guide his fingers. (If that works, try the same thing with his face.) Gradually, use your hands less and his more until you can let him fly solo. If having an orgasm while he's inside you is important to you (or him), use the techniques you develop during your masturbation exploration while he's fucking you.

There's no faster way to make sure you don't have orgasms than to put pressure on yourself. Or for him to put pressure on you. If your current lover is the kind of guy who wants you to come so he feels like a stud, find a different kind of lover. Your orgasms don't exist to bolster some insecure jerk's self-esteem. Give yourself permission not to come every time you try the masturbation thing or, once you're having orgasms, every time you have sex. It may take some time, stick with it!

Hey, Faggot:

My problem is rather serious. I've considered seeking professional help, but I'm a little embarrassed. I'm a well-adjusted female, except for one thing: I have been masturbating since age 11. I feel my masturbation habit is ruining my sex life. I believe I am unable to climax with a partner because I am so used to artificial climax. I've tried going without, but I just can't stop! Even when I had a consistent partner, I found myself masturbating once in a while to satisfy my urge for a climax.

I worry that this problem may lead to bisexuality, because I'm really losing interest in sex with men at this point. I have found myself picking my nails or watching television during intercourse! I'm confused because otherwise, I truly enjoy men, their sexuality, and what they have to offer me as a woman. Yet, I must admit I am curious to see what sex with a woman would be like. Am I totally ruining my sex life? Do I have bisexual tendencies?

Masturbator X

Hey, MX:

First, those orgasms you're having all by your lonesome aren't artificial. They're real. And if you can bring yourself off alone, you should be able to bring yourself off in the company of men. In fact, men would be good role models for you: Guys chase down their orgasms with a single-mindedness that women would do well to emulate. When a guy's fucking you, he maneuvers his dick around until he's getting rubbed just . . . so, and he keeps it up until he comes, right? When you masturbate, don't you do the same: rub yourself just . . . so, until you get off? Well, assert yourself! Communicate to the boyfriend exactly what is required to get you off and demand he do it: you know what it takes, you give yourself orgasms all the time! Show him how it's done!

Think of boyfriends not as people, but as large, sweaty sex toys with hairy bodies and weak batteries. Pleasure yourself with his body—that's what it's there for! Isn't that what he's doing with your body? When a guy fucks you, he's basically masturbating inside you, substituting pussy for fist. Well, turnabout is always fair play! If you masturbate humping pillows or going for long horseback rides, treat his thigh like your pillow, or his face like a saddle. Vibrator do the trick? Show him how to use it, guide his hands!

Too many girls (and boys) think that, if she has an orgasm at all, it has to be by happy accident: during intercourse, or as a result of the "right" amount of cunnilingus (read: until his tongue gets tired). But his orgasms? Whatever it takes: sets, costumes, livestock, laser light shows and trips to the emergency room if need be, he's gonna insist on it. So don't be demure! You insist right back!

And if he's too inept, or his face is too stubbly, or thighs are too squishy to get you off—DIY, girlfriend: Do It Yourself. He can still hold you, or make out with you, or play with your tits, or lick your ass, or register you to vote, or something, anything, while you bring yourself off! And the orgasm you give yourself with his loving assistance counts: self-induced orgasms in the presence of others are every bit as real as look-ma-no-hands orgasms.

Lastly, "overmasturbating" does not make people bisexual, or god knows, every last red-blooded American male would be bisexual by the time he turned 16. Should you decide to act on your bisexual impulses, your girlfriends will need as much direction as your boyfriends. If you don't learn how to communicate what you need to get off, you may find yourself lying under a girl picking your nails and watching television—and it'll be your own damn fault.

Hey, Faggot:

My question involves my present and ex-girlfriends, as I've had the same problem with both. Both say I'm a very good lover. Lovemaking sessions have lasted hours. However, neither could have an orgasm via intercourse alone. They can each come in a second by masturbation, and in minutes from oral sex. They say they've come very close during intercourse with me. They also say that I shouldn't worry. But if I didn't worry about it, wouldn't I be one of those guys women complain about all the time?

I'm beginning to get a complex. I wonder what I'm doing wrong. I wonder if they would be more satisfied if they had been with someone better endowed. During intercourse, I feel myself becoming discouraged: I think that she will never enjoy this as much as I do, and sometimes these thoughts have caused me to go soft in the middle of the act.

Please tell me what to do.

Brooklyn

Hey, B:

Your desire to not be "one of those guys women complain about" is commendable, but would be more so if you'd bothered to educate yourself about women's bodies and women's orgasms before you started fucking women.

News flash: most women are unable to "have an orgasm via intercourse alone." And why is this? Because the business end of her clitoris, which plays as central a role in her sexual pleasure as the head of your cock plays in yours, is located outside and above the vagina, not inside it. Are you with me? The clitoris is not a joy-buzzer at the top of the vaginal canal. It doesn't matter how hard your dick is, how big your dick is, or how far in her you manage to get it (okay, those things do matter, but for the sake of this argument, they don't): the clit's the thing!

While some women's clits are angled in such a way that simple bumping and grinding provides enough direct clitoral stimulation to get them off, most women's clits are not, and you actually have to go out of your way to make her orgasms happen. It never ceases to amaze me just how many heterosexual men don't know these basic vagi-facts!

But you needn't take my word for it. According to August's *Cosmo*—my reference for all questions regarding female anatomy, sexual response, and fashion—fully 70 percent of women need stimulation above and beyond vaginal intercourse in order to achieve orgasm. Now, it ain't science if the results of an experiment aren't repeatable. So we here at Savage Labs conducted our own study and, lo and behold, came up with the same results *Cosmo* did: of 10 female co-workers surveyed, seven required oral or manual stimulation in addition to, or in place of, vaginal intercourse to achieve orgasm.

Here's what some of our subjects had to say (listen up, boys): "It seems like the better educated guys are about sex, the less likely they are to think it's odd that I need other forms of stimulation in order to come. Whenever I'm with some young band boy, I've got to explain it to him." "Men who can't find my clit, or don't know what to do with it when I point it out, don't get invited back for seconds." "It's possible for me [coming from fucking], but it takes longer and it's less likely. Both at once—all sorts of stimulation at once—is the best way." "Direct clitoral stimulation, that's what I need. Sometimes I'd rather do that—or have that done to me—than fuck."

Imagine the flip side, Brooklyn: your new girlfriend pays no attention to the head of your cock during sex; the most she can be bothered to do is provide you with a little "indirect stimulation," casually nudging the side of your dick with her foot while you eat her to orgasm after orgasm. While you might enjoy this activity (especially if you're a foot fetishist), it probably isn't enough to get you off. Oh, you're havin' fun, but you're not havin' orgasms. Eventually, you pull your slimy face out of her crotch and ask her to pay some attention to your cock.

Now, imagine that after you ask for some much-deserved direct stimulation, your girlfriend recoils in horror, insisting that *all* her previous boyfriends could climax from indirect dick-nudging alone. "What is wrong with you?" she asks. Knowing boys, you tell her she's full of shit—delusional, in fact—and all of her previous boyfriends were liars. And you dump her, right? You wouldn't settle for indirect stimulation, would you? So why on earth should your girlfriends?

I'm going to let you off the hook just a bit: you're probably not entirely responsible for your predicament: the women you've been sleeping with up to this point have no doubt contributed to your appalling ignorance. A lot of women, when they first start having sex, believe they should be able to have orgasms from intercourse alone—cuz that's the way women's orgasms work in movies, porn, romance novels, and it's the way ill-informed boyfriends insist women's orgasms work. Consequently, some young women psych themselves out, convincing themselves they're having orgasms while their boyfriends huff and puff; others fake orgasms so their boyfriends won't think they're damaged goods.

Since inexperienced young women typically have sex with inexperienced young men, these psyched/faked orgasms can leave young boys like you with a false impression of just how women's bodies work and, sadly, of your own sexual powers. Bad-in-bed boys bop through their sex lives until the earth-shattering moment when they find themselves in bed with a woman who insists on a little hand action or a whole lotta oral sex; a woman who demands that her clit play as central a role in the sex act as the head of his dick. At this point, the boys, the dear, sweet, darling breeder boys, freak the fuck out.

They think the new girlfriend is some sort of psychotic nympho or, like you, they think their lovemaking skills have somehow deteriorated or their cocks aren't big enough. Of course, the new GF isn't a psycho-nympho, she's just not a doormat; and your lovemaking skills haven't deteriorated—they never developed in the first place. As for your cock, it may be too big, too small, or just right, but most women need stimulation in addition to fucking to achieve orgasm regardless of the size of their boyfriend's cock.

You fear the girlfriend "will never enjoy [intercourse] as much as I do," and that fear sometimes causes you to go soft. Well, fear not: she'll enjoy fucking as much as you do if you remember to pay attention to her clit while you're fucking her. If your arms aren't broken or bound, play with her clit while you bang away; encourage her to play with herself when you're fucking; try different positions to see if perhaps another angle might provide more direct stimulation to her clit, let her control the speed and pace of the grind; get her off with your mouth or your hand before you fuck; buy some "clit grapes" at a sex-toy store—the possibilities are endless. Make her pleasure a priority, and you won't be one of those men women complain about all the time.

Hey, Faggot:

Loved your advice for Brooklyn! I have a few suggestions for women "coming out" into better sex now that their boyfriends have read your column:

1. It's not dirty to touch yourself. In fact, men worth knowing grow increasingly hard when a woman places her hand on herself. Why do you think there's so much female masturbation in straight porn?
2. As Dan notes, God played a mean trick and positioned our clits outside and not inside where it could have received stimulation from the thrusting. So while your BF is thrusting, take your fingers and push your clit down against his shaft. His in-and-out will be your pleasure too!
3. Ask your BF to enter you high—that is, position himself so his crotch is high up on yours. When he enters, he'll go deep and perhaps catch your clit in the tight angle formed between his penetrating dick and firm torso. You'll get all the pressure you need—plus rocking and manipulation and presto: intercourse might work to make your climax happen, pleasing both your breeder boy and you.
4. Get on top. Intercourse in this position nearly always produces a climax. Granted, you won't whip in and out as fast as he needs for him to come, but you go first, slow and steady, you control the action, and remember to squeeze your Kegel muscles, which feels good to him but also makes your clit "erect" and firm, adding to its stimulation. After you've had 10 or 20 or so orgasms, let him take over the speed and let him enjoy his big O too.

The greatest thing, Dan, about your recent column is now that you've explained so wonderfully how all men can be great clit lovers, they all will be, and we women will stop falling so hard for the very few guys out there who can give us orgasms.

With more men capable of giving us O's, we'll be free to look for a few other qualities important to a caring relationship and friendship. Thanks!

Roberta

Hey, R:

You're welcome, girlfriend. I heartily endorse all your suggestions, though I have heard that #3 can lead to urinary tract infections in some women, so proceed with caution. I would like to add just one more to the list, though: what, under any circumstances, should you never do? Fake an orgasm. The boyfriend or husband you humor with fake O's today may be some other woman's boyfriend or husband tomorrow. He's not yours indefinitely. When he lands between another woman's legs, make sure you've done your part for sisterhood—which is powerful, you know—by not giving him a false impression of his own meager skills, or false expectations about women's sexual response.

Hey, Faggot:

I don't know whether to kiss you or kick your ass.

My girlfriend stuck your clit column under my pillow. I read it and we talked about her need for "additional clitoral stimulation," as you put it. So now I'm doing all I can to see that she gets hers, as per your instructions. I'd never seen your column until she showed it to me, and I don't have any interest in ever seeing it again. I'm not used to taking orders from fags, especially when it comes to pussy, but things are much happier in the sack since we "shared" your letter.

Thanks, I think.

Big-Time Breeder

Hey, BTB:

Don't know whether to kiss me or kick my ass? Split the difference and kiss my ass.

Hey, Faggot:

Fortunately for me, my current partner spent his high school and college years fornicating with women who taught him how to make them come while fucking—not by using his tongue and fingers, but just his five-and-a-half-inch white-ass penis. As you mentioned at the end of your response, angle is the answer! My boyfriend positions his hips close to my belly button. His penis gets much closer to my clit. I slowly or quickly buck or rock my hips so while he's coming up, I'm going down. My clit rubs against the root of his penis and . . . orgasm! It takes an amazingly short time.

Jill

Hey, J:

The position you describe—him riding high—may work for you, and many other women, but it is not a sure thing for all women. Much depends on the angle of your clit, whether your clit sits high or low. You're lucky to have a clit angled in such a way that altering the angle of penetration makes all the difference. But for most women, no amount of angle-play will result in enough prolonged, direct clitoral stimulation to result in an orgasm. But it's worth a whirl, girls.

Hey, Faggot:

"Bill" and I have been lovers on and off for five years. Lately we've been having troubles in bed. Basically, I was having a lot of trouble having an orgasm through our usual sex play and I wanted to incorporate my vibrator into our sex life. Bill refused to use a vibrator, saying it would take my attention away from him. Finally, out of sheer desperation, I told him that I had been faking most of my orgasms, and that while I enjoyed making love to him, a vibrator was necessary for me to achieve satisfaction. His response? "That's not something I'm really interested in doing, this is more about you, not about me."

Coincidentally your "Brooklyn" column came out two days later. Knowing that Bill reads your column regularly and respects your opinion, I thought I would send it to him with the relevant portions highlighted.

I'll briefly sum up Bill's response: In a six-page letter, he not only denied that the article had anything to do with our sex life, but also got personal: "I don't like the way you kiss, I never have"; he hinted that it would be easier to reach my clit during intercourse if I lost some weight; he doesn't like the way my pussy tastes/smells, he was only eating me because he didn't want to upset me; I need major therapy; and he told me not to call him again. He also threw in two "Fuck Yous" for good measure.

After a five-and-a-half-year relationship, I thought he would do better than hurl the same generic insults that men have been hurling at women since time immemorial. My question for you, Dan, is this: Is this sort of rejection typical when breeder boys are confronted with a woman who has the self-esteem to say what she needs and expects to get? Should I prepare myself for a lifetime of solitary orgasms?

Tuna Crotch

Hey, TC:

His defensiveness and hostility might have something to do with feeling humiliated by your deceit. Five years is an awful long time to let some poor schmo think he's been making you come. To abruptly inform him that he has not, in actual fact, been making you come lo these many years, in order to win an argument about a vibrator, was a little mean-spirited. I'd be angry too.

With any and all new partners, incorporate your vibrator into your sex play right away, and refrain from ticking off a partner's sexual shortcomings to win arguments.

Hey, Faggot:

I've been with the same man for a bit over a year now, and I'm pretty happy with him. He says he's crazy about me, and I believe him. But there's one problem—he won't eat me out! He says he doesn't like the way it tastes. On one occasion he said, "I won't eat something that tastes like chicken and smells like fish." One time, however, when he was insanely drunk, he went down on me, and it was glorious! Do you have any ideas or incentives for him to submit to pleasuring my nether folds with his beautiful tongue? I'm going insane over here!

Unlicked, Unsatisfied, Unhappy

Hey, UUU:

Encourage him to develop a cunnilingus-enabling drinking problem, or find yourself a brand-new lover. Personally, I don't think women should date men who think pussy is disgusting: why date someone who finds you, and your genitals, revolting? I wouldn't waste half an hour on a guy who wouldn't put my dick in his mouth. Most straight boys I know don't date girls who don't give head. Why do straight girls date boys who don't eat pussy?

Hey, Faggot:

The letter from the woman who has a boyfriend who won't eat her because she "tastes like chicken and smells like fish" caught my eye. I would agree that oral sex should go both ways and that it's a good idea to stop sleeping with a partner who is unreasonable about satisfying your sexual needs. But a fishy smell might be what turned him off, not oral sex in general.

There may be a very simple explanation for this couple's dilemma. Many sexually active women harbor an oftentimes asymptomatic vaginal infection called bacterial vaginosis (also known as gardnerella, or nonspecific vaginitis). The most common symptom of BV is the infamous (and disgusting) fishy odor. BV is not a sexually transmitted disease; however, there are two very effective prescription medications for women.

This is an embarrassing problem for a lot of couples. Please let your readers know that while almost all vaginal fragrances and discharges are completely normal, this one is not. Thanks so much.

Nancy

Hey, N:

Always happy to promote healthy attitudes about vaginal discharge and fragrance. While some twat-shy breeder boys cry "fish" out of sheer cunnaphobia, there are indeed instances where the woman does have an honest to goodness odor problem. Ladies: if your boyfriend adored eating out his last five girlfriends, but won't get near your pussy without a snorkel, maybe the problem is yours. Go to your doc and demand some of that BV-bustin' metronidazole, which according to a brochure Nancy was kind enough to enclose, "can be administered by mouth (i.e. tablets) or intravaginally," brouchure-speak for "Take this and stick it in your pussy."

Kink

Everybody is kinky.

That's not just my opinion as a sex advice columnist. In fact, I'd like to state for the record that this opinion has nothing to do with being a sex advice columnist—but if I were to form opinions on the basis of the thousands of letters that hit my desk, my opinion would remain the same: everybody is kinky. But as kinky folks are likelier to have problems, as their sex lives tend to be more complicated than those of non-kinky people, and therefore they are likelier to send me a letter, my sample could be called skewed. So I'm not going to point to my letters as proof that everyone is kinky.

Instead, I'm going to point to a much more scientific study, conducted over a longer period of time, involving many thousands more subjects. I refer to my own sex life. By most anyone's standards, I would be considered kinky—and no, I'm not gonna give you the details, so long as my mother is alive. But in the dozen or so years I've been out in the world having my way with men, I have yet to encounter one who couldn't be talked into doing just about anything, provided he wasn't enthusiastically into whatever-was-suggested to begin with. Or, as was often the case, provided he didn't beat me to the suggestion.

Also, let's remember that kink is a very subjective label. What Sue considers a freakish kink, Mary may regard as a common staple. Very often, when you talk to someone about what they like to do in bed, the bizarre things they enjoy aren't "kinks," they're "interests." Someone will tell you he's "interested" in bondage, feet, and Buddhists; but show him someone into spankings, armpits, and Baptists, and the bondage-freak foot fetishist with an "interest" in rimming the Dalai Lama will tell you that the Jesus-freak, butt-beating pit-sniffer standing over there is "kinky."

And, bear in mind, as you work your way through this chapter, that what's generally considered "kinky" changes over time. Two examples: Once upon a time, not too long ago, oral sex was regarded as the height of kink, and folks who were too interested in oral sex were considered freaks. Now, it's such a commonly engaged in sex practice that those who don't "do" oral sex are rightly regarded as freaks.

The same goes for bondage. People once thought bondage to be an almost unspeakable perversion, and anyone interested in bondage was sick. These days, outside my immediate family, it's hard to find someone who hasn't done bondage! Or doesn't want to give it a try! We live in a post-Madonna universe, where restraints can be purchased at sex shoppes in perfectly respectable shopping malls, and sexual exploration that does not involve minors, lasting bodily harm, rock videos, or the Speaker of the House of Representatives is generally considered pretty harmless.

So, as you read these letters, remember that in the last 20 years, oral sex went from taboo, to kinky, to normal. And bondage, lagging slightly behind, moved from unspeakable perversion, to serious kink, to good clean kinky fun. I don't think a day will come when folks who don't do bondage are thought odd, though I'm doing my best to make my boyfriend feel that way—bondage will probably always be regarded as kinky, but it is no longer regarded as sick. And that's progress, I guess. Today's unspeakable perversion is tomorrow's kink, is next week's good clean fun.

Finally, there are some kinks in this chapter that I hope remain taboo forever, like incest and dog-fucking. And bisexuality.

Why is bisexuality included in the kink and weirdness chapter? Well, because bisexuality is just the sickest, most depraved perversion imaginable, that's why.

Hey, Faggot:

This is a genuine sincere letter. I am not a frat row prankster or homophobe. What is "felching"?

Curious

Hey, C:

There's a town in Michigan called Felch, and one just north of Felch called Felch Mountain. For the definitive definition, I called the post office in Felch and spoke to Ken. Ken didn't know what "felching" was, but he guessed it would be "touring felch." Felch was named after the Governor of Michigan in 1846, Elfius Felch. Would a "felcher" be a kindred spirit of Governor Felch in the same way a sadist is a spiritual descendant of the Marquis de Sade? Ken wasn't sure. So I called Blomquist's Restaurant in Felch, thinking maybe somebody there would be able to help us. Donna, the waitress at Blomquist's, "had no idea" what felching was, "nope, I don't. None." If no one in Felch knows what felching is, how can I pretend to know? All I know for sure is that Felch is a city in Michigan.

Hey, Faggot:

Lecture me please: The topic is nipple rings. During my recent visit to Bondage A Go-Go in San Francisco, I was making a follow-up hit on a guy—I lost momentum after the first attempt—when I noticed that he was wearing a little silver nipple ring. My question: What does one do with those things sexually? What else can one do besides twist and pull?

Bondage Girl

Hey, BG:

Playing with tit rings is limited to variations of twisting and pulling, but you can keep the twisting and pulling interesting by making your variations interesting. You can hang things from his tit rings: padlocks look cool, they'll pull and leave your hands free to twist other things. If padlocks aren't to your taste—or if you're prone to misplacing keys or forgetting combinations— weights designed for hanging from tit rings can be purchased at sex-toy stores. Or loop some thin rope through his tit ring and tie it off on something—his balls, the bedpost, your nipple ring. However he moves, or any way you choose to move him, he'll be twisting and pulling his tit ring.

Hey, Faggot:

Recently I have heard about women shaving off other women's pubic areas as a sexual practice. Is there some significance or symbolism? Is it a fetish?

Just Curious

Hey, C:

Shaving off their pubic *areas*? I don't know about that. I know that shaving your pubic hair off isn't something only dykes do—a poll of the pervs around the office found that roughly 50 percent had shaved their own pubes off, or someone else's, at one time. Those who hadn't tried it weren't averse to giving it a whirl, though fear of ingrown hairs was cited as a deterrent.

Why do it? Well, why not? There's a certain because-it-was-there quality to erotic-shaving. Being suddenly pube-less is a weird sensation; it looks different, it feels different. People with a fetish for it generally fall into two camps: those who get excited by the look and feel of a hairless genital area, and those who get off on the actual act of removing their own, or their pal's, pubes. It's been my experience that the actual shaving part is tedious. It's messy, and you really have to concentrate: a knick on your leg or face is painful, but nothing compared to a knicked scrotum or pussy lip. And when the hairs begin to grow back, look out: it itches like hell and you can give someone a pretty wicked whisker burn.

Hey, Faggot:

I am a het chick who digs gay male porn. Am I sick? Am I alone in my secret passion? Am I really a gay man trapped in a woman's body, or just a fag hag? I'd like your opinion, please.
Confused

Hey, Confused:

Are straight guys who beat off to "lesbian" spreads in *Penthouse* dykes trapped in men's bodies? Of course not. You're a woman attracted to men so why wouldn't pictures of two naked men turn you on twice as much as pictures of one naked man?

Straight women who like to look at naughty pictures of men usually have no other option than porn manufactured for gay men. Consuming gay porn, you may have, over time, acquired a taste for images of men screwing other men.

Hey, Faggot:

I am totally turned on by women with hair on their arms, and especially if they have that line leading from their belly on down to their pubic hair. I don't mean guy-type hair, but normal, soft girl hair. My question: What percentage of men like hair, as opposed to men who like their women to shave down all their body hair?

DD

Hey, DD:

How the hell should I know? The percentage of men who like hairy women, women who have big clits, guys who like to be spanked, people who've fucked their mothers—even if I could produce these stats, what good would it do you? What does it matter if 8 or 80 percent of men prefer hairy women? It's what you like and it doesn't hurt anybody; that's all you need to know.

Not even Pam Winter, publisher of *Hair to Stay*, a magazine devoted to hairy women, could come up with a percentage. "If I took a poll of every person in the entire world, maybe I could give you an idea," she said. "But even if I did a poll, a lot of men won't admit they like hairy women for fear of being told something's wrong with them, or being called homos. Guys who like hairy women are made to feel like freaks, so a lot of guys who do won't admit it."

While she can't put a number on it, Pam can say this: judging by how many mags Pam moves in a year—more than 6,000—and the number of hits her Web site gets every day—over 2,500—you are not alone. "Lots of men like women with natural hair on their bodies. People are realizing that bleached-blonde, shaved, and siliconed look-alikes are not what everyone wants."

When I asked Pam if your particular thing—arm hair—was out of the ordinary, she said no. "In fact, after armpit and pubic, forearm hair is the leading fascination for men who like hairy women."

Hey, Faggot:

I have been attracted to female amputees for as long as I can remember. Have other people written you about this amputee attraction phenomenon? I get very excited when I come across a single-legged girl crutching along, or encounter a pretty young woman with an empty sleeve dangling where an arm should be. Do you know of any clubs or organizations that cater to such an interest? Are there many others with this attraction and where can I meet amputees?

AMP Fan

Hey, AMP Fan:

My dear old Catholic ma came to visit recently—for a whole week. Mom stayed with me at my new apartment, where she got to meet my new boyfriend. I bring up my mother not because she's an amputee but because it was my mom who taught me everything I know about giving advice. During my formative years, I spent countless hours listening to my mother tell her sisters, her friends, and ladies from the parish to get their shit together. So, since she was here, I thought I'd let the ol' gal have a go at this sex-advice gig. AMP Fan, here's Mom's advice for you:

"Go and do some volunteer work at a hospital. Work in a rehabilitation institute for people who've lost a limb in a car wreck or something." Sounds like ma's on your side. Did she really mean to say people attracted to amputees should lurk around hospitals? "Well, no, of course not. I just thought he could meet an amputee that way. I guess he'd be volunteering for the wrong reasons, like a pedophile working for the Boy Scouts." Or going into the priesthood, huh ma? "I'm not going to dignify that with a response. Maybe he should go see a shrink and find out why he's into this."

Hey, Faggot:

I read your recent Q&A with the guy who said he was attracted to amputees. I'm another "perv" who has the same interest.

You start out by comparing amputee-lovers to pedophiles. Well, maybe there's a parallel of sorts, but here's a big difference: The guy didn't say he was into amputee children, he didn't say he was into raping amputees, and he didn't say he was into making people into amputees. The guy said he was attracted to amputees. Why do you bring up criminal activity as a parallel? Sex between consenting adults isn't a crime, if you haven't heard.

There's an organization for amputees and the folks who love

'em called Fascination. It's run be a woman named Bette Hag-
glund, who's an amputee.

Joe

Hey, Joe:

First of all, I didn't compare amputee-fetishists to pedophiles,
my mother did. I compared pedophiles to Roman Catholic
priests. My mother's comparison was unfair. It was equally unfair
of me to imply that all pedophiles are Roman Catholic priests.
Some pedophiles are productive members of society.

Secondly, sex between consenting adults is illegal in roughly
half these United States—or hadn't you heard? In the 1986
Hardwick decision, the Supreme Court upheld Georgia's sodomy
law, ruling that, at least as far as gay sex is concerned, the
state has every right to regulate what consenting adults get up
to in their own bedrooms. While having sex with amputees, or
wanting to have sex with amputees, has never been illegal—
so long as the amputee is of one sex and the devotee is of
another—outlawing sex between consenting adults is one of
America's pastimes.

Thirdly, on your suggestion, I did give Bette a call. And what
a nice woman she is! Bette founded Fascination in 1984 to fill a
need: through a support group she was running for amputees,
Bette came to know men who were attracted to amputees (acro-
tomophiles), but were having a hard time meeting them. "So we
created an atmosphere where people with these feelings can
meet," says Bette.

In addition to organizing social events, Fascination produces
a quarterly newsletter that's "a combination of fiction, nonfic-
tion, and comments relating to the attraction." The newsletter
features photographs of amputees, but it is not pornography.
"Oh, no," says Bette, "definitely not."

According to Bette, most of the men and women involved
with Fascination are looking for partners. Has anyone met their
soulmate? "We've had several quad-amputees, triple amputees,
and double amputees who met men at our meetings and are
now married to them." How did Bette meet her husband?
"When I had surgery, many years ago—I'm not going to tell

you how many—there was an article about me in the paper. He saw the article and wrote me a letter asking if he could take me to dinner when I got out of the hospital. My roommate at the hospital knew him, he was her neighbor, so I went to dinner with him." How did Bette lose her legs? "I was born with deformed legs. As an adult, I decided to have them amputated. That's why there were articles written about me."

Are most amputee-admirers men? "Yes, but it can be the other way around. I've heard of some women who are attracted to men with disabilities, but more women are attracted to someone in a wheelchair, someone they could nurture and take care of." While no gay or lesbian amputee-admirers are involved with Fascination, "We haven't ever excluded anyone," says Bette. "We do have a couple of gays on the mailing list, though, but only a couple."

Hey, Faggot:

A poke in the eye with a prosthetic device for "AMP Fan." I'm a young woman with a myriad of attributes—some very desirable, some not. I am also an amputee. I have worked very hard to cultivate my positive natural qualities, to help define myself as a strong, whole person. "Amputee" is not high on the list of my "qualities."

I could just kick the hell out of some guy who is either jokingly or seriously seeking out young women who have lost limbs. He's targeting and fetishizing what a young woman may be missing at the possible expense of her long climb toward wholeness.

You're an insect, AMP Fan; spare me your parasitic shenanigans.

RSB, Seattle

Hey, RSB:

I shared your letter with Bette, and she leapt on your thoughtless ageism: "Why does she think only 'young women' are pursued? It's not true: the women who attend our meetings are 21 to 75 years old." And the Fascination boys, presumably, are in hot pursuit of all of them, from young amps to the AARP amps.

Bette agrees with your feelings about your missing limb: "Being an amputee is incidental, not a negative or positive quality." But Bette wanted you to reconsider your take on men attracted to you because of your stump: "All relationships begin with an initial attraction, and as far as men are concerned, the initial attraction is usually something physical—whether it's blue eyes, nice legs, fannies, etc. You can't base a relationship on being an amputee. But there is nothing wrong with it sparking the initial attraction."

Hey, Faggot:

I am an otherwise-typical gay male in my 20s, mostly satisfied with myself except for one bothersome condition: I am piss-shy.

I am unable to relax my urinary tract in the presence of others, no matter what degree of discomfort my bladder is causing me. Crowded and/or cruisy rest rooms are a formidable obstacle. Even after intimacy, I have to close the bathroom door so my partner can't watch me pee. I'm missing out on some great cruising opportunities, not to mention watersports. Do you have any advice that might be helpful?

Piss Shy

Hey, PS:

Here's a few pointers on getting the most out of cruisy toilets and watersports despite your "condition."

Say you're in a gay bar, hanging out with a few friends. There's this really cute guy on the other side of the room, and every time you look at him he's looking at you. Tell your friends you've "gotta go" to the bathroom and on the way, walk past the really cute guy. He may intercept you, or he may tell his friends he's "gotta go to the bathroom" too, and follow you. So what do you do when you find yourself in the john, with the cute guy, unable to make water? Stand at a urinal and pretend—unzip, haul it out, wait a minute, put it back, zip up. While you're making like you're making water is your chance to strike up a conversation: "Piss here often?" If the cute guy didn't follow you in, walk past the cute guy on the way back to where your friends are standing.

As for watersports: your sex partners can't all be pee-shy too, can they? You can enjoy watersports—at least as a bottom—while providing yourself with valuable non-pee-shy role models. (What's the opposite of pee-shy anyway? Pee-gregarious? Pee-forward? Pee-friendly? Pee-affable? Pee-cordial? Pee-social?) If you long to be the world's first pee-shy watersports top, you could step into the next room, pee into a water pistol, then join your friend in the bedroom, or the bathtub, and let him have it.

Hey, Faggot:

I am—or thought I was—a hetero woman who's been in a very satisfying relationship for the past 5½ years.

Here's my question/problem: I work for a very large company—we occupy a whole downtown high-rise. A few weeks ago, I went into the ladies' room and there was a woman in there (she must not have heard me enter) masturbating. At first I was disgusted and then I was fascinated! I waited until she was done and quickly left—I was extremely excited! Now every time my partner and I have sex, I relive the bathroom scene in my mind and try to imagine who it is. That's all I ever think about!

Am I a closet case? What's going on with me?

In the Bathroom

Hey, ITB:

If while you're making love to your husband, you're wishing you were on your knees in that bathroom stall with your head between the legs of the "mystery lady," then maybe you're some sorta latent bi/dyke jolted out of the closet by the sound of one woman masturbating.

But if what's running through your head is not "I want pussy" but "Gosh that was the freakiest thing that ever happened to me," then I'm guessing you ain't no dyke. You're just flying from the voyeuristic kicks you got that day, to say nothing of the delicious high of "getting away" with harmless naughtiness. So you're not a dyke, but a nice, polite straight woman with a nice, polite voyeuristic/exhibitionist streak.

Why not tell hubbie what happened? Tell him how it turned you on—share your high with him. Suggest he visit you at work for lunch—then sneak him into the bathroom and do him. Do him in the same stall she was doing herself in. Be naughty, risk getting "caught," or being "overheard."

Hey, Faggot:

I've been using one of those shower anal douches for about a year now and I've always wondered if there are any long-term side effects I should be aware of. Is using the douche once or twice a week too often? Am I washing away good bacteria? How do the prostate and colon fare during all this washing?

An Ass You Could Eat Dinner On

Hey, AYCEDO:

Anal douching—giving yourself mini-enemas—once or twice a week poses no health risks, so long as you're using lukewarm tap water and avoiding those nasty chemical douches sold in drugstores. As for your prostate: the water doesn't actually wash over your prostate, as your prostate is tucked safely behind the walls of the rectum. Giving yourself an enema—or having a friend give you an enema—places pressure on the prostate, which some people find pleasurable, but it doesn't "wash" your prostate. As for your colon, any poop or mucus you manage to flush out will be replaced in pretty short order—your body just keeps making more. So, not to worry.

The only risk you're running, actually, is the means to your end: that shower-attachment and doucher. You need to be very careful about the amount of water pressure you're putting on your guts. While those cyborg-douche shower attachments look dramatic, they're not the safest way to get water up your butt. Low-tech enema bags are easier to control and you're not going to bump the faucet and increase the pressure accidentally.

Hey, Faggot:

Call us ignorant, but could you please explain the term "scat" to us.

Two Clueless Ones

Hey, TCO:

Scat is slang for coprophilia—a fetish for poop. According to *The American Heritage Dictionary*, scat also means "to go away hastily." Precisely what you should do if someone you're dating announces they're into scat.

Hey, Faggot:

I have a fantasy I never heard of anybody else having. My fantasy is to have a girl flatulate in my face and mess her pants and I have to clean her and put her in fresh clothes. Do you know of any organization I could contact to find partners?

DW

Hey, DW:

The number of people interested in a particular kink has to reach a tipping point before clubs are formed. So far as I know, poopy pants fetishism has not yet reached the tipping point, and I would guess it isn't likely to anytime soon. But don't despair, DW, you are not without options. Volunteer at a nursing home. Or buy your next date a difficult-to-remove jumpsuit—something with lots of tricky belts, snaps, and zippers—and treat her to a delicious ground beef/fecal matter sandwich at your local burger chain. Then hope for the worst.

Hey, Faggot:

I feel the advice you gave DW about his fantasy of having a woman flatulate in his face and mess herself was rude, insensitive, and condescending. I am not remotely interested in that sort of thing, although I do know there are a lot of people who are. First of all, advising him to volunteer at a nursing home?! That's just plain fucked-up. When I am 90+ years old, I don't want someone getting off on my shit!

Basically, there are a lot of people with odd fetishes. Obviously, he was reaching out to you, and aside from the fact that we may think it's weird, he needed someone to anonymously answer his questions. You just made him feel like an ass (no pun intended). You should have told him that if he needs to, there are lots of dominatrixes who will do that. And what about the Internet?

ME

Hey, ME:

Oh, the Internet—of course! If you're into shit, there's no better place to find it than on-line—the Internet is full of shit!

Hey, Faggot:

Tell me I'm normal! I'm a 26-year-old straight man with sexual tastes leading toward the bizarre. My ultimate fantasy is to lie in an empty tub and have a woman defecate on me. How do I meet a female who shares my interest?

Bill

Hey, Bill:

You're not normal, and there are no social clubs in North America for men who love poop and the women who'll consent to crap on them. Your best bets are personal ads or twice-yearly jaunts to beautiful Amsterdam's accommodating red-light district.

Hey, Faggot:

Your recent "advice" confirmed a long-standing suspicion of mine: you are about as qualified to give sex advice as Ricki Lake is to give advice to fat people. To tell a man, straight or gay, that he is not "normal" because he wants to have his lady or boy friend poop on his chest or whatever confirmed yet another: that lefty fags of your ilk are just as fascist as the rightest of right-wingers—and just as intolerant. What to you is so shocking is simply the breaking of a capricious moral code; another taboo shattered.

It seems to me the only "unfortunate fetish" your readers are guilty of is looking to your column for advice!

Rev. Frank

Hey, Reverend:

"Fascists" with something against coprophilia are unlikely to recommend, as I did, personal ads, or trips to Amsterdam. No, fascists with a thing against coprophiliacs would, if the behavior of the 20th century's true "fascists" is any indication, herd them into camps, and gas them. Why do so many radicals—political radicals and sex radicals—fall into the squish-brained habit of labeling everyone who disagrees with them—usually on some minor point—a "fascist"? It takes the piss out of a word we may need again soon, and it trivializes the sufferings of those who've actually lived and died under fascism.

Bill's shit-fetish is "unfortunate" only because not a lot of other folks share his tastes and, consequently, he's going to have a hard time hooking up with other poop-fans. People into shit simply aren't as common as, say, people who wanna get spanked. The easier it is to indulge whatever fetish you're saddled with, the happier you'll probably be. For instance, a fetish for lingerie: what reasonably accommodating lover would refuse to dance around in something from Victoria's Secret? I'd do it. Poop? That's a harder sell, Reverend.

Hey, Faggot:

I have a question concerning a certain sexual proclivity of mine. I am a healthy, hot professional babe in my 20s. The thing is, I love when a guy talks dirty in bed; when he uses nasty language and is slightly physically abusive. I've really only dated one man who was into it, and he turned out to be a bit of a headcase.

Socially and professionally I'm pretty aggressive and opinionated. I only enjoy mistreatment in bed. Is this a problem worthy of therapy? My parents were pretty abusive and very neglectful.

Chicago

Hey, Chicago:

"It's going to be a lot easier for her if she just calls what she's interested in SM," said Dossie Easton, author of two books on SM (*The Bottoming Book: How to Get Terrible Things Done to You by Wonderful People* and *The Topping Book: Or Getting Good at Being Bad*). "If she doesn't like thinking of it that way, if she avoids the SM community, she isolates herself from the books, the groups, the ads, and all the other ways that people meet so they can share their sexual fantasies in safe, sane, and consensual ways."

Easton, a licensed marriage, family, and child counselor with a private practice in—where else?—San Francisco, has been into SM for almost 25 years. Before she came out about her desires she found herself in a similar situation to the one you describe. "I spent my idle youth hunting down rough trade in the streets of New York, and I finally wound up with a first-class batterer. So I'm not surprised she found somebody who was really exciting, who turned out to be a 'headcase.'"

It's like this, Chicago: if you bop through life hoping to meet men who by chance happen to share your desires, or if you encourage the men you're involved with to be "slightly physically abusive," you may well find yourself with men who will use your desires as a pretext to abuse you. A man who is openly into SM, who has thought about it and read about it and is involved to some extent in the SM community, is a much safer bet. He's likelier to know what boundaries and limits are; to possess a vocabulary that allows him to articulate his desires and help you articulate yours; and to understand where fantasy ends and reality begins.

As for your abusive parents, Easton says, "There are many people into SM who experienced abuse, and many who have not. I am an abuse survivor myself, and SM has not made me sicker than my parents did. If anything, it's made me healthier. I've been bottoming since 1974, and I just get stronger all the time, and more assertive." If the abuse and neglect you suffered as a child trouble you, Easton strongly suggests you find a therapist, one who is "trained in working with child abuse, but is not prejudiced against SM. Your local SM group will know who those people are.

"Too many therapists will say your desires are sick and you should just get rid of them. Not only is that not possible, but what I found in my 25 years of SM is that the experience is very empowering for me. I'm in control of it, making conscious decisions. My friend who plays the dominant has my safety as his chief concern. I can ride this roller coaster knowing it has been safety-tested. SM has made a major contribution to my healing from child abuse, and I have seen it in other clients I've worked with."

Hey, Faggot:

I'm a young handsome male with a problem. I like to be tied up and wear lingerie, and need to find a female friend who shares my interests.

Unfortunately, I know very little about the bondage scene. I've tried everything I can think of, including personal ads and hanging out at fetish clubs. I met some dominatrixes who showed some interest in me, but they were also heavily into SM, an activity I don't particularly enjoy, and seemed unwilling to give me the bondage without the discipline. I could respect where they were coming from, but this brought me no closer to finding someone I could share my appetites with.

I'm not sure where to proceed from here. Any advice?

Breeder Bondage Boy

Hey, BBB:

Kinky straight boys have it kind of rough; there just aren't as many kinky straight women as kinky straight men. Read the personals—there's ten kinky straight boy ads for every kinky girl ad. Kinky straight boys often have no choice but to resort to professionals to get there kinky rocks off.

But you're mostly into bondage, so you shouldn't have trouble finding a girl who's into it or willing to give it a whirl. God, everyone does bondage these days. Bondage isn't kinky! It's music videos, it's sitcom jokes, apple pie. Find a girl you like, date her, and if things click for you two sexually, ask her to think about incorporating bondage into your sex lives. Shouldn't be that big a deal. Then wait a week and spring the lingerie thing on her.

It sounds like you want to meet a girl who'll tie you up on the first date. You may meet someone like that at a fetish club or through a personal ad, but if you're out "shopping" for a girl who'll fulfill your laundry list of fantasies (1. make me wear your underwear, 2. tie me up, 3. don't hit me), you better be flexible about the fantasies she needs fulfilled (like the dominatrixes you've met). If you're just looking for someone, anyone, to plug into your fantasy scenario for the evening and not for a three-dimensional person with fantasies and needs of her own, maybe you ought to hire somebody and leave the nice dominatrixes alone.

Hey, Faggot:

I love to give myself up to my boyfriend for bondage, flogging, and whatever else he sees fit. I have some concerns, however, over the possible long-term effects of our play:

1. Can repeated bruising of the same area (i.e., my ass) cause any permanent harm?
2. Will the clamping of my nipples for long periods of time cause any problems in the future with breast-feeding?

Rachel

Hey, R:

1. Oft-flogged skin, especially in a "fleshy" area like the buttocks, can become mottled or spongy and begin to sag. If your boyfriend gives your butt enough time to fully recover between floggings, you can avoid this fate.
2. According to a leather-dyke pal of mine who recently had a baby ("I'm Pat Robertson's worst nightmare"), she had no trouble breast-feeding. In fact, since her nipples had already been toughened up by years of abuse, she was spared the tenderness some women experience when they begin to breast-feed.

Hey, Faggot:

I'm in a good relationship (three years), but the sex is kind of boring. Before this relationship, I was in and out of bad relationships with great sex. The difference? The old, bad relationships involved light SM.

I get off on being spanked, tied up, whipped, etc. There seemed to be a negative head trip that carried over from acts of kinkiness into the rest of those relationships and colored them bad. I don't want that to happen with my boyfriend now—he's willing to experiment—but I know what works for me. Any tips?

Pup Luck

Hey, PL:

Before we get to your main issue, how to have SM sex with your boyfriend without negative energy spilling over into the rest of the relationship, let me just say this: having kinky sex with someone who isn't into it—and by "into it" I mean "someone who digs your particular kink as much as you do, as opposed to someone who's giving it a shot to please you"—doesn't usually work. Nothing is a bigger turnoff than feeling indulged, having your kink "put up with" by a "long-suffering" or "understanding" partner. Its not easy getting your kinky rocks off when the whole time your lover is (a) stepping on you, (b) diapering you, (c) spanking you, you've got the sneaking feeling they're thinking to themselves, "How did I end up married to this sick fuck?"

It's especially troublesome if the person who's "giving it a try" is topping you in an SM scene. If your thing is, say, getting pissed on, that doesn't require much imagination on your boyfriend's part: you get in the tub, he thinks about waterfalls and open taps and raindrops on roses, and voilà, he's a watersports pro. But SM? For a person to be a "hot" SM top, they need to have a feel for it. Someone who's topping his boyfriend by request will almost certainly lack the erotic spark a top must possess to keep safe-sane-consensual SM sex crackling.

Having said that, here's my advice for you: teach your boyfriend to top you. "Training a top" requires more than showing him how to tie knots, or flog you without hitting your kidneys. No: your mission, should you choose to accept it, is this: to instill in your boyfriend the erotic imagination required of good SM tops. Buy your boyfriend some SM porn—books, not videos. Read them out loud, talk about what turns you on; ask him what, if anything, turns him on. If you can get his dick hard talking, reading, and fantasizing about SM sex before you guys actually start having SM sex, he may end up being one of those rare people introduced to SM by a lover who winds up digging it.

Once you get him going, you can guard against inappropriate SMish vibes in the nonfantasy realm of your relationship by establishing—everybody, all together—Clearly Defined Boundaries. SM sex should have an obvious beginning and an obvious end; something like, "Our kinky fantasy sex begins and ends with you putting a dog collar on me." If he violates those boundaries, if he starts treating you like his slave when you're not having sex, don't bottom out: call him on it. Say, "Excuse me, but I'm not wearing a dog collar right now, and unless I'm wearing one, I'd prefer you didn't treat me like a dog."

Hey, Faggot:

Any tips for bondage beginners? My girlfriend and I are ready to give kinkier sex the old college try. But neither of us has tied a knot more complicated than the ones we accidentally put in our shoelaces. Any tips?

New to It

Hey, NTI:

You're in luck: a friend of a friend of a friend of mine just happens to be the editor and publisher of *Bound & Gagged*, which is, with the exception of *Christian Family Today*, the finest special-interest kink lifestyle magazine in America today.

B&G features reader-written accounts of real-life male-male bondage experiences, "from Cowboy-and-Indian kids' games to college frat hazings, to adult erotic bondage experiences." When it comes to tying up boys, *B&G*'s editor and publisher, Bob Wingate, is an expert. Since tying up a girl really ain't all that different from tying up a boy, I turned your letter over to Mr. Wingate.

Here are Bob's bondage-for-beginners pointers: "To my mind, there are three types of rope bondage: too tight, too loose, and just right—just like 'Goldilocks and the Three Bears.' Just right is snug without turning the extremities cold." For equipment, clothesline will do, "the kind that doesn't have a wire or plastic string running through it. Nylon rope, which is softer than cotton, is also good, as are neckties and stockings. It is not a costly game, or it need not be a costly game."

When it comes to knots, "the ones you put in your shoelaces should do the trick. It's not a question of how you make the knots, but where you put them." Bob doesn't understand why bondage beginners are intimidated by the prospect of tying knots, or tying each other up at all. "Cowboys and Indians is a game children play. If children know how to tie each other up, adults should be able to do it. You never hear one child say to another, 'Oh, I don't know how to tie a knot!' "

Hey, Faggot:

My girlfriend, who is 29, wants to explore leather/SM. We have been going together for six months. Soon after we began having sex, she suggested I tie her to the bed and have my way with her body. I did so. She loves it, and I must admit I like the power I have over her.

Now she wants us to attend a "bondage night" in a night-club, and she wants me to lead her around on a collar and leash. The bed routine is not all that normal, as far as I am concerned, but at least it is in private. But doing what she suggests in public? Will she want to go farther into territory that I find strange and kinky? And why would she want such public humiliation?

What should I do about this?

TW

Hey, TW:

Have a frank conversation with her about the extent of her SM desires. She wants public humiliation because why? Because it turns her on, du-huh. What should you do about it? Set aside your reservations and give it a whirl. Visit that bondage nightclub, but just observe. Then, if you feel more comfortable, go and play.

Hey, Faggot:

I'm not sexually experienced, but I am totally in love with my new man, and I want to please him in every way possible and drive him wild with desire. I want to blindfold him and tie his hands, maybe even handcuff him. But then what? We are not into pain. I feel so dumb! Besides honey and all that good stuff to lick off him, what else is there? What can I do to drive him crazy? He's excited that I want to tie his hands and blindfold him, so I want to make this good. But this is not going to happen 'til I get some ideas.

SQ

Hey, SQ:

For some ideas on tying up straight boys—not that I don't have ideas of my own—I shared your letter with Mistress Matisse, who has a bit more experience ropin' straight boys than I do. "If she wants to do a sexy femme top scene with no pain, I would suggest sensory deprivation combined with a lot of suspense and mindfucks." Now, without SM jargon: "Get dressed in sexy lingerie or something fetishy. Tie him up, blindfold him, and gag him." Get real restraints if you can afford them. Handcuffs hurt, and badly done rope bondage can lead to burns, pinched nerves, and amputated limbs. Restraints buckle on like belts, are practically foolproof, and are easier to remove if the boyfriend freaks.

Then if you can't beat him, scare him: "Start talking to him about all the things you could do. My rap goes like this: 'You know, baby, it's so-o-o sexy having you all tied up and helpless—I could do anything I want to you, and you can't stop me. . . .' Say this slow and thoughtful, like you're considering some very evil shit. Then tell him you're going to leave him there alone while you go get some 'things.' Walk to the bedroom door, open it and close it, but don't really leave the room (never actually leave anyone tied up alone). Stand very quietly and watch him. Is he struggling? Is his dick hard? Wait a minute, then quietly approach him and whisper in his ear, 'Are you thinking about me?' But don't get too close—if he jumps you'll bang heads.

"Alternate different sensations on his body, like a feather, your fingernails, and your mouth. I don't recommend the honey thing—looks good in movies, not all that exciting in real life. [I agree: Licking gooey crap off people is vastly overrated fauxnaughtiness, boring breeder kink.] You can take things a little further on the sensation scale: get a utility candle (white, no fragrance) and try dripping it on different parts of your body until you get a feel for it. Dripping warm wax on his skin and following it with a trail of ice can give quite the endorphin buzz."

You might also consider bringing in a professional consultant. Pro doms don't generally make house calls, but most will do couples in their own spaces, and would happily show you the ropes. "She would get to see someone experienced in action, someone who could show her a few tricks," said Mistress Matisse. "And she would get to see the attitude, which is the most important thing."

Hey, Faggot:

I am a single female. I have a special desire which I have never fulfilled due to shyness.

I have always wanted to hurt a man sexually. I want to see a man scream and writhe in pain. I need this satisfaction to cure a rage in me to physically hurt them. My long-standing fantasy has been to tie up or cuff a man and stick his body, including his penis, with a million stickpins. I want to draw blood. I want to see him scream and beg for mercy. I have always been fearful of expressing this desire, but I want this now. Can you understand the meaning of this? Why must I do this? Have you ever heard of this?

Joan

Hey, J:

"Properly channeled and marketed, she has a big career in professional dominance ahead of her," said Mistress Matisse. "There are many men who would love to have her do these things to them." As for your specific fantasy—sticking someone full of pins—it is not unheard of in SM, though sterile surgical needles are preferred over stickpins. "Temporary or 'play' piercings are considered an extreme form of SM by some wusses—I mean people," said Mistress Matisse. As for the meaning of your desires—the why—Mistress Matisse had this to say: "She sounds like a sadist. I am a bit of a sadist myself, and some of my friends are sadists. Doing these things will not 'cure her rage.' It's like food or sex—you want more. The thing is to find people who want you to do these things to them, and then learning how to inflict pain skillfully and safely. Sticking 22-gauge hypodermic needles under someone's skin and watching them yelp is fun—accidentally poking an arterial vein and having to call 911 is not." To find a willing victim, try the personal ads, join an SM club, look around on the Web—there are men out there paying Mistress Matisse cold hard cash to do what you're willing to do for free.

Hey, Faggot:

Strangulation is a big turn-on for me; both giving and receiving. However, I have a lot of scary scenarios in my head about going into a coma or giving somebody brain damage or something. Could you please give me and anyone else who needs to know the lowdown on how to give good choke without landing in the emergency room?

Breathless

Hey, B:

Folks with strangulation fantasies need to proceed with caution. Hands are best, and unlike rope, they're easily removed. And while rope or a belt may look more dramatic, it's harder to judge just how much pressure you're placing on that bundle of arteries, veins, and nerves that pass through the neck. You can give "good choke"—erotic asphyxia—without actually exerting all that much pressure, and you can better judge how much pressure you're using if you're using your hands. Maintain eye contact with your partner, and don't do choke drunk or high.

I should mention, however, that exerting *any* pressure on someone's throat can collapse certain nerves, and result in *swift and sudden death*! Really. So, be very careful. A better, safer way to play "breath control games," as the SMers like to call them, is to purchase a gas mask with a hose attached to it. Pinch off the hose, and you can "strangle" your partner without having to lay a finger on them.

Hey, Faggot:

You don't mention us transsexuals too much—at least not like we're real people—but I got a problem here that's freaking me out! My girlfriends are "stumped" by this one too, so maybe you can help. I'm passing, I look fine. Guys ask me out, we go through the dating game, they get told about me, nearly all of them say they can handle it. So we get intimate, and they try to suck my dick! What is with these "straight" guys? Is everybody latent?

Stop Trying to Suck My Dick

Hey, STTSMD:

A guy who dates a chick with a dick ain't no straight boy—which explains why your dates are diving on your cock. If it bothers you, get your dick cut off. Nobody can suck a cock you don't have.

Hey, Faggot:

We're a straight couple who enjoy tremendous sex and snuggling together. Lately we've been joined in bed by . . . our dog. He's a sweet puppy, one year old and neutered, and a willing partner in both foreplay and cleanup, and does amazing reaches with his snout when we fuck. Very fuzzy.

Since we all respect each other afterwards, and he seems to enjoy what pleasure we can give him, our question isn't moral, but practical: Are there any pathogens in his mouth that you know of that could result in yeast infections or other genito-urinary afflictions?

More Than Just Puppy Lovers

Hey, MTJPL:

Your question is outside my various and sundry areas of expertise. So I'm passing this one off to a specially assembled squad of experts: a vet (Dr. Kari Johnson), a sex therapist (Elizabeth Ray Larson), and a spokesperson for People for the Ethical Treatment of Animals (Kathy Savory).

Here's what the vet had to say: "Dogs have quite a bit of bacteria in their mouths. They lick their butts, they lick their genitals, they lick other dogs' butts, they eat poop—and it's very common for dogs to have E. coli in their feces; it's the most frequent cause of urinary tract infections in dogs. I wouldn't want that in my mouth or my genital or rectal area. There are millions of organisms in a dog's mouth that could cause urinary tract infections, yeast infections. There's staphylococcus, streptococcus, proteus, mycoplasma, pseudomonas.

"The male human could get prostatitis (infection of the prostate gland), and testicular infections—draining tracts of pus around the testes—which can result in serious damage to the testes; fibrosis (scarring) and sterility."

What would the doctor do if she learned that a dog under her care was being used for sex? "I'd do what I could to see that the animal is not returned to the person."

Here's what the sex therapist had to say: "Many people derive comfort from simple physical contact with their animals—we live with these animals most intimately. Erotic contact with dogs and cats is a widespread practice. Some people are in total denial and some are in total recognition. He sounds conscious of what he likes, he doesn't seem to have any moral conflicts."

If a patient were having sex with a dog, our sex therapist would "tell them to think it through. Anytime you're doing something controversial in your culture, you need to be clear about it. Is this harming you? Harming the dog? Just going with your feelings, going with your desires, is irresponsible unless you include your brain, your judgment, before you make the decision to proceed."

Here's what PETA had to say: "We're against animal exploitation in any way, shape, or form. This is definitely something PETA would be against. The animal doesn't have any choice in the matter, they're taking advantage of the animal. If this couple has a great sex life with each other, leave the dog out of it. Spend quality time with the dog in some other way."

Hey, Faggot:

What is the harm in a woman fucking a dog? Obviously, the male dog has to be showing some serious interest in order to consummate the deed, so it's not as if it's rape or abuse, right?

While in Amsterdam, I was able to watch videos of women getting down and dirty with man's best friend. Here in Portland, the only way I get to witness my favorite fuck act is at a video arcade. They have rooms where you can flip through several channels of smut for a pocketful of quarters. I can watch it there, but according to the guy at the counter, I can't rent it because it is illegal.

Does this make sense? I don't own a dog because they aren't allowed in the complex I live in. So where can a person indulge in such acts? Is it as uncommon as I am led to believe, or is it that it's way too taboo to speak of?

Horny as Hell

Hey, HAH:

The vet: "Dogs get erections at anything—when they come to the vet's office, when you walk them down the street—their erections can't be interpreted as the dog consenting to a sex act. Someone who says, 'Well, the dog has an erection and that means the dog wants to do this,' isn't very familiar with dogs."

The sex therapist: "As people go, the Dutch are a very healthful people. But women who have sex with animals, for the most part, do it for the money. And there's money in it because guys like Horny find it compelling."

If watching dogs screw women is important to you, return to Amsterdam—for good: "Have you ever noticed how much dog shit there is in the red-light district? Live in Amsterdam. If you pursue this here, you're going to get in trouble. Don't think you're entitled to your fantasy materials simply because you found them in Amsterdam."

PETA: "Forgive me for sounding flustered, but in a year of working this position, this is the first time it has ever come up. Look: Keeping pets is okay, dogs and cats have been so far removed from their natural state, they rely on us. But we're against having sex with them, even if they appear to enjoy it. This cannot be considered part of a normal human interaction with a pet."

Dan here: You make it sound like the hard part is finding a willing *dog*.

Frankly, I don't understand why people would want a dog as a pet, let alone a sex partner. All they do is eat and shit, eat and shit. It's like having an enormous, hairy, severely retarded child that never grows up, never gets any smarter, and can't be institutionalized. Worst of all, if you have a dog, you're required to watch it pinch out turds twice a day, and in a lot of places you're required by law *to pick those turds up with your own hands*! I wouldn't pick up my own turds, or my boyfriend's, so why would I put myself through canine scat scenes?

Hey, Faggot:

One of my fetishes is to have my boyfriend piss up my butt. He's resistant, thinking its most unsanitary. Aside from the obvious exposure to STDs, is there any other reason I shouldn't let him piss up my ass?

Fixated on Piss

Hey, FOP:

Here's what my old pal, Dr. Barak Gaster, had to say: "Yuck." After assuring him that entertaining your question isn't the same as endorsing your interests—don't I know it—he went on to say this: "Well, um . . . urine is pretty sterile. Unless someone has a urinary tract infection, there are almost never bacteria in urine. There is a question of whether the waste products, such as urea, would irritate the rectal mucosa. But other than that, it's probably no big deal. It's not a 'safe sex' practice: the HIV load in urine is pretty low, but the virus is present [in the urine of HIV-infected persons]." As long as your partner doesn't have a urinary tract infection, isn't HIV-positive, or suffering from any other STDs, this peeing-up-your-butt stuff is apparently kosher. Gross, but kosher.

Hey, Faggot:

My girlfriend and I only see each other on weekends. To overcome the overwhelming desire to jerk off during the week, I have discovered that I get great pleasure urinating on myself. I don't know how this happened—one morning I just did it. Now about twice a week, I lie down in the bathtub and direct a clear stream of urine all over my body. Then I pull my briefs back up and soak them. I keep my eyes closed, but do I need to worry about any long-term effects on my hair or skin? Is there anything wrong with me? My girlfriend knows nothing about this. I have no intention of telling her, and I don't want to be urinated on by anyone else.

Wet

Hey, Everybody:

We get a lot of letters here at Savage Labs. While everyone's dumb-ass problem is unique in its own very special way, patterns do emerge, and Wet's letter is a good example of a certain type of letter we get. The kids in the mailroom like to call them HTHs, or "How'd That Happen?!" letters.

You see, Wet is doing this completely wack thing—pissing on himself in the bathtub as a substitute for masturbation—and like a lot of folks doing wack things, Wet has some wack concerns. He has questions about the advisability of this wack behavior—Will urine damage my skin? Is there something wrong with me?—so he writes a letter. Something that he thinks took courage. But in composing his letter, Wet chickens out: he fails to take responsibility for his actions, casting himself as a passive player in this bathtub drama. He may pee on himself, but it wasn't his idea—he writes: "I don't know how this happened, one morning I just did it." How'd That Happen?!

I've been taking unsupervised baths for 27 years, and in all that time I never "happened" to pee all over myself. The times I have pissed in the tub or shower, it was on purpose—I was too lazy to get out of the shower, or there was someone else in the shower with me and I was fulfilling a special request. But it never just happened. I did it.

So, Wet, while I'm happy to answer your questions—no, it won't hurt you; yes, there is probably something wrong with you, something terribly, terribly wrong—your unwillingness to take responsibility for your actions is what disturbs me most about your letter. Come on, admit it: you're into piss, you like it, for its own sake, and not as a masturbation substitute. Repeat after me: "I like piss. I'm into golden showers." You're a perv—cop to it, fer Christ's sake.

Hey, Faggot:

I was dog-sitting my friend's dog, and I fell asleep on the floor in my T-shirt (no underwear). When I awoke, the dog was licking my pussy, and to be honest, it felt so good that I didn't stop him until I came like I never have in my life. I was totally embarrassed and disgusted with myself, but the next night, it happened again. I was so embarrassed and disgusted with myself. My questions:

1. Can I get infected in any way by dog germs on my pussy?
2. Is this harmful to me in any way?
3. How sick am I to fully enjoy this?

I am too ashamed to ask a single soul in the world these questions. I wouldn't even ask a doctor these questions. I'm so afraid I'm going to catch some kind of infection from his tongue. Please answer me, because I need to know. I feel sick and ashamed.

Help Me

Hey, Everybody:

Here's another "How'd That Happen?!" letter. The setup—Help Me wakes to find the dog lapping away at her pussy—sounds an awful lot like an urban myth (sans peanut butter), or a letter to the *Penthouse* Forum. She fell asleep on the floor, wearing only a T-shirt, and "awoke" to find the dog lapping at her pussy? What probably happened was this: she was dog-sitting, feeling horny, and Mr. Dog was doing those wack horny-dog things horny dogs do (sticking its nose in her crotch, following her around, humping her leg). So similar was the dog's behavior to the behavior of males of her own species, Help Me was intrigued, tempted. So she did this wack thing, and it felt really good, so she did it again. And now she's freaking out.

So she writes me a letter, but just can't take responsibility for her actions, just can't bring herself to write a letter that begins, "I fuck dogs. . . ." So, she writes her letter in such a way as to make it sound like the dog fucking wasn't something she did, it was something that happened to her. HTH. She was innocently taking a nap on the floor, with no pants or panties on, and woke to find the dog between her legs—why, that could happen to anyone! Twice!

Not by a long shot, Help Me. Anyway, in answer to your questions:

1. Yes.
2. Yup.
3. Pretty fucking sick.

Hey, Faggot:

I'm a 200 percent straight guy, married with children. About six months ago, I went to a masseur who finished things with a terrific blow job. If you wonder why I didn't stop him, the truth is, I couldn't, because he was massaging my asshole with his thumb while blowing me. It was so good that I've been going back to the guy just about every week, not for the massage but for the blow job. Now I'm starting to worry that this might label me as gay. I have no interest in blowing this guy, but I wonder if the guy who gets the blow job is as guilty as the one who does it.

Unsigned

Hey, Everybody:

This is my personal favorite of all the "How'd That Happen?!" letters we've ever received. Mr. 200 Percent Straight Guy couldn't stop the big, bad masseur from giving him a blow job because the masseur had his thumb up Mr. 200 Percent Straight Guy's butt. Is there a system-override switch in straight men's butts? Can't . . . move . . . thumb . . . in . . . ass . . . send . . . help. Please! But Mr. 200 Percent can't admit that he liked it, that he didn't object because there was nothing objectionable about this blow job—that he let the masseur continue because he was diggin' it—or that he might have sought it out (just where did you find this masseur?). So he comes up with what has to be the lamest excuse in the long, sordid history of blow jobs: he had his thumb in my butt, Your Honor, what could I do? HTH. Of course, this does not explain why Mr. 200 Percent Straight keeps going back for more blow jobs. Did the masseur leave his thumb in his butt?

Hey, Faggot:

You bioboys think you've got problems . . .

I'm a female-to-male transsexual who, since my accession to sentience, has been wild about boys. For years I tried to be happy as a straight female, but it never worked. I wasn't a female and I wasn't straight. What I was, and am, is a guy who is into gay SM/leather as a master/top. I've been on testosterone a year and a half and pass as male most of the time, and in daily life my gender is not problematic. I'm small and boyish (think Michael J. Fox) and while I'd like to be taller, lots of big guys get off on being topped by a smaller guy. And since

I'm also a drag queen, I like being able to still look good when I go out en femme. Deep down, I think I'm a she-male dominatrix trapped in the body of an FTM tranny.

Here's my problem. I haven't been able to afford surgery, having been on disability for five years. I'm working again now, but saving is difficult, and my insurance, like most, excludes sex reassignment surgery. Even if they did, phalloplasty (weenie surgery) sucks: it gives you a non-erectile, usually non-orgasmic flesh-toned garden hose for the low price of 70 grand. With the aid of a penis enlarger pump, this leather-Master wannabe has managed to grow himself a 2⅝ inch dick. I have some hope of being able to afford breast reduction and scrotoplasty (conversion of labia into balls, with testicular implants). But in the foreseeable future, pending advances in genital reconstruction surgery, I am the proverbial Needledick. Now, don't get me wrong, my mini-dick is a very cute pint-sized version of an uncut dick, head, skin and all, and in sensitivity and orgasmic capacity is an 11 out of a 10. It's just that, in an SM scene, whipping it out and ordering a slave to worship it is sort of, well, anticlimactic.

Friends tell me I shouldn't let being phallically challenged interfere with my sense of sexual self, but then they are either FTMs who are bottoms, or bioboys with standard-issue dongs. At this point, I consider myself bi and enjoy topping sub females, and females are much more accepting of physical imperfections. But my primary erotic interest is hot raunchy, male/male leathersex, and I understand that gay men want a partner with a dick.

Any suggestions or observations you might like to make are welcome.

Dickless in Frisco

Hey, DIF:

Wow: a female-to-male tranny sadomasochist bisexual dickless drag queen. Just wait till conservative pundits George Will (*Newsweek*) and John Leo (*U.S. News and World Report*) hear about you: they're always harping on the divisiveness of gender and identity politics, on how they pull people apart, instead of bringing them together. Things were simpler when men were men and women were women, and they stayed that way. But in your case, gender and identity politics aren't pulling you apart, it sounds like they're all that's holding you together. Play your cards right, and your three-inch diclit could get you an outraged writeup in *Newsweek*.

You can't afford a frankencock—and you're right about those sex-reassignment cocks being a waste of money and fatty thigh tissue—but who says that the cock that gets worshiped in one of your hot fag leather/SM scenes has to be your own? Many Leather/SM relationships are many-partnered. Hook up with another top, and then the two of you get out there and find yourselves a bottom to share. When it's time for a little cock worship, give the order to your bottom-boyfriend-slave to worship your top-boyfriend-Master's cock. And everybody will be happy.

Except, of course, for George Will and John Leo.

Hey, Faggot:

I'm a straight person and my situation is this: my boyfriend has a fetish; he likes arms. Forget T&A—the bigger the arms the better.

Running is my workout of choice, but a few months ago, I also began working out at a gym (my idea, not his). I don't like gyms. I don't like the people, the sweat, the stench, the uncomfortable workout wear, or the attitudes. What I do like is the effect it has on my boyfriend.

However, when we aren't having at it, I don't like my big, bulging biceps. And I have disappointed myself by altering my body to please him. I'd always thought women who dye their hair a color they don't like or get plastic surgery merely to please a man pathetic. Yet, here I was doing just that. So gradually, I stopped going to the gym, and my arms are now back to their thin regular selves. My boyfriend loves me and my arms regardless, but I often miss those wild afternoons, and I was wondering if I should hit the bench press again.

I suppose my real question is this: how far in changing your body and appearance do you go to please a lover before sacrificing your own identity and self-respect?

Firm Butt, Puny Arms

Hey, FBPA:

If changing your body pleases you, by all means change. Get tattoos, poke holes, dye your hair, muscle up, nip here, tuck there, get fat—whatever. It's your body.

If changing your body pleases your lover, well . . . we all do things to please our lovers. We buy their favorite cookies, put up with their pastimes, indulge their kinks—but we should pause before doing something as drastic as altering our bodies to please someone else. If having big arms made you feel bad, avoid the gym. But if you felt neutral about having big arms, and you enjoyed the attention—then hit the bench press.

Hey, Faggot:

I'm a "normal" girl. Not too bright, not too dull, not too weird, not too mundane, but I have one little problem: since the age of five or six, I've had these not-so-normal fantasies. I've alternately fantasized that I was being molested by an adult, or I was a child accosting an adult, or an adult molesting a child. Now, I have other fantasies from time to time, but for some reason these are the only ones that can make me come *really* hard. I have never been raped, molested, sexually assaulted, or unwillingly accosted in my life, nor have I ever done such a thing to another person. I thought that once I lost my virginity and was having regular sex with only one person, these thoughts would go away. But I've been in a steady and wonderful relationship for over a year now, and though "Jack" is a terrific lover, I am still plagued by thoughts of little kids.

This obviously is not normal. Am I doomed to be a dirty baby-fucking pedophile? Do you think I should get a shrink to examine me and my very tiny pocketbook in minute detail? I'm scared that a shrink will say I'm a risk to my kids—when I have them—and take them away as soon as they're born. Or do you think this is just a classic case of "desire for the forbidden" or "dominance/submission" and that I should just ignore it as long as I never actually *do* anything?

Baby Pedophile

Hey, BP:

On your behalf, I contacted a shrink—Laura Keim—who has done absolutely amazing work with the most disturbed young man I have ever known: my glue-sniffin', pill-poppin', fact-checkin' research assistant Kevin. Predictably, Kevin's shrink suggested you see a shrink. "I would suggest," Laura suggested, "that this young woman talk to somebody." Kevin's shrink did have some pretty good reasons why you might want to talk with "somebody" about your problem: "It can be really therapeutic to get this kind of heavy stuff out. Talking about it will lift a burden off your shoulders." To protect your tiny pocketbook, Laura recommends you seek a therapist who "works on a sliding fee scale. And you needn't fear that a therapist will turn you in to the Department of Children and Family Services when you have a kid: "The time to report would be if this person had a child and came in and said, 'I'm molesting my baby,' or, 'I'm beating up my baby.' Then a therapist is required by law in most places to report the crime."

On to your problem: your fantasies are not all that uncommon. In my opinion, child molestation fantasies do not make you an evil person—so long as they remain fantasies, so long as you can be satisfied pretending to be a child while having sex with your boyfriend, or vice versa. In the same way that Mistresses don't really have slaves, but only pretend-slaves, you can safely *pretend* to molest "children" in role-play scenarios *with other adults*.

Laura the shrink disagrees with me, however: "It's one thing if a fantasy is about adults, but if it's about kids, even if they're not there in the room, that concerns me." Laura worried that you might have trouble "keeping this a fantasy. And if somebody keeps having that fantasy over and over, maybe something else is going on. What does it say about what you're needing in your life? Nurturance? Feelings of control? Is it about being lonely?"

Or is it about what makes you come really hard? The problem with the "what's really going on here" approach to taboo desire is that it only deals with half the problem: your molestation fantasies could be about all the things Laura mentioned, and more—but they're also about what makes you wet. A shrink can help you explore "what's really going on," but those explorations are unlikely to erase your fantasies. The tape is still playing in your head. So what do you do with the desires?

"It's not a very healthy turn-on," Laura observed, and I agree. But all sorts of people with "unhealthy" turn-ons—incest, murder, torture—can and do safely explore their fantasies through consensual role-playing. Men and women with rape fantasies, for example, are told that it's okay to act out their fantasies with partners willing to play at rape. Rape is also wrong, at least as wrong as child molestation—which is itself rape—so it seems inconsistent to tell people it's okay to play at rape with consenting adult partners, but not okay to play at child molestation with consenting adult partners. The difference is, of course, kids. Folks fear that by fantasizing about kids, you're stepping onto a slippery slope that leads directly to becoming a dirty babyfucking pedophile, and that people like me need to be careful not to create more child molesters by giving people like you permission to indulge your fantasy. But the slippery slope argument isn't applied to folks with rape fantasies, even at the risk of "creating rapists."

Hey, Faggot:

This letter is in response to Baby Pedophile. I am also a normal young woman with what might be considered very disturbing sexual fantasies. If you can imagine it, I've probably fantasized about it. Although I've found my thoughts odd, I never thought they were abnormal, because, as you wisely pointed out, we've been told for years that there's nothing wrong with fantasies. Just because you think about being raped doesn't mean you want to be raped. Or in my case, just because I think about raping doesn't mean I want to rape. I would like BP to know that I've had a happy and healthy sex life keeping my fantasies to myself (my fantasies are not the kind of shit a guy wants to hear when he asks what you fantasize about). I would also like her to know that I have worked with pre- and grade-school children for many years, and have never once had any urge or sexual feeling whatsoever toward them.

My fantasies are a completely separate part of my life, and I accept them as such. I hope my letter makes BP feel a little less alone. I know there must be more of us out there.

Another Baby Pedophile

Hey, Faggot:

I was interested in the letter from Baby Pedophile about her supposedly abnormal fantasies, and wanted to assure her that she's not as unusual as she thinks. I too am a normal 31-year-old woman who's fantasized about kids and teens with adults for over 20 years. As far as being doomed to a life of pedophilia, give me a break! In my experience, the things that are the most intensely erotic in fantasy life turn out not to be a bit erotic in real life. Here are some examples from my personal life:

Fantasy: Getting caught by parents. Ooh-la-la!

Reality: What a drag!

Fantasy: Being raped by a stranger.

Reality: A sexual assault by two strangers was no fun at all.

The same holds true for kids, for me and probably for Baby Pedophile as well: fantasies about them get me totally wet, but real kids don't arouse me at all. Nothing, nada, zilch—not even the tiniest twitch of the arousal meter when I'm around a kid. Now, I'm not saying that real-life people whose real-life behavior with children is a problem don't have fantasies about them, but that doesn't mean fantasies lead to behavior.

My advice: Treat real people as they deserve to be treated, treat fantasy characters (including yourself) however you like, and keep your mouth shut. You may have plenty of fellow travelers, but who's going to admit it?

Cheaper Than a Shrink

Hey, Faggot:

I have a fascination with women's periods. I am a breeder male who did not have any sisters, and growing up I learned what little I know about women from the "experts" at school: my equally misinformed classmates. For reasons that I don't understand, the smell drives me nuts, and plunging into a hot, bleeding pussy is the ultimate turn-on for me.

However, some women are extremely uncomfortable with this. My last girlfriend would not even let me touch her during the event.

My questions: I have never eaten a woman during her period. Is this safe? Can I get some kind of disease, like AIDS, from this? Second, how can I go about convincing my partner (I don't have one at the moment, unfortunately) that I would like to do this? I would also like to share in the event by changing her tampon. Can you ask your hetero women friends what they think about all of this, and how I should go about raising the issue when I do get a new girlfriend?

Red-Hot

Hey, RH:

At your request, I shared your letter with a few of the fascinating hetero women at Savage Labs, and here's what they had to say about their fascinating periods:

Janet loves having intercourse during her period. "My sex

drive goes up when I'm bleeding, and I want sex more. In my experience, it's usually the guy who has a problem with it— bloody condoms freak 'em out, I guess." No one has ever gone down on her during "the event," and while it doesn't turn her crank, she might let a guy do it, "if he really wanted to." Donna also enjoys having sex during her period, but unlike Janet, doesn't feel any more or less horny than usual. "I guess for me it's like, 'Why not have sex?' It's no reason to, but it's no reason to avoid sex either." Hazel, on the other hand, avoids sex during her period. "It's not that I think it's gross, it's just that I have a really heavy flow," and Hazel doesn't want to drown anyone.

When it comes to convincing a partner to let you go down on her during her period, all three felt the best approach would be a subtle one. "He should keep his mouth shut," said Donna. "If he has a girlfriend, she's going to have periods, so there's no need to creep her out by explaining in too much detail how you wanna eat her when she's bleeding. Just eat her." What about letting someone change their tampons? "Well, it would depend, I guess, on the guy—how close we were, how long we'd been together," said Donna. "I might let him if I felt close to the guy, but I wouldn't let some guy I hardly knew who just wanted to do it for kicks." Hazel about spit up at the thought: "No way. It's not something I enjoy doing myself, so I'm not going to let someone else do it for me, especially some creepy freak getting a boner off it."

Finally, Red-Hot, of course it isn't "safe" to go down on a woman during her period! Her "hot bleeding pussy" is bleeding blood, ya moron. Unless you're certain your girlfriend does not have HIV, and that she isn't suffering from any other blood-borne illness (such as hepatitis), then lapping up her blood can't be called "safe."

Hey, Faggot:

I am a straight-acting bi guy with a girlfriend that I love a lot. However, I also have a humongous crush on this guy I see working out at the gym. He is a blond Adonis, and I would sell my soul to the devil just to be butt-fucked once by him. (God, I'm getting hard just thinking about it!) I haven't approached him yet, but the way he looks at me in the locker room makes me think he'd be into being my fuck-buddy. I have this incredible fantasy about being butt-fucked by him while I butt-fuck her. Do you think I should suggest a ménage à trois? My girlfriend doesn't know I'm bi.

Between a Rock and a Hard Place

Hey, BARAHP:

Someone once told me that "straight-acting" wasn't homophobic—just short for masculine. Since there are 14 letters and one hyphen in "straight-acting," and only nine letters in masculine—thereby making the former long for the latter, not short—I didn't buy it. "Straight-acting," like "discreet," is usually code for closeted, as is the case with you, my bisexual friend. You're a "straight-acting bi guy with a girlfriend that I love a lot," only she doesn't know you're bi. Love her a lot? Love her enough to lie to her? Cheat on her? Run around behind her back? You're a fucking scumbag.

But let's talk about your problem: though your fantasy ménage is pushing you toward revealing your sexual orientation—and not any sense of, oh, decency or right and wrong—you might want to tell your girlfriend you're bisexual before proposing a three-way. She might need a little time to process this new information about you before she's ready to play choo-choo with you and the Adonis from the gym.

Now, even if Girlfriend goes for it, don't assume Adonis will: even if he's into you—and that's a big if: every straight-acting-bi-guy/twisted-closet-case I've ever met has operated under the delusion that gay men all wanna be his fuck-buddy—he may not be into her, or he may not be into three-ways, or he may not, like me, be into bi guys. Especially closeted ones.

Hey, Faggot:

Why is it every time a bisexual, or someone experiencing same-sex fantasies, writes you a letter, you holler "closet case" and tenaciously maintain that they're really gay?

You, of all people, should be able to understand the magnificent scope and diversity of human sexuality and the many fetishes, fantasies, and desires contained therewith. Can't a person experience or think about a sexual happening that strays from their normal routine without having a label thrown at them? And why do there have to be labels for everything?

I personally believe everyone to be ambisexual, to some degree, no matter how "straight" or "gay" they claim to be. I'm sure even you—his royal gayness—has had, at some moment in your life, a hint, a smidgen of a dash of a trace of curiosity of what sex would be like with—eek, gasp, argh!—a woman.

Sexually Objective

Hey, SO:

When I called the bi guy a closet case, I didn't mean he was a closeted gay man, but a closeted bisexual. "I am a straight-acting bi guy with a girlfriend that I love a lot. . . . My girlfriend doesn't know I'm bi." He's in the closet—not about being a fag, moron, but about being bi.

In defense of labels: most people are heterosexual; if gays and lesbians do not identify as gay and lesbian, we are assumed to be straight. We either have to label ourselves or be inaccurately labeled by others. Without those labels you dislike so much, we'd be swallowed up by the assumption of heterosexuality and we wouldn't be able to find each other. If we can't find each other *we can't get laid*. If labels make you uncomfortable, tough shit. Given a choice between your discomfort and my sex life, I'm going to chose the latter.

And I have had sex with women. It was smooshy.

Hey, Faggot:

One constantly hears the awkward phrase "gay/lesbian/ bisexual/transgender community." As a more-or-less hetero- sexual woman who doesn't like her men too straight, I would like to know where all these alleged "bisexuals" are.

Horny in San Francisco

Hey, HSF:

Since the majority of bisexual men seem to be closeted, many "bi" men can be found hanging out in gay bathhouses, cruisy parks, and toilets, having anonymous sex with other men—adding to straight people's mistaken impression that all "gay" men are indiscriminate sex-crazed risk takers—before dashing home to wife and child. Out bi men, on the other hand, are plagued by that pesky "bisexual invisibility," which goes something like this: you see two guys holding hands, you assume they're gay; you see a guy holding a girl's hand, you assume he's straight. All three boys could be bisexual, ya just can't tell by looking at them.

Hey, Faggot:

What can you do for us "proud to admit it" bisexual men/ boys who have been criticized by the male homosexual crowd?

Tell me where the clubs, coffee houses, and bars are where bisexual people can go. I used to go to gay bars, but I would always end up in a big debate over whether there is such a thing as bisexuality (or is it latent homosexuality or simply being afraid to admit to one's homosexuality due to social pressure). When I was finished debating, I no longer had an interest in meeting anyone. So, tell me, where are those clubs, coffee houses, bars, organizations where bisexual people can go and enjoy the company of others like them?

Bi-Male

Hey, BM:

Personally, I can't imagine anything more excruciating than the company of bisexuals. Addicted as bisexuals are to complaining about the treatment they get at the hands of mean monosexual homos, it's no wonder you idiots can't scrape together the time to open a decent dance place or a few clubs of your own. If bi's want their own clubs, bars, and coffee houses you're going to have to get off your butts, stop whining about how you get treated by *gay* people in *gay* bars, and open a few of your own.

Hey, Faggot:

Why do you give bisexuality such a bad rap? What could be better than being able to love and make love to both sexes? Before I came along, my husband enjoyed relationships with both. I myself have feelings of love and physical attraction toward females. While I support wholeheartedly people's choice or natural predisposition to be homo or hetero, I suppose I have a special admiration for those who can experience the delights of both sexes, and I have a feeling bisexuality is the natural "norm."

Blurred Boundaries

Hey, BB:

I also admire those who can enjoy the pleasures of both sexes. What I don't admire is bi-whiners who complain when the gay people don't applaud every time one of them wanders into a gay bar with a chip on his shoulder. I'm sorry you've fallen for that tired old bi-propaganda about bisexuality being the "norm." All us heteros and homos are damaged goods then, right? How sad that we cannot achieve the elevated spiritual/emotional/sexual plane inhabited by the mystic bisexuals who deign to walk amongst us. Bi-Supremist bullshit.

Hey, Faggot:

After reading Bi-Male's letter about the social tribulations of bisexuality (V-day issue), I was shocked to find the tone of your response so vituperative. It disgusts me that you berated (and belittled) an expression of a sexuality that, like gay sexuality, is also embroiled in a difficult struggle for political and social recognition. Why didn't you discuss the real tragedy underlying the letter: the bigoted debate over whether there is such a thing as bisexuality?

CM

Hey, CM:

"Vituperative"? Listen, Scrabble Champ, you apparently didn't read my column very carefully. The "real tragedy" is not whether bisexuality exists. It does. I never called the existence of bisexuality into question. The tragedy for bisexuals is that there will never be a "bisexual community," and therefore, no bi-bars, clubs, discos, or restaurants, because the vast majority of bisexuals are in straight relationships, and belong to and identify with the "straight community."

Hey, Faggot:

My sexual history has pretty much proven me to be about as bisexual as one can be. I'm 26, and have had meaningful, long-term, monogamous relationships with a handful of "people." I enjoy sex with either gender equally, and for different reasons. It's really what's on the inside of a person that turns me on.

My gay friends all tell me I'm a closet case and just can't accept my homosexuality. My straight friends tell me that no self-respecting female would ever want to have anything to do with a man that has "jumped the fence." Now I'm wondering why my gay friends (who seem to want everyone to accept them the way they are) have such a hard time accepting me for the same reasons. And as for my straight friends, who among them hasn't at least had a same-sex fantasy?

In my mind, a relationship is with a "person," not genitals. I've been espousing this view to my friends repeatedly but they seem incapable of seeing my point.

                                                    Gender-Blind

Hey, GB:

You identify as anything you want—straight, gay, bi—but it doesn't mean anyone has to believe you. And maybe your friends aren't able to see your point because when you say your relationships are with a "person, not genitals," you're saying that their relationships are with genitals, not persons. So you have relationships with persons, GB, and I have relationships with what? Cocks? Bisexuality is a sexual identity, not a higher calling, yet good luck finding a bisexual who can talk about their sexuality without launching into infuriating "person, not genitals" crapola. And bisexuals wonder why they have such lousy reps.

Hey, Faggot:

I'm a 26-year-old male who has been having a three-year affair with my aunt. I'll spare you the prurient details, save to say that, like many a "normal" relationship, we began as good friends (more kith than kin) and ended up in bed together. We love and respect each other; sex is exciting and fulfilling; and despite a slight age difference—she's 34, my mom's baby sister—we are on the same "pop cultural" level.

Because of the taboo nature of our relationship, we see each other sub rosa, keeping separate residences. However, the overwhelming desire to move in together and openly declare our mutual love to family and friends has reached the boiling point. We don't fear their wrath, and we hope they'll eventually accept us, but we do fear the judiciary system. Is our particular incestuous relationship punishable by law? I know that incest between minors and adults is a serious offense, but we are consenting adults who just happen to be in an odd situation.

Wondering

P.S. Don't mention where we're from. We don't plan to have kids, I had a vasectomy.

Hey, WN:

According to the various prosecutors I spoke with—including one in the county you live in—incest between consenting adults is perfectly legal. "In regards to criminal law, incest is mostly covered in child abuse statutes," a prosecutor in your area told me. "If the nephew is an adult, and the aunt is too, well then it's fine—well, not 'fine.' Just not criminal." Give my regards to Geraldo.

Hey, Faggot:

A few weeks ago, you printed a letter from a man having a torrid but loving incestuous relationship with his mother's sister. You probably didn't intend to become "Incest Info Central," but since you were able to answer his question, perhaps you would be so kind as to answer mine.

In am 32 and my mother is 51. For the last 10 years, we have engaged in a mutually agreeable sexual relationship. Before I make my request to you, may I make the following points to your readers:

1. Stop grimacing. This is not a TV-movie scenario. It's a reciprocal thing.
2. Here's why we do it: Simply put, we are very good-looking people and we feel attracted to each other. If not for those simple facts, we would not be together. In fact, I could not imagine this type of relationship if my mother were a matronly-looking lady. She's a babe.

3. It's just sex. As my mother says, "You're here, I'm here. So why not?"

Here is where we need your help. My mother and I have combed the planet looking for others like us, but to no avail. We're not looking for a swingers' club. Rather, we feel it would be wonderful just to talk openly and freely about our lifestyle with other incest couples who feel the same way.

If a nationally known sicko organization exists for men who love boys, is it not possible that another sicko one exists "out there" for mother/son (or other partner) incest?

Looking for Company

Hey, LFC:

Sometimes I think I should boil my mail before reading it.

My brother Eddie is a total stud—but I don't have sex with him. By your reasoning, when Ed's there and I'm there (weddings, funerals) we oughta slip away from the reception or the casket, and . . . just do it? Just cuz he's cute? Your casualness about this 10-year (!) affair with your mother rings false. In all that time, have you never paused to mull over the emotional consequences of schtoopin' yer ma? Or have you been hiding behind "Well, we're good-looking!" all that time, like that's all the thought you need give the subject? You want someone to talk with about your relationship? Here's an idea: Get a shrink.

But hey, you're consenting adults: If you wanna bone ma, and she wants to bone you, well, more power to ya. I am afraid, though, that I can't offer much in the way of an answer to your question; you two have combed the earth in search of others like you, to no avail. And as I'm not inclined to back-comb the earth on your behalf, you'll have to settle for what I can come up with off the top of my pointy head. Which is this: form your own sicko organization.

Hey, Faggot:

Could you address brother-sister incest in one of your columns? I have a gut feeling it is quite widespread. But figures to verify that are very hard to come by. Perhaps your experience and expertise could shed some light in this area.

An Interested Reader

Hey, AIR:

My experience with brother-sister incest is nonexistent. But I do have two older brothers and one sister, all straight: maybe they have some "expertise" in this area. So I called them:

Younger Sister Laura: "Sex with my brothers. No way! That's sick. With their friends maybe, but not my brothers!"

Older Brother Eddie: "Never did it, never thought about it, and don't want to think about it. Cousins maybe, but not siblings."

Even Older Brother Billy: "Sorry, no. That is the single most disgusting idea I've ever heard in my entire life, without exception. But, of course, none of us liked each other as children. If we'd liked each other, God only knows what might have happened."

Hey, Faggot:

I have a reason to think my fiancé's genes may be defective— he's a product of incest. I have noticed that his come is always chunky and thick. Is this normal? Men I have known in the past have had easy-flowing come of comparatively normal consistency. Please help!

Scared Stupid

Hey, Scared:

Some men spray skim, others spurt whole, and a few spew chunky monkey. The consistency of your boyfriend's spunk tells you nothing about possible "genetic defects." Your children, when and if you have them, are no likelier to be born with flippers or claws or tails or connected eyebrows than children fathered by a guy with runny spunk.

Hey, Faggot:

A couple of months ago, I went to Iowa for my aunt's funeral. At the funeral, I saw my cousin Bill, her son, who I had a crush on when I was younger (I'm 27 now). Well, Bill's had a double dose of heartbreak, as his wife filed for divorce right when his mother died. So one night, while offering comfort, we ended up in bed together.

Bill and I actually have a lot in common: neither of us wants kids, and it's hard for us to keep our hands off each other (though we are trying to until his divorce is final). Do you think we can make this relationship work? Should we even try? What if our family tries to keep us apart?

Jane

Hey, J:

You're 27, and if he's old enough to have a dead mother and a divorce, you're both old enough to do what you like. While there are laws that prevent first cousins from marrying, they don't prevent first cousins from screwing. Your family can disapprove, they can disown you and make your lives unpleasant, but legally, there isn't anything they can do to separate you. As far as making it work, so long as you don't want to have kids, you're reconciled to never being able to marry, and you're braced for chilly receptions at reunions, weddings, and funerals—in short, if you can handle the pressure of being gay—then I'm sure you'll be able to make this relationship work.

Hey, Faggot:

Usually your info is right on the mark, but your reply to June—in love with her cousin Bill—contained errors.

First, and most importantly, first cousins are allowed to marry in 25 of our 50 states, and these marriages are honored as legal in all of them. Doctors have also begun to revise their opinions on the "high risk" of first-cousin procreation. The risk is higher than it would be if you weren't first cousins, but many first-cousin pairs have had healthy babies. Just see your friendly neighborhood genetic consultant before you start trying.

As far as "chilly receptions at family reunions" are concerned, that's not inevitable either. When I first became romantically involved with my cousin, the relatives' reactions ranged from indifference to enthusiasm. Only a couple of family members actively disapproved, and even they are coming around now that we've been together for a couple of years and will be marrying quite soon. One big plus: You'll never have to argue about whose family gathering to attend on holidays!

Of course, some family members and friends may give you a hard time because there's a lot of ignorance on this subject (even Dan Savage was misinformed!). One thing you can mention if anyone gives you the "only uneducated trailer-trash types marry first cousins" line is this: both Albert Einstein and Charles Darwin married first cousins.

A Happily Kissing Cousin in the Enlightened
State of New York

Hey, Faggot:

I went out with this guy for a few months. Upon getting to know him, he expressed that he has "bi" tendencies. It somehow turned me on and it became a strong fantasy for me to see him with another man. The thing is, he suddenly lost interest in me—no calls anymore, nothing! I feel rejected and almost feel like being a woman is "boring." I couldn't satisfy him? How can a guy walk away from his girlfriend (me) knowing she's (I'm) interested in the "bi-ness"? Most women would be disgusted. Not me.

Unsigned

Hey, U:

You feel rejected, sugarcube, 'cuz you were rejected. You weren't threatened by the bi thing—so what? Bisexual guys break up with women for lots of different reasons; even supportive girlfriends sometimes get dumped. He may have weighed your bi-supportiveness in your favor when he was deciding what to do: "Gee, she is okay with my being bi, but she has really bad breath, and lousy table manners—guess I'll have to dump her." That's the way it goes.

Hey, Faggot:

My husband walked in on me in the bathroom as I was preparing to take an enema. He started to excuse himself and I told him that it was okay. He asked if he could help, and I suggested that he hold the bag for me. He did that. Then he asked me if I would let him do the whole thing. I taught him how to do it. Afterward, he told me he was aroused while he was giving me the enema. He said that my naked body seemed so fragile and vulnerable in that position. Since that time, he continuously offers to give me another enema. I turned it around on him the other day and asked if he wanted me to give him one. He declined and was embarrassed.

Any comments on this fixation he seems to have now? Is this a common thing? I myself am not aroused by enemas. It has, however, crossed my mind that I might find it erotic to be the giver and to be in the controlling position.

Overflowing

Hey, O:

Your husband has already given you a pretty straight-forward explanation for this fixation: your naked body, fragile and vulnerable. Seems perfectly reasonable.

While having a thing for enemas isn't all that common, it is common enough to have its own listing in *The Encyclopedia of Unusual Sex Practices*, and special-interest videos, Web sites, and Internet newsgroups. But your husband doesn't sound like an honest-to-goodness enema freak: he saw you in that alluring position, was intrigued by the power and the glory of filling you up, and wants to mess around. Simple. Indulge him! As this isn't an organic kink, he'll probably wanna play enema doc for a while, and then he'll lose interest.

And don't give up on him. He probably declined your offer to enemize him because most straight men don't want to appear too eager to put anything in their butts, for fear of being called homos. Make him an offer he can't refuse: "Honey, I'll let you give me ten enemas, if I can give you one." He'll bravely submit to that single enema—not because he wants to, oh no: he *has to.*

Hey, Faggot:

I recently placed an ad in your paper's personals section under the headline "Horny White TV." I received quite a few responses but one in particular stood out because of his extremely sexy voice and what he said he wanted to do to me. He said he was totally straight but had a fantasy of being with a TV. Anyway, to make a long story short, when we finally met at my place—I was dressed to the nines and more than ready to be fucked—alas, he told me he couldn't go through with it. My question to you is: What can I do to convince him to give it another try? He's really cute and I'm a virgin as far as being penetrated is concerned and I would really like him to take my cherry. What's a girl to do?

Horny White TV

Hey, HWT:

Meeting people through personals ads is a gamble. When you meet in a bar or at a party, physical attraction is established first and then you feel each other out, discovering whether your sexual interests jibe. But when you connect through the personals, especially kink personals, mutual sexual interest is established first, then you have to meet and see if you're physically attracted to one another.

You met on the phone, talked, and established mutual sexual interests. Then he came over to your house, probably fully prepared to go through with it, but discovered he wasn't sexually attracted to you, and bailed. When he told you he "couldn't go through with it," he was telling you a lie to spare your feelings. He meant, "I can't go through with it—with you." There probably isn't anything you can do to convince him to give it another try, so don't waste any more time on him. What's a girl to do? Take out another ad.

Hey, Faggot:

I'm a guy who grew up hiding my TV tendencies. Only in the last few years have I gone out in women's clothing, but I can pass and love to dress very revealingly. I was surprised to discover how excited I became when a man hit on me. We ended up in a secluded spot where I blew him. After some soul-searching, I accepted the fact that I enjoyed it and wanted to experience more.

But while men are the majority of people attracted to TVs, I would prefer to build a long-term relationship with a woman. Are there any out there? Am I twisted, or what?

Wild Side

Hey, WS:

Are you twisted? Yes, you certainly are. But your twist is relatively straightforward: you're a cross-dressing bisexual guy with hetero leanings—what could be simpler?!

In finding a mate, you have two options: search high and low for a woman whose sexual tastes are compatible with your own—personals ads, TV/TS organizations, fetish clubs. If by some miracle you meet a woman with whom you're emotionally as well as kink-compatible, you're set. Your second option is to find a woman with whom you're emotionally compatible, date, fall in love, get married, etc. Then, very slowly, break the bad news to her: she married a twisted guy.

Hey, Faggot:

I have recently added the use of sex toys to my playtime. What's with the warnings about the use of vibrators and "unexplained thigh or calf pain"? Is there some kind of weird medical condition that could develop with the use of a vibrator?

Kid with a New Toy

Hey, KWANT:

According to Mary Martone, who works at Seattle's sex-positive, woman-owned sex toy emporium, Toys in Babeland, the warning is there to keep you from accidentally killing yourself. "You can get blood clots in your legs. If your calf is sore, you might go, 'Hey my leg hurts,' vibe it, and loosen a blood clot. Then the clot zips up to your head, and that moment of calf-soothing pleasure is followed by a stroke."

Martone thinks there must have been a dislodged-blood-clot lawsuit at some point in vibrator history. "Someone died massaging mysterious thigh pain and the family sued, got a huge chunk of change, and now every vibrator has to have that do-not-use-on-unexplained-thigh-and-calf-pain sticker on it. Tragic, but that's product liability for you."

Hey, Faggot:

I am 57 years old, and I can't get pussy. I am kinky, bold, and tattooed all over. I am looking for a young, kinky female—

bi would be nice, someone who likes strange things. Where are the young women who might be interested in me?

AM

Hey, AM:

Nevada.

Hey, Faggot:

During the summer I had a part-time job working in a lingerie store. It is the company's policy to let men who wish to do so try garments on. I happened to wait on one, and accidentally got to see him dressed up in the fitting room. At the time I found it somewhat disturbing, but the more I think about it, the more exciting I find it.

My questions are: Is this "normal"? Also, how can I ask my boyfriend to wear some of my clothes sometimes without offending him?

CMD

Hey, CMD:

Normal? No. But so what? "Normal" is very rarely "exciting," and it is the potential excitement factor that's making you want to cross-dress up the boyfriend, right? So don't sweat normal. How has he responded to other, perhaps less out-there requests in past? Is he generally open to new things? Has he ever asked you to indulge him in something freaky? If the answers to the above questions are yes, he'll probably go for it. So why ask? Just tell him about what you saw, hand him a few sexy thangs, and he'll know what to do.

Hey, Faggot:

Recently my boyfriend has been putting ice in my vagina during sex. It is pleasurable for both of us. I am wondering if there's any danger to this? Is there danger of contamination with something? We use the kind of ice you buy in "Party Bags" at the grocery store, if that makes a difference.

Catherine

Hey, Catherine:

Ice is water. Can you put small amounts of water in your vagina? Sure. Can you put small amounts of ice in your vagina? Sure. As long as he refrains from packing you full of ice—it's a twat, not a sno-cone—you should be fine. And while you're popping cubes, why not slide a few up his ass?

Hey, Faggot:

This is in response to the girl who enjoys ice cubes in her vagina during sex. She asked if it was safe and you said ice was water: of course it's safe. Well, if the water were clean and pure, of course it would be safe, but unfortunately, all the chemicals that are found in our water (including those found in party ice) which are put there to kill "living organisms" (what the hell are we?) are anything but safe and can have serious long-term effects on our health.

I recently began working with an environmentally conscious company and have learned some disgusting facts about the effects of chlorine on the body. It is one of the leading causes of breast cancer in women, intestinal cancer, skin cancer, blah, blah, blah. Unfortunately, most people aren't aware of this. I suggest she invest in a water filter treatment system. A good one goes for about $200. After that, she can ram cubes up her twat for the rest of eternity; I just wouldn't suggest she do it now.

No Name Please

P.S. Bottled water isn't really an alternative either. It's not as clean as the media would like us to believe.

Hey, No Name:

I hadn't realized that bottled water was a media conspiracy. You've opened my eyes. Thanks for writing. As for tap water, I'll take a little chlorine over a lotta cholera any day.

Hey, Faggot:

I have a rather tricky situation on my hands. I'm 25 years old, and have a 27-year-old boyfriend. We've been dating for almost a year, and I like him a lot. The problem is I have a secret sex life on the side that he doesn't know about.

I have a Master. He's from Amsterdam, and only comes to town every three months or so. While he's here I'm his total sex slave. I met my "Dutch Master" at a regular bar four years ago. He took me back to his hotel room and kept me tied up all weekend (with my consent)! I loved it! When he comes to town, I tell my friends (and now my boyfriend) that I'm going away for a few days. Really, I'm tied up at my Dutch Master's hotel. My friends would die if they knew anything about this four-year thing (my longest relationship ever!), and needless to say, I haven't told my boyfriend about it.

Here's the problem: Before he comes to town he sends me instructions—when he's going to arrive, what I'm to wear, how long I have to go without masturbating. Well, in his last letter he said he's going to pierce my cock on his next trip, and put a ring in the head—a Prince Albert—so I will always know he owns my dick, even when he's not around.

Sooooo, what do I tell my boyfriend when he asks about the PA I got "visiting my aunt in Pittsburgh" for three days? Or my friends (who I go to the gym with)? I'm not the piercing type, and I don't run with a pierced crowd. My boyfriend has on many occasions expressed disgust for leather and SM (for no apparent reason—I never bring it up) and I'm afraid if I tell him about my secret life as a sex slave, he'll dump me.

Rock and Hard Place

Hey, RAHP:

Tell your boyfriend the truth. Use your impending PA as a conversation starter, and get all those cards on the table. As for your friends, tell 'em too. They'll be jealous, impressed, or scandalized—and what's so terrible about that? And how many can say they've had a four-year relationship with anything other than a hairdresser or a collections agency?

Lastly, your boyfriend's unsolicited comments about SM sex may be his way of sounding you out on the subject. He could very well be interested in exploring kinky sex, and too ashamed to come right out and admit it. So he broaches the subject by making negative comments to see how you react. So, tell him. If he dumps you, he dumps you. But he may want to tag along on your Dutch Master's next visit. Enjoy your piercing.

Hey, Faggot:

Mine are fantasies I believe many women have—to be a stripper, skin mag model, prostitute, porn star, truck-stop waitress in lingerie—you name it. I guess they stem from a need to be desired by men. I've dreamed of being a *Playboy* model since the age of six. I'm often tempted to buy a *Playboy* just to look at and maybe masturbate to. But for years, I've just been too embarrassed to buy it in public. I'm not a lesbian, although I would fool around with a woman once if given the opportunity.

I enjoy going crazy alone: dressing in kinky clothes and playthings (nothing store bought) and masturbating in wild positions. Even so, I remain unsatisfied. I'm worried there must be some better way to take advantage of my youthful sexuality while my breasts are still perky. I fear I'll be a perverted old woman coming on to teenage boys if I don't come to terms with these frustrated fantasies now. Trouble is, I'm not sure I could live with myself if someone found out about my desires. I'm afraid to own a dildo or porn magazine because what if I become ill or die and my family members look through my stuff and find traces of my intimate thoughts? Maybe I'm a frustrated closet nymphomaniac. I just want to learn how to temper/satisfy these fantasies and still maintain my dignity.

Fantasy Crazed

Hey, FC:

Let's say you go crazy and get yourself a subscription to *Playboy* magazine (oooh), and not only that, but you also run out and buy yourself something really naughty, like a vibrator (aaah). And three months later, you drop dead, struck down by a vengeful God, who then casts your everlasting soul into a lake of fire. While your perky breasts roast on a spit over a fiery pit in hell, your mom sorts through your personal belongings, finds your mags and your sticky, still-damp vibrator and . . . so what? *You're dead!*

You need to find yourself a nice, respectable, sexually adventurous boyfriend (or girlfriend), who can help you explore your rather run-of-the-mill truck-stop fantasies. Buy the lingerie, buy the dildos, have the sex, and if you're really worried about it, store the goods at your lover's apartment. That way, should God strike you down, Mom will never come across your dirty secrets.

And you know what, FC? Last weekend, I was going through some boxes when I came across a diary I kept for a few months several years ago. There was stuff in there—three-ways and rope burns and saturated fats—that I had completely forgotten about. It shocked me! And I did it! And what did I do with that incriminating diary? Burn it, for fear my mom or my boyfriend or my as-yet unborn grandkids should find it and discover the shocking truth about what went on in the Calberer Hotel Supply Building? Not on your life. I put it back in the box, with a bookmark at the best passage: Roger's rubber shorts. You see, when I die, I want whoever has the odious, backbreaking job of sorting through my shit to find that diary and know that I lived, damnit, *lived!* And so should you.

Hey, Faggot:

I'm a 27-year-old gay male. I spent the last two years working in Italy and Germany. As you might know, almost all males in Italy and Germany are uncircumcised. To my surprise, I found intact cocks to be more sexy and exciting. I love the way they look, smell, and taste. I feel angry at my parents for taking my foreskin away from me.

My question to you is, where can I meet uncircumcised guys? I don't mind bars, but I do not like personal ads. Help! I love sex, but I dislike circumcised cocks.

Intact Lover

Hey, IL:

You can join a gay gym, hang out in the showers, and present intact men your phone number on laminated cards. Or you can ask guys who flirt with you if they were brutally mutilated by crazed surgeons when they were defenseless little baby boys. But you're going to hear "Yes" most of the time, making this approach both time-consuming and frustrating. Or you can save yourself a lot of time and trouble (and a gym membership) by giving the personals a whirl.

You don't dig personal ads, but like anyone else who feels strongly about something that cannot be ascertained at first glance ("My lover *must* be into watersports!" "My lover *must* enjoy spanking my bottom!" "My lover *must* have a big ol' cheesy foreskin!"), then for Christ's sake save yourself and your prospective partners time and trouble by spelling out your wants in advance in the personals.

Hey, Faggot:

I'm a gay man who has a foot fetish. My problem: I don't know when to tell my partner of my attraction to his feet. Should I tell him before we go to bed together, while in bed together and expressing our sexual interest, or should I get to know a person first through dating, then tell him? This dilemma causes me anxiety every time I meet someone. I know my anxiety is related to my fear of rejection over the issue, but I feel if I were more confident about the timing I would be more relaxed and better able to communicate my needs. What is your advice?

KC

Hey, KC:

Hand your next sex partner this book, and tell him one of the letters in this section is from you. He'll be so relieved you're the foot fetishist—so relieved that you don't want him to fuck a dog, or piss up your butt, or take a shit on him—that he'll let you do anything you like with his feet. As fetishes go, yours is pretty harmless.

Butt Sex & Blow Jobs

Questions from Men and Women, Straight and Gay, About My Two Favorite Contact Sports

Why a separate chapter for butt sex and blow jobs? Well, over the years, I've answered a lot of questions about both these subjects. In fact, a healthy chunk of my mail every day comes from men and women, straight and gay, asking me for tips on butt sex and blow jobs—two sex acts that gay men, rightly or wrongly, are strongly identified with, and commonly regarded to be rather expert at. It's my considered opinion that straight people are extremely hungry for butt sex and blow job tips, judging from my mail, and by putting all my butt sex and blow job tips in one place, it'll be easier for straight folks to find, read, and digest 'em.

But that's only half the reason why I've decided to segregate these letters from the others in this collection. Partly, I'm doing it as a favor to my dear ol' mom. She can't stand to read about butt sex, and thinks my blow job advice, while sound, is a little too graphic. Also, the only time I've ever mentioned my mother in my column in such a way that made her angry was in a question about blow jobs. By putting all my best butt sex and blow job advice in one place, instead of scattering these letters throughout the collection, my mother can easily avoid these questions while she reads this collection. She can just skip this chapter.

Also, my mother is very proud of me, and clips my columns and sends them to my far-flung relatives. Except for the ones about butt sex. I know she wants to send the book to my relatives, so by putting all these letters in once place, she'll be able to simply rip this chapter from the books she presents to my relatives as gifts. If I didn't put all these questions and answers in one place, Mom would have to go through the entire book, ripping out every other page, making a mess of my great aunt's copies.

Hey, Faggot:

What is the difference between cocksucking, blow jobs, and fellatio?

Unsigned

Hey, Unsigned:

"Cocksucking," is what my boyfriend's good at; "blow jobs" are what my sister gives; and "fellatio" is what my mom does.

Hey, Faggot:

I enjoy performing oral sex on men, but I'm not very adept at having a penis rammed halfway down my throat. What other techniques are there for giving a good "blow job"? Do men enjoy having their testicles licked and fondled as well as their penis? Thanks.

Pen-Pal

Hey, PP:

Gag reflex or not, he shouldn't be ramming his penis down your throat. It's not polite. Unlike getting fucked, where the fucker usually controls the "speed and depth of penetration," the person giving head should control the S&D. You're in charge: only take him in your throat every now and then, every ninth or tenth thrust. If he starts bucking, bite him. Or put in a speed bump: wrap a fist around the base of his cock, thereby shortening it, and let him thrust away, moving his dick in and out of your fist and mouth—then it won't go far enough back to gag you.

And remember: just 'cause you put him in your mouth doesn't mean he gets to stay there. It's a blow job, not a lease. Take frequent breaks. If you pull him out of your mouth, keep your fist moving up and down on his cock. Have a breather—you've earned it! While you're resting and pumping, nuzzle his balls. I hope I'm not letting the cat out of the bag here, but most men enjoy having their "testicles licked and fondled." When he starts coming round the mountain, sacrifice—even if you're starting to get a little sore and uncomfortable, it'll be all over soon enough.

Hey, Faggot:

Any advice on how to manage that pesky gag reflex? To make fellatio a more enjoyable experience for me and for him? I await your reply on this, and any other tricks of the trade as well.

Girl Gettin' It

Hey, GGI:

See above.

But here's one more pointer: don't give head kneeling in front of your lover. The classic blow job position is not practical—for the most part, hard cocks point up and, if you're kneeling, that means it's pointing up at the roof of your mouth. Unless you've got a cleft palate and can "deep sinus" your man, this snot won't fly.

Get him in a position where his cock is hard but pointing down—hang him from the ceiling by his ankles. Or if that's too much work, have him lie on his back, get on top of him "69" style, and straighten out your throat. Then, like a circus sword-swallower, you'll be in the perfect position to let him slide down your throat, nice and easy.

Hey, Faggot:

Is there a trick to deep-throating? I have this fantasy of being forced to take something big all the way until the pubic hairs are scratching against my lips, and I'd like to know how to do it before the opportunity presents itself. So I tried practicing on inanimate objects. I was able to take a long cooked asparagus way down and pull it back up, but when I tried it on a banana—after putting a condom over the banana, of course—I started gagging when it got to the back of my throat. When I tried to put it deeper, my stomach went on automatic and started to heave. I pulled out fast.

Is there some way I can overcome this? Or does deep-throating necessarily include vomiting? I've never thought of vomit as a turn-on.

Closet Submissive

Hey, CS:

If you choke to death on a condom-covered banana, your family won't be able to keep a straight face at your funeral. Practice on something with a wide base, something that you can easily remove if you begin to gag, something along the lines of, oh, say, a man.

Practicing with fruit and veg, or even a dildo, isn't really going to do you much good when push comes to shove—penises, unlike bananas, have men attached to them, and men are less predictable than bananas. Bananas go right where you put them, and only as fast as you want them to. Men, on the other hand, go places you don't expect and speed up without warning. The best deep-throat practice is done with a considerate guy, a guy who wants to help you realize your submissive deep-throat fantasy. Train on his cock, and work up to deep-throating. When you've got it down, when you can take him in and out of your throat without chucking in his lap, give him permission to dominate and "face-fuck" you.

Hey, Faggot:

Can you get hemorrhoids from anal sex? I've got to know before I do it!

Roscoe Pee Cold Train

Hey, RPCT:

My father has hemorrhoids, I don't. My father doesn't have anal sex, I do. My immediate family's experience would seem to indicate that not only doesn't anal sex give you hemorrhoids, it actually prevents them.

Hey, Faggot:

My boyfriend has recently become fixated on my anus. My anus enjoys stimulation as much as the next erogenous zone, but not all the time. He's also very well endowed, and it can be a bit painful. It seems as if he would rather go "there" than encounter the softness of my womanness.

Should I be concerned about his sexuality? He says once my vagina becomes wet it's not as pleasurable, which sounds like a justification for his anal fixation. Don't get me wrong—we have great sex, but I prefer vaginal intercourse to anal. Isn't my love box enough to get his rocks off?

Given the Slip

Hey, GTS:

Apparently not. If you're worried that your boyfriend's fixation on your anus means he's gay, understand this: being gay is not about fixations on anuses. It's not like we wake up one day and shout, "Hey, I want me some butt! Boy butt, girl butt, dog butt, sheep butt! Any butt will do!" You're a girl. He's a boy. He wants your butt—girl butt. Gay men don't want girl butt, we want boy butt.

Hey, Faggot:

I have to get my two cents worth in the fray about butt-fucking. I'm a very normal-looking 46-year-old working grandmother who has been anally active for as many years as most of your readers have been alive! I think anal sex is to vaginal sex what Prime Rib is to hamburgers! It is soooo sexy! You know, there are quite a few more nerve endings in the rectum than there are in the relatively numb environs of the vagina!

In order for my lover and me to enjoy the experience fully (without the embarrassment of fecal matter or odor) I usually "enemize" myself, then shower with my lover. A lovely prelude to full butt-intercourse is a hot, wet, soapy finger (mine or his) inserted repeatedly into the rectum while I or my lover rubs my clit. Not only does it get the area pretty clean for foreplay (i.e., rimming) purposes, it relaxes the sphincter in preparation for a much larger object. A practice I highly recommend. I also enjoy finger fucking my lover in the shower while jerking rapidly on his cock with my fist or sucking him. Needless to say, he likes this too!

Also, though my lover and I are HIV-negative, we use a condom for anal sex because I don't like a load of seminal fluid in my exit. It's not comfortable.

Now, I realize I'm not telling you gay butt fuckers anything you don't already know. But to those reluctant hets out there who, for whatever reason, have not tried anal sex, I believe you are missing out on what is a very nice occasional treat. Just take precautions, follow my advice, relax and enjoy yourself. Ooo—I made myself horny!

Granny

Hey, Faggot:

I am a het woman. Is it terribly unusual to hate giving head? At best, it's uncomfortable, difficult, and tastes disgusting; at worst, it's degrading. To me, sex is love for another individual (I don't know why, but it's guys for me) carried over into a physical dimension. Sorry, but when your chin is against a hairy anus and your jaw is dislocated and all you can see is a stomach going up and down, thoughts for the individual seem a little obscured.

Every guy I've ever been with has reacted angrily when I've told them that I don't enjoy giving oral sex, then pretended they were joking. False facetiousness, that lifesaver. Why do men feel compelled to stick it in everything, in every orifice a woman has? If our ears were big enough, they'd stick it in there too! I just don't like using my means of communication, eating, and breathing as a masturbation machine for large, smelly, long, rock-hard veiny things that spew sticky stuff down my throat.

Not Liking It

Hey, NLI:

All the problems you mention are solvable: if the guy smells bad, he needs a bath; you don't have to let him come in your mouth if you don't like the taste; you can control the speed and depth of penetration. If the real reason you don't want to give head is that you simply don't like giving head, and are unwilling to learn to like it, then say so. Don't work up rationalizations about what lovemaking is and isn't, about what's degrading and what's not, or about how icky and disgusting men's genitals are. Don't like men's genitals? Sleep with women.

And what of the discomfort? Being on the insertive end of oral, vaginal, or anal intercourse sometimes results in fleeting moments of physical discomfort, yet we endure these discomforts out of a hopefully genuine desire to pleasure our partners. There are times when I'm blowing my boyfriend where, okay, maybe my jaw is tired, but he's having fun, and I'm fond of him, and so I . . . endure. If I'm in pain, I'll call a halt, or take a break, and when I'm simply not up to it (headache, passed out, jaw wired shut), he goes without. But the idea that enduring momentary discomfort somehow degrades me, or anyone else who hangs in there while the boyfriend (or girlfriend—cunnilingus can be exhausting too, ladies) finishes up, is frankly bullshit.

As for why men want to "stick it in everything," well, speaking as a man, we like sticking it in things because it feels good. If my boyfriend's ears were big enough, I'd fuck them. Finding a man willing to go without head isn't gonna be easy—and why should it be? We all have the right—male and female, gay and straight—to good head. And, hey: love me, love my hairy anus.

Hey, Faggot:

I am writing in response to the woman who hated giving head.

With my first two boyfriends, oral sex wasn't a large part of our sex lives. Neither liked eating me much, and I didn't offer to suck them much. My third boyfriend was inexperienced, but had great enthusiasm for everything. He loved eating me, and I quickly learned to love being eaten. I also tried to suck him off, out of feelings of fair play. I'm sure you can predict the results: monotonous blow jobs that rarely led to his having an orgasm.

I had been struck by the amazing difference between eager (him) and dutiful (me) oral sex, and I wanted to give my next boyfriend eager head. When my current boyfriend came along, I was ready to try out my new attitude, anxious to make him feel good.

Our first sessions weren't very successful, until he told me the incredible magic secret no one had ever told me: *You can stop when you get tired!* You don't have to set your jaw and suck him till he comes. Try long licks up the shaft, sucking the balls, a little handjob action. When you're ready, dive back in there with your mouth. Do something for as long as it's fun, and switch when it isn't! The difference is amazing. Wanting your boyfriend to get head you enjoy giving, and relaxing when you give head—these two things make all the difference in the world!

Exciting New Treats

Hey, Faggot:

Can you provide any safe-sex guidelines for ways of improving the taste of a latex condom? It pisses me off that food stores carry every half-assed revolution in panty-shield technology, but nobody sells a good condom designed for oral sex.

Rubber Chick

Hey, RC:

Do not despair, Rubber Chick, the marketplace has responded to the demand for a decent-tasting condom. Lifestyle's Taste O' Mint and Straub's Vanilla Trustex are both condoms "specifically designed for oral sex." In a blind taste test—I closed my eyes—one out of one sex advice columnists preferred the vanilla to the mint, but sadly, neither tastes very good. But here's a safe-sucking tip from Savage Labs: put the condom on your lover's cock, spit into your hand, and stroke your lover's condom-covered cock. Repeat. Then suck. By the time you put his dick in your mouth, it shouldn't taste any worse than your very own spit.

Hey, Faggot:

I have given a lot of blow jobs in my day, but recently a very strange thing happened. I was with a new fellow, and the morning after I delighted him orally, I had really appalling diarrhea.

I figured it must have been something else I ate the night before. So we had oral sex three more times that day, and the next morning I was intestinally distressed again. Monday rolled around, he went back home, and my belly returned to normal.

Then I went to visit him three weeks later and the same thing happened!

So what's up? I have given blow jobs to men before and after this particular gent, and I've never experienced anything like this. Is it an allergic reaction? A hex put on me by his girlfriend? (I know, I know: infidelity is wrong and dangerous, but she hasn't fucked him in over a year and we're both HIV-free and it just seemed like the thing to do, you know?) The only thing I have been able to come up with is that he, being an adventurous vegetarian, eats a lot of curries and stuff my tender tummy can't handle.

Blown Away

Hey, BA:

It's highly unlikely your reaction to his spunk had anything to do with curry. According to my ol' pal Dr. Barak Gaster, "The components of curry that might cause an intestinal reaction in some people are unlikely to be transmitted to sperm—it's unlikely that any food allergen would be transmitted in this manner."

So what caused your intestinal distress? "One of the causes of human infertility is antibody production by women in reaction to a particular partner's sperm. And there are women who produce antibodies to all sperm. This raises the possibility that people can also be allergic to a particular individual's sperm. From what she's describing, it sounds possible that she is having a food allergy to his semen."

So, what do to? "Food-type allergies are very subjective and hard to sort out. The only reliable way to identify a food allergy is to keep a food diary, recording food intake and symptoms. Look for consistent correlations. If repeated exposures seem to cause repeated symptoms, there isn't much to do beyond avoidance."

Hey, Faggot:

I know this is going to sound like I don't have a problem, but I'm worried about what my boyfriend might think.

I'm not sure exactly how it happened (we'd been drinking, so I guess I wasn't paying much attention at first), but while we were making quite passionate love, all of a sudden I realized we were having anal sex. It wasn't rape or anything—I was on top!

It was great. I had a wonderful orgasm, and "Todd" did too. The thing is, I don't know if he remembers! He is the last person in the world I would expect to want to have anal sex. I really want to try this again sober, but knowing him, sober he might think it was dirty or slutty. Should I forget about this and fondly remember the "accident"? How can I approach him without scaring him?

Kinda Kinky

Hey, KK:

The boyfriend knows what happened. Ass and pussy are very different sensations, and any guy too drunk to tell the difference is too drunk to get it up in the first place. So he knows. Maybe he's convinced that, since you were drunk, you have no idea what happened. There's probably a letter from him in the mail asking how to approach you: "My girlfriend was so drunk, she had no idea I was fucking her in the ass! She's the last person in the world who would want to have anal sex. How do I tell her? . . ."

Hey, Faggot:

I am a 25-year-old that enjoys a satisfying sex life with the woman of my dreams. Occasionally during sex, I like her to put her finger in my ass. I've asked some of my friends and they think I'm a freak. Is this normal? Is this dangerous? Please let me know.

Druff

Hey, Druff:

Normal? No, normally women's fingers are not found in their boyfriend's butts. Dangerous? Only if she forgets to remove her rings or trim her fingernails. And what does normal have to do with anything? It feels good, you like it, she likes it—everybody's happy. Who cares what your friends think?

Hey, Faggot:

My wife and I have always enjoyed a healthy sexual relationship, but this has taken a new twist. After watching a very kinky movie in which a man was having sex with a very attractive she-male, my wife and I had great sex.

A couple of days later, my wife came home with stockings, panties and suspenders which she insisted I put on, which I did. Next came the biggest surprise: she walked into the bedroom wearing a strap-on dildo. She slowly inserted the dildo in my ass and fucked me. This is an experience we have repeated several times and we both enjoy it. My question is: does this make me gay or bisexual or something? I'm not attracted to men.

Lacey and Butt-Plugged

Hey, LABP:

Straight men, listen up: it's past time that heterosexual males forged themselves a positive sexual identity. As it stands now, being a "man" means *not* being a woman, and being a straight man means *not* being a gay man. Straight men who do something perceived as feminine—like have a feeling—or perceived as queer—like get fucked in the ass—feel like they aren't straight men anymore.

So long as being a straight man is defined by *not* being a woman and *not* being a gay man, straight men who like to have their butts played with—from a little fingering to being ass-fucked by their wives and girlfriends—are going to worry they're turning "gay." This wouldn't be so bad, except straight guys in Am-I-a-homo? panics tend to overcompensate; they beat up their girlfriends or queers; they invade Hungary or Afghanistan or Grenada or Panama or Kuwait; they open fast-food franchises, all in a desperate attempt to prove to themselves that—their enjoyment of anal sex notwithstanding—they're still real men.

So, LABP, your wife's a woman, right? You're a man. That's amore—heterosexual amore.

Hey, Faggot:

My boyfriend is very open-minded about trying new things in bed. However, one fantasy I have always had is to be the one with the dick. I would like to wear a dildo and fuck my boyfriend up the butt. I suspect many women are curious about what it feels like to fuck someone instead of being fucked. I don't think I'm being unreasonable. But my boyfriend won't even consider the idea. What do you think?

Fantasy

Hey, F:

Did you attempt any other butt-play with the boyfriend before stomping in and announcing you wanted to ream his straight-boy butt with a big ol' strap-on dildo? If not, no wonder he balked! Unenlightened breeder boys have a hard enough time with women fingering their buttholes! Taking pleasure from anal play is as good as becoming a fag in many straight boys' minds, so imagine how tweaked your boyfriend must have been by the idea of having his virgin butthole "played with" by the business end of a big greasy ol' rubber cock!

You need to bring him around gradually! Start small—fingers and tongues—working your way up to une petite butt plug. A butt plug is a wonderful "transition toy" for straight boys, as it neither looks nor functions like a cock. They look like Lava lamps, and once they're in, they stay put—no in/out fucking dynamics·

to work his nerves. After he's come to see his butt as a source of sexual pleasure, explain why you want to fuck him. Reassure him that your interest is in the mutually pleasurable aspects of anal sex: his newfound enjoyment of his butthole is one selling point, the base of the dildo pressing on your clit as you grind away is another. And reassure him that it's still "straight" sex. And explain to him that his prostate gland is a gland just like your boobs and the knob on the end of his dick, and it responds to stimulation in a similar fashion.

And here's one last tip: instead of "fucking" the first few times you play with your strap-on, try "frottage" instead. Place the dildo between his legs, right under his dick, have him clamp down his thighs, and "fuck" him—lots of thrusting, no penetration. You'll still derive the pleasure of grinding your clit against the base of the dildo, and "get to do the fucking." He'll have his perineum massaged, his butthole teased, his mind opened, his ego insulated, and his sexual identity left intact.

Hey, Faggot:

Regarding het men and anal play: If it feels good, do it! My wife and I both love it. All those paranoid guys out there need to get a clue from our homo-brothers. There's a pleasure button up there as well as a sexual nerve center. We recently tried a strap-on dildo—sold to more hetero couples that dykes—and I had one of the most intense orgasms I have ever experienced. I think the strap-on is the great equalizer, physically and psychologically. So bend over guys and give your lady the power tool that will drive you nuts, not gay.

PKP

Hey, PKP:

You're not telling this gay buttfucker anything he doesn't already know about pleasure buttons and nerve endings. But your claim that strap-ons are "sold to more hetero couples than dykes"—rang false. So I went to the experts.

According to the salesgirls at San Francisco's Good Vibrations, a sizable chunk of strap-on sales are to hetero couples, but nowhere near the majority. They estimated the dyke to het dildo sales percentage at 70/30, but growing. Without prompting, Rachel at Toys in Babeland in Seattle cited the same ratio—70/30 dykes/breeders. "It's more fun to sell dildos to breeders," Rachel added. "There's a special sweetness to a straight guy trying to pick out a dildo. It's cute." And Nelson at the Pleasure Chest in New York City cited the exact same numbers Rachel and the Good Vibrations gang did—70/30 dyke/straight! Nelson, unlike Rachel, gets no special thrill selling dildos to straight couples, but he has noticed that breeders are less likely to chat or comparison shop. "They're usually in a hurry. They just buy it and get out the door as soon as possible."

Hey, Faggot:

I'm a straight male with a diet high in legumes, grains and spicy curries, leaving me as flatulent as the next guy, at least. Given that I'm cursed/blessed with a fair amount of body hair, I sometimes feel . . . you know, not so fresh. What I'm wondering is this: would a gay man, such as yourself, with a presumably greater familiarity with anal hygiene issues than a straight man, have any tips to pass along that would leave me feeling confident and fresh as a summer's eve the next time I'm rimmed? This doesn't seem to be an issue straight men discuss much, if at all.

Buttrock

Hey, Butt:

For the sake of my breeder-sisters everywhere, I'm hoping soap and water aren't hygiene tips only gay men are aware of. If rimming is on the menu, move the action into the shower and scrub those buttholes! Or sneak a moment alone in the bathroom, give yourself a few swipes with a soapy washcloth and tiptoe back into the bedroom.

For extra credit, you might also want to keep those pesky

butthairs of yours neatly trimmed. Leave about a quarter of an inch to spare yourself stubble down there, to say nothing of sparing your partner the heartbreak of butthair-induced whisker burn.

Hey, Faggot:

I have been entertaining having anal sex, without a condom, with my girlfriend. However, I would like your advice on the following:

1. How come in all those pornographic anal penetration movies, the penis always comes out "clean," with no fecal matter smeared on it? What's the secret?
2. When a man and a woman engage in anal sex without condoms, what is the risk of the man getting an infection, and what type, if any?
3. How about giving your partner a deep "rim job"?

LCB

Hey, LCB:

1. The secret is making sure your butt, or the butt you're buggering, is good and empty. Some lucky folks have a sixth sense about when they're "clean." Lesser mortals have to take an extra-credit dump, or have a quick enema or anal douche. Poop-smeared dicks caught on video during porno shoots doubtless wind up on the cutting-room floor with the cunt farts, blow job–induced retching, stray pubic hairs, etc.
2. If the woman you're butt-fucking without a condom has a sexually transmitted disease—rectal gonorrhea, syphilis, HIV, etc.—you could have it too by the time you pull out. If you have any doubts about your partner's health or rectitude, use a condom. And, hey, there's an added bonus to condom use: if your dick does emerge from her ass "smeared with feces," the shit's on the condom, not your dick.

3. Rimming is not a first-date/mystery-date activity. Add hepatitis, intestinal parasites, E. coli, and other bugs to the list of STDs you have to worry about.

Hey, Faggot:

I am writing to ask your advice on a rather embarrassing subject. A year ago I had my first experience with anal sex. Right when my boyfriend stuck his member up my ass, my butt let out the most embarrassing suction/farting sound. We stopped for a few minutes and I asked him if that usually happened. My boyfriend said he had never heard of that happening before, which added to my humiliation.

I had been feeling kinda gassy before we started, but was too embarrassed to "cut one" right in front of him, and maybe that's what caused it. Or maybe it was caused by reasons similar to "queefing" and not because of gassiness. Anyway, I haven't had anal sex since then even though I enjoyed it, because that first experience really traumatized me. I'm afraid of it happening again! Have you ever heard of this, or am I a freak? Is there any way to prevent such an embarrassing situation?

STF

Hey, STF:

What can you do to prevent farts? You could get a cosmetic colostomy, I suppose. Or you could remember that it's a butt-hole first, and a fuckhole second. The butthole is attached to the digestive tract's terminus, eliminating poop, gas, undigested kernels of corn, and condoms filled with heroin, as need be. When it comes to anal sex, sometimes gas (or worse) just . . . happens.

Your mistake was, having sensed you were gassy, not excusing yourself from the bedroom for a moment alone in the toilet. It is common butt sex etiquette to prep, whether your prep is a bowel-clearing dump, an extra-credit enema, or a few moments on the bathroom floor in the pregnancy antigas position. (Kneel, bend forward, place your chest on the floor, with your head resting on your hands, and your ass in the air—gas rises.)

Once upon a time, a new love was screwing my freshman-in-college rear end and I committed the exact faux pas you did. I wanted to die, but my older, wiser, and cuter boyfriend said, "Hey, don't worry about it—that comes with the territory." He was right.

Hey, Faggot:

I am a 24-year-old het woman and I need some info.

This guy I started sleeping with wants to have anal sex. I have had fingers in there during vaginal stimulation, but I've never had only anal stimulation from a penis. The reason for this? It hurts like hell! I just can't get past that panic of "Oh, shit! I'm being ripped right open!" to relax enough to let it happen. Does that panic go away? I would like to try anal sex—please share some advice and/or pointers that us het women wouldn't normally hear.

Boyfriend Knocking at the Back Door

Hey, Back Door:

Besides having what would be a terrific drag name if she wasn't an actual woman, Carol Queen is the manager of San Francisco's Good Vibrations, a sex-toy and erotic-book store by and for women. Carol had some pointers for you.

Carol thinks you're uptight: "The level of fear she's bringing to her exploration is guaranteeing the pain, like a self-fulfilling prophecy. If she can learn to relax—the pain will go away." If you're lying there thinking, "It's gonna hurt, it's gonna hurt," it's probably gonna hurt. How can you relax? Carol had several suggestions. "Practice anal sex by yourself, when you masturbate." You won't feel under any pressure to perform, and you won't feel like you're letting your partner down if you bail. Have a beer, a glass of wine, smoke some pot, lock yourself in a dark room in the middle of the night, and experiment on your own. When you want to give it a go with your boyfriend, Carol suggests you "completely control the pace, speed, and depth of penetration." Have your boyfriend lie there and not move. Get him worked up and then sit on his dick. "Being in complete control will lessen her panic. When and if she tells him to move, he should begin to proceed slowly."

You may find you can only last a few minutes the first dozen or so times your boyfriend penetrates you anally. Don't feel like you've failed if you have to move on to some other activity—but don't go from butt-fucking to vaginal intercourse without giving his dick a good scrubbing. And you are using lube, aren't you? Lots of it? "If she only used a little lube the first times she tried it, it's no wonder it hurt!" said Carol. Use huge sloppy handfuls of lube and reapply (pull it out, put some more on it, put it back in) two or three times during anal sex.

Hey, Faggot:

I'm concerned with your recent "suggestion" that someone interested in experimenting with anal sex "dash home, have a beer, a glass of wine, smoke some pot, then lock yourself in a dark room in the middle of the night and experiment on your own." Drugs, alcohol and sex do not mix, especially in this age of AIDS. Other satisfying suggestions are: hot baths or showers to relax the strong rectum muscles, nice fragrances to arouse calmly our desires, soft music to guide us with rhythms.

Carlos

Hey, Carlos:

Drugs, alcohol, and sex do not mix? Really? Get out much?

Not all substance use is abuse. Drugs and alcohol used in moderation can be a wonderful social lubricant and, in a metaphorical sense, they're pretty terrific sexual lubricants as well. Getting seriously fucked-up before having sex can place you at greater risk of just about anything—from stumbling in front of a speeding bus to having unprotected sex to not being able to have sex at all. No one should get so seriously fucked before sex that they can't remember how to use condoms.

But telling the grown-ups out there who can drink a beer or smoke some dope and still manage to behave safely that "drugs, sex and alcohol do not mix" is bullshit—patronizing, condescending horseshit. High does not automatically equal high risk, any more than sober equals low risk. Plenty of morons have unsafe sex stone-cold sober, and plenty of people have safe safe sex completely fucked-up.

Hey, Faggot:

I am a lesbian and have been with my partner for five years. I love her with all my heart and we have really great sex, but I yearn for something more. I have, in previous relationships, enjoyed butt-fucking, both giving and receiving, but she refuses to participate.

As a Butt-fucking Guru, what advice can you give to help me convince her to loosen up and at least try this pleasure with me?

Tastefully Wanting

Hey, TW:

When you addressed me as Butt-fucking Guru, I thought, "It is not I she means. I am only a poor country girl. Dr. Jack Morin, author of *Anal Pleasure and Health*, is twice the Butt-fucking Guru I am!" So I gave Dr. Morin, a sex therapist in private practice in San Francisco, a ringy-dingy. After listening to me gush like a schoolgirl, Dr. Morin graciously consented to come down off the mountaintop and answer your letter.

Dr. Morin feels you should proceed slowly: "For the one who is more experienced, it's really important, especially if your partner is reluctant, that you are patient. Pressure is the worst thing, it makes a person more tense, and tension is the enemy of anal pleasure." So if you can't pressure or rush her, what can you do? "Find out from your partner what makes her uncomfortable, what might make her more comfortable, and what might make anal intercourse more appealing.

"She may feel it's dirty and yucky. If that's the issue, you could address how to make it less yucky. If encountering shit or smells is a concern, as it is for a lot of people, showering together and anal douching could help." If all else fails, you may need to reconcile yourself to a butt-sex-free partnership. "Maybe your partner just doesn't like anal stimulation. There are people who explore, get to know the area, are able to relax and it still turns them off."

Hey, Faggot:

A friend of mine just came out of the closet. I asked him a lot of questions, but he did not answer some of them because he felt uncomfortable. I am curious about gay sex. How do gay men . . . do it? I mean, doesn't it hurt? If a condom is not used, doesn't the come . . . leak out? How can you receive any pleasure and orgasm from this?

Sickly Concerned

Hey, SC:

Gay men "do it" lots of different ways, many of them similar to the ways straight people "do it." Judging from your letter, you seem to think gay men only have anal sex. Not true: we have oral sex, anal sex, we masturbate together, and sometimes we masturbate alone. There are gay men who don't like or have anal sex, just as there are straights who do like and do have anal sex. Anal sex hurts if you do it wrong and, as with vaginal intercourse, the insertee may experience discomfort bordering on pain at the start, but this can be overcome with patience and practice.

If you don't use condoms, the come will "leak out," but come leaks out of vaginas too. And mouths, and armpits, and nostrils, and just about any place you put it—it is a liquid, after all. As for pleasure, well, again, that's highly subjective. Take eating pussy. My straight male friends swear by it, while I'd rather—well, I know this sounds like I'm exaggerating, but really, I'm very serious—I'd rather die.

Hey, Faggot:

I stumbled across a video titled *Blow Your Own Horn*. It featured guys who could suck their own dicks. I went home and attempted to do this. It didn't work. I'm only three or four inches away from pulling this feat off. Is there some special technique or do you just have to be hung like a horse?

Kevin

Hey, Kevin:

You need to be limber. Start a stretching regimen, take a yoga class, and one day you may be able to suck yourself off. In the meantime, find a cock to practice on—imagine how disappointed you'll be if after months of hard work you can finally reach your cock only to discover you give lousy head.

Hey, Faggot:

I'm an 18-year-old and I have a question: I've heard stories about autofellatio and I've even read one account of the activity, so I want to know from an expert: can a man really suck his own cock? If so, please tell me how. Thank you for your time.

Graham

Hey, G:

At some point in adolescence, most men throw their legs over their heads and try to suck cock. Most of us discover, to our crushing disappointment, that we can't. The few who can are usually blessed with limber upper bodies or longer-than-average cocks, or both. Those who can't autofellate have no choice but to leave the house and sweet-talk other people into doing it for us.

But you don't know until you try. Give it a whirl: lie down on your back, lift your legs straight up into the air, place your hands on your lower back for balance, and slowly bring your knees down to your ears.

Hey, Faggot:

I'm a hetero male that enjoys sucking his own dick. I came home one night very drunk, horny, and alone. I started a consolatory wank, when I flashed on a story I had read of a well-hung man that liked to suck himself off. My body is flexible from years of yoga and I thought I'd give it a try. The result was fantastic. Apart from the less-than-pleasant taste of semen, I'd never had a better blow job in my life.

This is not something I do often. I have a normal sex life and truly enjoy women. In no way do I consider myself gay, but I know the pleasure of having a live cock in my mouth. I fantasize about giving another man head, but I don't really fit into the gay lifestyle.

I must admit, I'm clueless and confused as far as asking a man if I can go down on him. I guess I'd like the best of both worlds.

Any suggestions?

J.H.

Hey, J.H.:

March up to the next straight guy you see, and tell him what you told all of us: "In no way do I consider myself gay, but I would like to suck your dick. How about it?" I'll bet you wind up with something in your mouth—definitely your foot, maybe his fist, or, if you're extremely lucky, his cock. Best of luck, Straight Boy.

Hey, Faggot:

While my buddy—straight, I thought—was out East for Xmas, I stayed at his apartment so his place wouldn't be empty. I made myself at home. I drank his beer, I ate his food, I watched his movies. I also watched his homemade pornos: him and his two girlfriends. I know it was wrong, but he said to make myself at home!

Here's the weird part: There was a video of him curled up sucking his own dick! This one got me excited. Okay, so here are the questions: Is he gay? Is he bi? Would a straight guy do this? Is this a common ability, straight or gay, or is he one unusual dude? He doesn't know I saw his tapes.

Mr. Nosey

Hey, N:

You watched a videotape of your best friend sucking his own dick, which "excited you," and you're wondering if your buddy is queer? *What about you?* You're the one turned on watching videos of him suck his dick. *Projecting* much? Are you wondering if your buddy's bi, or are you hoping he is?

For the record: Giving yourself a blow job doesn't make you any gayer than giving yourself a handjob. Consider: a guy giving another guy a handjob is doing a pretty gay thing, but a guy giving himself a handjob might be doing a gay thing, and he might not. It depends on what he's thinking about: is he pretending his right hand is Luke Skywalker's hairy blond butt, or Princess Leia Lipsmacker's more generous rear end?

I will concede that a gay guy with limber/length working for him is likelier to suck himself off than a similarly endowed straight boy, if only because the gay boy isn't afraid sucking his own dick is going to make him gay—he's already gay! Straight boys, on the other hand, often let homosexual panic keep them from all sorts of pleasures. Like getting fucked in the ass, for instance. You don't have to be gay to enjoy getting fucked in the ass, but it helps.

Hey, Faggot:

You told Mr. Nosey his buddy was unusual in his ability to suck himself off. Speaking from personal experience, I'm inclined to think it's not as rare as all that. While I am in good shape, I am only slightly more flexible than most and my erect cock is not quite 6". A lot of guys I've observed stretching out at the gym are more limber than me and probably have longer dicks. Yet I am able to get my lips around the head of my penis, and I enjoy getting off like that once or twice a week.

If I can do it, other guys can—and do. I recall reading in Kinsey that 3 percent of men admitted to fellating themselves. The actual figure today must be much higher, because we are in better shape, and more open to the idea of self-fellatio than the guilt-ridden self-polluters of Kinsey's time.

Here's my technique in case you want to give it a go: I lie on my back with a couple of pillows under my neck, and throw my legs over my head. It's important that the pillows are under your neck, and not your head, and it helps to brace your feet against the wall. The more you do it, the easier it gets.

Because I Can

P.S. I'm straight—and I've never told or shown any of my girlfriends that I can do this. I prefer their blow jobs.

Hey, Faggot:

Sucking your own dick can be dangerous. I know. I put myself in the hospital doing it—or I should say, trying to do it.

There were warning signs that it wasn't a good idea—cricks in the neck and shooting pains—but I was young and horny and alone and I figured they'd pass. They didn't. I finally pulled something. I'll spare you the details. Suffice to say that I was immobilized and in pain and in the hospital for a week, followed by a long recuperation, physical therapy, and to this day, years later, there's still occasionally pain in my neck and shoulders.

Painful experience has taught me that unless you're uncommonly well endowed, it's best to get out and find someone to suck your dick for you.

Hey, Faggot:

Please explain the difference between a "dildo" and a "butt plug." I'm pretty naive.

Clueless

Hey, C:

Dildos look like dicks, go where dicks go, and do what dicks do, without getting you pregnant or spreading STDs. Butt plugs, on the other hand, look like Lava lamps and go in your butt.

Hey, Faggot:

I'm a curious male breeder with a question: I recently heard from some of my bi-friends that orgasms are longer and of greater intensity when the prostate is stimulated in addition to the penis. What's your take on this?

Also, what would you recommend as a good way to get started? I've heard butt plugs are good. Please tell me.

Virgin Prostate

Hey, VP:

Your bi-friends are correct: applying pressure to a man's prostate gland while he's fucking, or getting sucked off, or jerking off will, if his prostate is "wired," enhance orgasm. Enhance probably isn't strong enough a word: a little prostate stim can mean the difference between come-dribbling-on-your-stomach or come-flying-over-the-top-of-your-head. Unfortunately, most straight men are too scared of their butts to allow themselves this pleasure!

The prostate gland is just inside your ass, underneath your bladder. The most effective way to stimulate that li'l gland is by sticking something in your ass. One of the beauties of being male is the ability to be both insertee and inserter simultaneously. You would think that would be enough to convince scaredy-cat straight boys to go for it—if she sticks something into you, you can compensate by sticking something into her. Since her insertion is canceled out by yours, no sexual identity crisis! But from the reports I've had from straight women whose boyfriends freaked out when they got within fingering range of his rear end, most straight men aren't willing to go there, not even for an enhanced orgasm!

You, VP, sound curious, and butt plugs are a fabulous way to satisfy your curiosity. Since they're wide in the middle, narrow toward the bottom, and have a flared base, your own sphincter muscles hold the plug in your ass, leaving your hands free for other activities: jerking off, fingering her ass, knitting, writing advice columns. And since butt plugs, unlike dildos, don't look like cocks, they're a very good beginner's butt-toy for insecure straight boys.

P.S. The above Prostate Propaganda may give the impression that possession of a prostate gland is a prerequisite to enjoying anal sex play, or that prostate stimulation is the goal of all anal sex. This, of course, is not the case. Women do not have prostate glands, yet many women enjoy anal sex play. While the prostate is a major player in anal pleasure for men, there are millions of nerve endings hanging around your ass that, in the absence of prostate stimulation or a prostate, make anal sex play worth your time and effort.

Hey, Faggot:

I am a breeder boy who at one time gave scant thought to the use of cock rings and butt plugs. Actually, I regarded these things as reserved for the gay and SM crowds, or for folks "wilder" than me. My girlfriend is very sexy and exciting, but I began to question our sexual activity. Honestly, it was becoming as predictable as my morning dump, so we started wandering into "toy" stores.

Please allow me to speak for a moment to the many het guys reading this column:

Boys, if you can find the nerve to cinch an adjustable ring

around your meat and push a lubed, mid-sized silicone plug into your hole, you're going to come like a gorilla and see stars. None of this is painful—in fact, the opposite—and I've never been faced with a poopy butt plug when the fun's over. As I come longer and louder, so does she. Our toy experience has made us happier and more comfortable with our bodies, our holes. Gentlemen, if you're too chicken to discover your butts, *yer a bunch of suckers!*

PTM

Hey, Faggot:

I would like to fist my friend's cute little waiting butthole. I know some of the nuts and bolts—use gloves and lube, cup your hand at first, make a fist inside—but what I want to know is this: I read somewhere that yer supposed to clean yer butt out first. What exactly does this entail? Shitting first? An enema? A bidet? Why might it be a good idea to have a clean butt?

Fly Bi Knight

Hey, FBK:

The reason it "might" be a "good idea" to clean out your butt before someone puts their arm up it should be obvious. That you're even asking makes me think your letter isn't serious. But in case it is: a bidet cleans the outside of your butt. If your pal has a bathtub, you don't need a bidet. Shitting first is always a good idea, whether you're going to the movies, for a drive in the country, or having sex. Shit first. After a good dump, most people's butts are clean enough for all practical purposes. For advanced butt-hijinks, such as fisting, an enema is always a good idea. And trim your fingernails.

❤ Life & Death

Birth Control, Death Control, Babies, and Other Sexually Transmitted Diseases

Sexually transmitted diseases and unplanned pregnancies are bummers.

While I've never knocked anyone up, I have had an STD. Like a lot of folks, I caught the clap in my teens. I discovered my problem on a Friday night, when I was 19 years old. I was in a movie theater, at a mall near where I was going to college, watching Disney's animated *Jungle Book*, of all things. I excused myself to go take what would turn out to be a life-changing leak. Stepping up to the urinal, I hauled out my dick and assumed the position. If I'd looked down, I would immediately have known something was wrong. But in high school, I'd learned that if you really want to get out of public toilets in one piece—or with your one piece—you look straight ahead at all times, don't look at other guys' bare necessities, and avoid making eye contact.

So, because I was looking straight ahead, I didn't see the Technicolor pusworks that had soiled my tighty whities. A split second after I'd given my bladder the go-ahead, the most excruciating burning sensation I'd ever felt—like I was pissing ground glass suspended in napalm—shot from my dick to my brain. Um, like, ouch. There was a guy on either side of me, and I somehow managed to stifle a yelp and keep looking straight ahead. I pinched off the flow of urine, stopping the torture for the moment, and stood there waiting for the other two guys to leave. When I was alone, I stepped away from the urinal, and looked down at my dick. What looked like greenish-gray soft-serve ice cream was coming out of my piss-slit, and my undies was full of the thick, pussy discharge we'd been warned about in sex ed. I still had to pee, so I stepped back up to the urinal, feeling like a man who was about to stick his dick in an electric pencil sharpener—for a second time.

The next day, I went to the University Health Clinic, learned I had nongonococcal urethritis, or NGU, and was given a shot and a lecture. Feeling like I ought to, I called the only guy I'd slept with in the previous two months. When I explained that I thought he had given me the clap, he said I must be mistaken, it had to be someone I'd "tricked" with at school. But I hadn't "tricked" with anyone at school. There hadn't been anyone since him, I'd been good since I got to the dorms—it just had to be him. I didn't scream, or freak out, I was only calling because I thought he should see a doc too. He'd never had an STD in his life, he told me, and slammed down the phone. What a stupid thing to do.

I did something stupid too, though. I'd just met a boy, and we were getting close to getting it on. I was afraid if I told him I had an STD he'd think I was a sexually transmitted disease–spreading tramp (STD–ST), and dump me, so I avoided sex for as long as I could, but then the time came to put up (fuck him!) or open up (tell him!). And . . . I fucked him. I'd had my shots, I was taking my pills—maybe it would be okay. It wasn't. To his credit, he didn't kill me. He was upset, but he was also older (23!) and wiser. He explained that I shouldn't have been ashamed of having an STD, or have been afraid to tell him because he wouldn't have dumped me. He was very nice and very adult about the fact that I was, when it came right down to it, a sexually transmitted disease–spreading tramp (STD–ST).

Are you following this? Ashamed of myself for having contracted an STD, and afraid my boyfriend would think I was an

STD–ST if I told him the truth, I spread an STD! This experience is a common one. Folks are so ashamed of having an STD that they can't tell their sex partner about it, and since taking precautions would clue their partner in, they take risks instead . . . and they give their sex partner an STD! Which is a much more dramatic way of telling someone you have an STD. It should work like this: having an STD is nothing to be ashamed of, taking precautions while you have one is nothing to be ashamed of. The only thing people should be ashamed of is giving someone else an STD. Less shame would mean fewer transmissions, because people would be able to tell the truth and take precautions without having to worry about being dumped.

Ultimately, the boyfriend—Mr. Wonderful—didn't reject me, though there were some tense moments. He went in for shots, and we waited a couple of months for the all-clear before we started going at it again. Even a negative experience—I really hated having NGU—can often have a positive outcome. My experience with my freshman-year STD was ultimately positive, for it taught me a valuable lesson about what to do when or if I contract an STD, and how to treat a partner who has an STD. And guess what? I've never had one again.

This section contains a sampling of the letters I've answered from folks wrestling with the serious side of being sexually active, the "consequences." Most of the questions are about birth control (how to use it, where to find it) and death control (how to avoid HIV infection), and a few are about children. Alert readers will notice that HIV, as an issue, tends to swamp all other issues—questions that start out about, oh, birth-control pills, have a way of landing on AIDS.

Hey, Faggot:

I need your help fast! I am going overseas to visit my lover, whom I have not seen for four months. We are deeply in love and when we get together we are going to hump like bunnies! The problem is that, for a variety of reasons too complicated to go into, we are unable to use any real effective birth control.

Pills are out, condoms prove excruciatingly painful, and she is not in a location where a diaphragm or—heaven forbid—an IUD is a possibility.

Originally I thought we would be satisfied with mutual oral gratification, and maybe even a little backdoor action. But I started having powerful fantasies about filling up my lover in the way only intercourse can. Which is riskier, my being in her early on and bringing her to orgasm fairly quickly and then retreating; or her going down on me, bringing me off and then my entering her while still stiff and wiped clean?

Fearing Ecstasy

P.S. She is more than willing to take the risk. She has been tracking her ovulation to see when we can best avoid high fertility, etc.

Hey, FE:

Since your girlfriend is somewhere she can't get her twat on a diaphragm or—heaven forbid—an IUD, it's safe to assume she's also somewhere that lacks an abortion clinic. Which is unfortunate, since she could very well be pregnant by the time you get back on that plane.

Look, I can't grant you absolution. You rule out just about every birth control method there is, and then want some reassurance that the rhythm method is gonna save your ass. Well, as the son of practicing Catholics who had four kids in three and a half years, I can tell you that the rhythm method doesn't work. I'm walking, talking, typing proof. Neither does pulling out, putting it in "just a little," or putting it back in.

Anyway, what's so "excruciatingly painful" about condoms?

Hey, Faggot:

Permit me to respond to the question you recently posed to Fearing Ecstasy: "What's so excruciatingly painful about condoms?" For most folks, there's no pain at all involved in using regular condoms, but in this instance, I would hazard a guess that FE's gal pal is one of us fems who happen to be allergic "down there" to the latex used to make the damn things. My hubby and I are unable to use rubber rubbers for the simple reason that within a minute or so of having a Trojan-covered jimmy whipping in and out of me, I'm in utter agony.

However, FE could try using the option that cleared up the problem completely for me: natural lambskin condoms. No pain, no irritation, and the answer to his prayers.

LR

Hey, LR:

When I jumped all over FE, all I heard was yet another straight boy claiming that condoms "didn't work" for him. And I overreacted. And I'm so very sorry. Maybe his partner is allergic to latex, and maybe they should try lambskin condoms.

But, please note: while effective birth control, lambskin condoms do not provide the same level of protection against STDs that latex does—bugs that can't pass through latex can pass through sheep gut. Another option for the latex intolerant is polyurethane condoms, sold under the brand name Avanti. They keep sperms and bugs at bay, and as they're not latex, you can use any ol' kind of grease you want to for lube, including, for you retro butt-fuckers, Crisco.

Hey, Faggot:

I wanted to comment on a particular kind of condom you recommended for use by those that have either a dislike or an allergy to latex, Avanti polyurethane condoms. My boyfriend and I tried Avantis. We usually engage in fairly normal, hetero intercourse and although he is above average in size, my partner does not rival John Holmes, if you get what I'm saying.

On two separate occasions when using Avanti condoms, they broke. This was, mind you, with ample lube, correct application, etc. The first time we thought, well, this can happen to anyone. After the second time, we decided a new addition to the family was not worth avoiding the extra application of lube now and then (which keeps latex condoms comfortable for us).

I asked around and found that I was not the only one who had experienced difficulty with these guys. Anal sex would certainly give these little jobbies a run for their money if my relatively tame hetero sex did.

Concerned

Hey, Faggot:

I'm a 26-year-old het guy. When corporate stress gets me down, I like to relax by scoring a soothing hand job or titfuck from an escort girl/"masseuse." Does this put me at risk for exposure to HIV? If not, how risky would it be to get a blow job from an escort using a condom?

Gold Coast

Hey, GC:

Neither of the activities you're engaging in with your escorts—handjobs, tit-fucking—place you at risk of contracting HIV. None whatever. Zip. Zilch. Getting a blow job while wearing a condom is also completely safe—though blow jobs will cost you more. Even getting a blow job without wearing a condom is pretty much a no-risker. That's *getting* a blow job; *giving* a blow job places you at some small risk, provided the dick you're sucking is attached to an HIV-positive person. So your "masseuse" is wise to use condoms: she needs to protect herself from whatever bugs *you* may be carting from escort to escort.

This is an entirely unsolicited opinion, as titfucking isn't the issue here—safety is—but, hey, it's my column: were I into women, I would doubtless be into titfucking. But it has always seemed to me that the person doing the titfucking must look absolutely ridiculous to the person providing the tits. Look up, and there's this guy squattin' over you, huffin' and puffin'. Look down, and the head of his dick is popping in and out of your cleave like a spazzed turtle or, I don't know—something. Then the turtle pukes all over your chin. I don't think I'd be able to keep a straight face. Unless I was being paid to.

Hey, Faggot:

I am a 24-year-old heterosexual female. I do my best to practice safe sex, and I have remained STD-free so far.

I enjoy anal sex very much, though I understand it is a very risky type of sex. My question is, how risky is anal sex with a condom and lubricant in regards to STDs? Is it more or less dangerous than vaginal intercourse without a condom? Thanks.

Likes Her Backdoor Man

Hey, LHBM:

Because butts are, generally speaking, tighter than twats, screwing is harder on condoms and butts than it is on twats: condoms are likelier to break during rigorous butt-fucking than equally rigorous twat-fucking, and your anus is likelier to suffer wee abrasions if you're not using enough lube. For these simple reasons, and a few others, protected anal sex does carry slightly higher STD risks than protected twat-fucking—it's protected sex, remember, not fail-safe sex.

But, my fellow butt-fuckers, a little extra vigilance is all that's required to negate the slightly elevated risk of condom failure during anal sex. You see, very often it's not the condom that fails us, but we who fail the condom. Use stronger latex condoms for butt-fucking—don't use "maxithins"—and keep the butt being fucked well lubricated. Check periodically to make sure the condom is still on and in one piece. After your partner comes, he should grip the base of the condom while he pulls out, in order to avoid a spill.

It should go without saying—but I'm going to say it anyway—that anal sex *with* condoms is *less* dangerous than vaginal sex *without* condoms.

Hey, Faggot:

Is there an HIV risk to the person getting his dick sucked? I am asking because I recently took a walk on the wild side and "swung" with a married breeder couple, and the husband sucked my cock for a few minutes. I was not wearing a condom, and did not cum. Did I put myself at risk for HIV?

First Time Swinger

Hey, FTS:

Sucking places a person at some small risk of acquiring HIV—provided he or she is sucking HIV-positive cock—but getting sucked presents no risk, stud.

Hey, Faggot:

I am an HIV-positive gay man with some input on the recent banter over oral sex and risk. Taking come in your mouth is pretty much agreed to be a "high-risk" behavior, while sucking cock without taking come in your mouth is considered "low risk." But, still, the risk is there, even if the guy you're blowing doesn't pop his load in your mouth.

When my partner and I met, he was negative. Now he's not. He had tested negative for years, and did so after our only episode of protected anal sex (he was the "top"). His only risk for exposure to HIV came after we decided that oral sex without a condom was okay, as long as there was no come. The messages available seemed to support that the risk of spreading HIV in this manner (assuming a mouth was healthy) was virtually nil. We took that risk and now he is HIV-positive. Which sucks.

We throw around "high risk" and "low risk" like we are talking mutual funds or something. If you take a cock in your mouth—even if he doesn't come—you are taking a chance, a risk. You can't be certain you won't get infected with HIV. It's that simple. If you're the one who ends up infected with HIV, it really doesn't matter how "high" or "low" the risk was.

Unsigned

Hey, Faggot:

In the past month, four different tricks—um, I mean gentleman friends—have offered me poppers as part of sex. I have always declined on the grounds that they give me a headache. But, Dan, I thought poppers were incredibly passé and that there existed a possible connection between them and Kaposi's sarcoma. Am I behind the times? What's your opinion of inhalants?

Curious About This Phenomenon

Hey, CATP:

You're a bit behind the times. . . .

Poppers are amyl or butyl nitrites. When inhaled, they cause dilation of the blood vessels and certain muscles to relax, including the anal sphincter. Poppers became popular with gay men because "they decreased pain sensitivity, prolonged orgasm, and facilitated penetration," according to a sex educator I spoke with. You can get yourself some over the counter in Canada and Europe and Mexico. But sales of poppers were banned in the U.S. in '88 because of a suspected link between popper use and AIDS.

Almost all early AIDS victims were heavy users of poppers, and some early studies demonstrated a correlation (not the same as causation) between poppers and Kaposi's sarcoma, but as more studies were done, that correlation was found to be unreliable. In other words, studies thought to show a "link" were actually showing a coincidence. Should you accept the next time a guy offers? Maybe, maybe not. While not the cause of AIDS, poppers are definitely bad for your health. "Any responsible health official or doctor is going to urge you not to use them," said the responsible health official I spoke with.

Being neither responsible nor professional, I am going to tell you to use them. Even the responsible health educator agreed that popper use, in moderation, may be no worse for you than moderate use of other drugs or alcohol.

Hey, Faggot:

I'm a 20-year-old male intent on having children. Recently a friend of mine mentioned that bubble bath will cause a man to be sterile. Is this true? Are there any other commonly used products which I should avoid? The worst nightmare of my life would be the inability to have a child of my own.

Bubble Bath Boy

Hey, BBB:

I showed your letter to Jennifer, my 20-year-old intern, and said, "Anyone who thinks bubble bath can make them sterile is too stupid to have children." She replied, "Anyone who is 20 years old is too stupid to have children."

Hey, Faggot:

Hello!?! Do the words "dental dam" mean anything to you? A het male recently wrote in to you with cutesy little tips about eating pussy [see The King of Oral Sex's letter in "Gettin' Together"] and you remained silent! I know I don't need to tell you that HIV exists in vaginal fluid as well as semen. What's the deal?

EM

Hey, EM:

Hello?!? Does the word "seroprevalence" mean anything to you?

I am aware that HIV is as likely to be present in an HIV-positive woman's vaginal secretions as it is in an HIV-positive man's semen. I am also aware that there are far fewer HIV-positive straight women out there than HIV-positive gay men. If the population you draw your partners from does not have a significant percentage of HIV-positive individuals, the odds of going down on an HIV-positive person, and thereby risking exposure to HIV, are significantly less than if the population you draw your partners from has a higher percentage of HIV-positive individuals.

Are you following me?

According to some data from the Centers for Disease Control, we can conservatively estimate that of the one million people with HIV in the United States, 40 percent (400,000) are gay men, and 18 percent (180,000) are women. (These numbers are speculative and the CDC acknowledges that they underestimate the numbers of infected gay men, but for the sake of argument, we'll go with them.) At first glance, those numbers look pretty dire—for every two infected gay men, there's one infected woman. Why, pretty soon the number of infected women will catch up with the number of infected gay men, and (drumroll, please) we'll all be at equal risk, right?

Wrong.

Gay men, depending on whom you want to believe, make up anywhere from 0.5 to 5 percent of the population. Women are 53 percent of the population. Work it out: If there are 132,500,000 women in this country, and 180,000 of them are HIV+, the straight guys who wrote in about cunnilingus have a 1 in 735 chance of finding their noses tucked in the twat of an HIV-positive woman. Of the 1,175,000/11,750,000 gay men in the country, 400,000 (probably more) are HIV+. Gay men have between a 1 in 3 to 1 in 30 chance of finding themselves in bed with an HIV-positive person. In New York City and San Francisco, half of all gay men are infected, bringing those odds up to 1 in 2! Even if the odds of a straight man finding himself in bed with an HIV-positive woman were halved—most HIV-positive women also live in major urban areas—the odds for him are still relatively slight: 1 in 368. How many straight men sleep with 368 women in a year? Hell, in a lifetime? Some gay men sleep with 368 other gay men over a long weekend.

So, I ask you, who's at greater risk of acquiring HIV from a new partner? Gay men, or straight men (not that women aren't also at risk, but we're talking about whether or not to advise straight men to use dental dams)? Who has to be more careful? Take more precautions?

Factor in that most HIV-positive women in this country are, sadly, the geographically and economically isolated partners of IV drug users, that men are more likely to infect women than vice versa, and that we're talking about the less risky practice of oral sex here, and not vaginal or anal intercourse. When all those points are taken into consideration, your average straight man's risk of acquiring HIV during oral sex with your average straight woman shrinks to almost nothing.

Now, I know HIV looks like a lot of fun to those of you who may never have the honor of being memorialized in that heap of grief pornography, the AIDS Memorial Quilt, and it must seem terribly unfair that HIV isn't subject to equal opportunity laws—I'm all in favor of giving HIV quotas—but AIDS doesn't pick on everyone equally. Gay men are at the greatest risk, followed by IV drug users and their partners. African Americans are at more risk than Euro Americans, but again, the African Americans getting HIV and AIDS are largely gay/bi men, IV drug users, and their partners.

We all weigh the risks, and hopefully make educated choices about our sex lives and the risk we're willing to accept. Whether or not AIDS groupies or AIDS educators like it, people are making up their own minds about the degree of risk they're willing to accept. Straight men and their sex partners have plenty of STDs to worry about—syphilis, gonorrhea, genital warts (HPV), herpes, chlamydia—but, for the most part, HIV isn't among them—and are making choices accordingly, and I give advice accordingly.

Hey, Faggot:

I'm a bi girl. Let me clue you in on a few facts-o-life among the pussy lickers.

Pussy juice contains as high a concentration of HIV as jism.

So I'm as much at risk when I lick unprotected HIV-positive pussy as I am when I suck unprotected HIV-positive cock, and HIV-positive pussy can't pull out of my mouth before it comes. In my case, since my gums bleed if you wink at them, I'm at risk from fluids in my mouth.

Now let's talk about the way statistics are kept. My wife is HIV-positive. In fact, she has AIDS. Say I lick my wife's pussy three times a day for a year, using no barrier. Say during the same year I let my HIV-positive boyfriend come in my mouth once with no condom and I gulp it all down. If at the end of the year I test positive, the CDC [Centers for Disease Control] will record me as having become infected through heterosexual transmission because that is "more likely."

You are probably right about the likelihood of running into an HIV-positive man as opposed to an HIV-positive woman. But if people assume, as you seem to suggest, that all women are HIV-negative and may be slurped with relative abandon, it will increase the chances of it being equally risky in five years as more of us convert.

By the way, I have a great time. And if I use clear Saran Wrap on my gal—colored Saran Wrap has this weird flavor, like bad sheet cake—I *can* taste my gal. I *smell* her, even though what I'm actually tasting is my own saliva, but what my tongue perceives is *her* taste. One of my gals tastes tangy, like a subtle vinaigrette. One tastes like potato leek soup. Another tastes like molasses. Yummy! Now if only there were a decent way to safely suck cock that didn't taste like latex. Sigh.

Love and Pussy-Lip Kisses

Hey, LAPLK:

By my count, you have five regular sex partners, two of whom you know to be HIV-positive. Not only are you a rather accomplished slut (I mean that in the most sex-positive sense of the word; if an alternate spelling existed to indicate nonpejorative usage, I'd use it), but you're a smart slut. I applaud you for your devotion to latex—condoms for blow jobs, Saran Wrap for pussy licking, and I assume, condoms for fucking. You've accurately assessed the level of risk in your sex life (high), you're using common sense (and latex), and you're proceeding with caution. Bravo, girlfriend. In your shoes, lesser vigilance would be suicide.

But not everyone is in your shoes: not everyone has multiple sex partners, is married to an HIV-positive person, or has gums that bleed so easily. Not everyone is running the same risks you are—so not everyone needs to take the exact same precautions you do. I am not going to sit here and lie to people: "Use condoms and latex every time you have oral sex or in five short years *you'll all be exposed*!!!" That is bullshit. We're fifteen years into the AIDS crisis, three 5-year cycles, and in that time the vast majority of sexually active adults in America—gay, bi and straight—have rejected latex for oral sex. And guess what? *Everyone is not HIV-positive.*

As for those CDC stats: I'm no fan of the CDC, but according to the woman I spoke with on the phone, they don't "credit" one method of transmission over another when it comes to someone who, like you, falls into "multiple risk groups." They acknowledge they can't be sure whether your infection was due to that one hetero contact or those one thousand lesbian contacts. If they were studying woman-to-woman transmission of the HIV virus via oral sex, your case would be excluded from the study. Have these standards resulted in a slightly skewed picture of woman-to-woman transmissions? Yep. Is it a conspiracy to trick women who have sex with women into letting down their guard? Don't think so.

Hey, Faggot:

Great Answer to "Love and Pussy-Lip Kisses" about evaluating personal HIV risk and going down joyfully! As a woman who loves to eat pussy, I feel insulted by all the "shut up and dam it" propaganda. It sounds too much like "Good girls know sex is dangerous." Thanks for your sex-positive female-intelligence-positive advice.

Horny, Brainy Femme

Hey, Faggot:

For as long as I can remember, I've been subject to what I think is some type of oral herpes. Any time I bite my lip hard enough to break the surface, and sometimes during periods of high stress, I develop mouth sores. These sores are like little craters, and they last for about a week, maybe a week and a half. At first they are very painful, but hard to see. Then they feel fine but look hideous: covered in white goo. They usually reside far enough inside my mouth that passersby or interlocutors cannot spy them. But sometimes not. Ugh.

What is this malady I suffer from? Can it be cured? Or can healing be sped up somehow? Is this contagious? Can it be passed through kissing? Through oral sex (of either variety)? Would I be more susceptible to catching STDs during one of these bouts?

Humorous Moniker

Hey, HM:

I am not a doc, and haven't had a look in your mouth, so take this advice with a grain of salt and consider having a real, live doc check your mouth out. But it is my considered opinion that you are not suffering from oral herpes. What you got goin' on is boring ol' canker sores. Oral herpes, aka cold sores, usually appear outside the mouth, on the outer edge of the lip, and they're caused by those pesky Herpes Simplex Number Something Or Other viruses. Oral herpes can spread from the mouth of an infected person to the genitals of an uninfected person, and it's a big ugly bummer, though by no means the end of an afflicted person's sex life.

Canker sores, what you're suffering from, appear inside the mouth, usually as the result of a break in the skin, like when you bite yourself. They can also be caused by an allergic reaction to something you ate, or by stress. They're small, very painful, and a few days after appearing, they're usually covered or filled with the whitish gook you describe. The good news:

canker sores are not contagious—you can't give them to your partners. The bad news: there is no cure, and as you suspected, you are more susceptible to picking up STDs via, say, oral sex with an infected partner while you have a canker sore in your mouth. Luckily, canker sores are pretty freakin' painful, and usually located on the parts of your mouth and lip lining that move across your teeth. Giving a blow job or eating pussy with a canker sore in your mouth will cause the sore to grind against your teeth—a painful reminder that you probably shouldn't be engaging in unprotected oral sex at the moment.

Hey, Faggot:

I'm a breeder chick who's about to breed. If we have a son, I don't want to circumcise him. My partner, however, feels that we should circumcise him because of cleanliness issues and the humiliation the only uncircumcised kid in his high school gym class suffered.

I'd love to hear your thoughts. Is circumcision genital mutilation, or are there legitimate hygienic reasons for doing it? How do your readers feel? I'd love to hear from men, women, gays, straights and everyone in between.

Lynn

Hey, Lynn:

If it's a boy, have him cut. It's cleaner, no one will make fun of him in the locker room, and circumcision builds character: if you survive getting the end of your dick chopped off, you can survive almost anything.

And, mom, his lovers—be they male or female—will bless the memory of his mother every time they go down on him. I say a little prayer of thanks when I give head to a circumcised guy. Occasionally I even light a candle in memory of all the moms who've had their son's genitals mutilated for my head-giving pleasure.

Hey, Faggot:

Your attitude towards circumcision is in total alignment with Rush Limbaugh and the status quo.

The present circumcision rate in the United States is 60 percent; almost half the peers of Lynn's child will be intact. In ten years her son may ask one of two questions: "Why didn't you circumcise me?" or "Why did you?" Lynn has to decide whether she would rather answer, "We didn't think it was necessary. When you turn 18, have it removed if you like," or "We wanted you to look like your dad so *he* would feel more normal. Besides, we didn't think you could be taught to clean yourself." Lynn doesn't need advice from you or me. As a mother, she only has to trust her natural desire to protect her baby from harm. Don't back down, Lynn!

Frank Cranbourne
Executive Director, National Organization of
Circumcision Information Resource Centers (NOCIRC)

Hey, Frank:

I'm pro-circumcision because I prefer sucking circumcised cock. I doubt that Rush Limbaugh, if he is pro-circumcision, is pro-circumcision for the same reason I am!

Hey, Faggot:

Enclosed is a news item from the *New York Times* about a circumcision—add the possible transmission of HIV to the arguments against this barbarous ritual whose roots are in sexphobic religions. In the Jewish and Muslim faiths, circumcision is a ceremony performed by persons who are not physicians. Are these people licensed? What precautions do they take?

Kenneth

Hey, Ken:

The article Ken refers to is about an infant who was infected with HIV in a New York City hospital. The kid "underwent 99 procedures that involved the use of needles or contact with mucus membranes," including "obtaining blood specimens, putting a tube in the bladder, putting a needle in the spine for a lumbar puncture and inserting an intravenous tube." And the kid was circumcised by a "circumcisor who tested negative for HIV."

And we're supposed to believe it was the circumcision that resulted in the kid's HIV infection? Please.

And, Ken, according to Carol Starin at the Jewish Educational Council, rabbis who perform circumcisions are nationally certified by the Conservative Jewish movement. Carol and a rabbi I spoke with had qualms about your description of circumcision. Far from being a barbaric ritual, "Jewish circumcision is a service and a ceremony welcoming the child into the Jewish community." And—yow!—what a welcome!

Professional mohels (rhymes with goyls) do "jillions" of circumcisions, many more than doctors do. They're trained in Israel and, according to Rabbi Simon Benzaquen, "We do a better job than the doctors do, our methods are better than theirs. We've had this tradition for thousands of years, since the time of Abraham, as a covenant between God and the Jewish people. It's not just a fancy thing we like to do. We've studied, there are whole books of Jewish law, outside the Talmud, about circumcision."

Hey, Faggot:

Routine unanesthetized circumcision of male infant newborns is an extremely painful experience. There can be complications to circumcision as there can be with any surgery, from botched jobs to death. The hygiene argument is absurd. If soap and water can make the anus a possible place for oral pleasuring, they can certainly do the same for the penis and its foreskin.

Nature designed the whole penis very well. The loose skin of the foreskin on an unmutilated penis acts to preserve lubrication during intercourse. When flaccid, the foreskin acts as a protective covering which keeps the glans of the penis moist and very sensitive. As circumcised men, we are not aware that we have lost any sensitivity: we never had a chance to experience our intact penises for comparison.

Matthew

Hey, Faggot:

I am a 21-year-old straight guy who was not circumcised. I was teased relentlessly through high school and am now socially dysfunctional—*not!* If and when I have kids, I would not circumcise a boy. The skin acts as a protectant to the sensitive head. Without it, the head becomes callused.

Uncut

Hey, Faggot:

Circumcision is physical mutilation and, when done to a child, it is child abuse. There should be a law against doing it to children. Doctors who do it should be put in prison and parents who allow it should lose custody of their children.

Dean

Hey, Faggot:

Who do these anti-circumcision guys think they're fooling? I don't have calluses, I don't have lubrication problems, and as for the claim that circumcision makes it less sensitive, if it were any more sensitive, I wouldn't be able to go for a walk without losing my load.

I won't think twice about having my kids cut. It has nothing to do with cleanliness or aesthetics: rather, it worked out fine for me and I don't see any good reason why junior shouldn't be like dad. As for Lynn, the woman who started all of this, why won't she trust her husband on the one subject where he knows perfectly well what he's talking about and she doesn't know squat!

Content with the Cut

Hey, Faggot:

When my son was born, I refused to have him cut. I thought it was cruel and unnecessary. But by the time he was two years old, his foreskin was very tight and difficult to push back enough to clean. I asked an uncut male friend about this; he said his foreskin loosened up when he hit puberty and started getting erections.

My son's skin was so tight, I could only see two options: his little penis could get pretty damn funky over the next ten years, or I could put in enough time manipulating it to get and keep the skin loose. Neither option struck me as appropriate, so I gave in and had him cut. So far he hasn't complained—he's 19 now.

Breeder Momma

Hey, Faggot:

I am 23 years old and I have quite a few relatives ranging in ages from three months to seven years old. I do a lot of baby-sitting, and bathing is part of my duty. I know how to clean a young boy's penis, yet when he reaches four or five, I allow him the privacy of doing his bathing alone. Sometimes they forget, or may not clean themselves properly and an infection may occur. One of my cousins did get an infection in which the foreskin was stuck over the head of his penis. The doctor gave us two options: circumcise him or forcibly pull the foreskin back.

Could you imagine the pain of having your foreskin forced back every time you have to bathe? On the other hand, the pain of circumcision is quickly forgotten.

Now for the view from a sexually healthy and safely active young woman: all the talk of calluses and lessened sensitivity is a load of BS. I've had more than one sex partner and in my honest opinion, those who've been circumcised are more appealing and I've never had a complaint regarding "sensitivity."

LW

Hey, Faggot:

So, I'm in Peepland in a feelie booth and I give the girl five bucks to let me put my fingers in her pussy. With her juice still wet on my fingers, I continue to wank with the same hand. Is that safe? Could I have transmitted something? Should I be losing sleep?

Horndog

Hey, H:

It's unlikely you contracted anything dreadful. While theoretically possible, it would be extremely difficult to pick up HIV from whacking off with a tiny schmear of her juices still on your hand. But if she had warts or herpes or both, you may have picked those up. Get an STD screening if you're losing sleep, and if you're partnered—if you brought that skanky dick home to a wife or girlfriend after dragging it through the peepshows—get screened because it's the right thing to do.

Hey, Faggot:

I'm noticing a real depressing trend among the lovers I encounter lately—namely, losing their erections when it comes time to strap on the old condom. I'm speaking of a range of men, from their 30s to 50s. I do what I can to overcome the problem (I'm a very attractive woman, and understand the delicacy of the male ego), but honestly, in my heart I'm just aching for a fully functional penis for a change. It's a problem that I began noticing when I made my commitment to safe sex, after losing a loved one to AIDS. Does safe sex mean going without a lot? Or am I calling it wrong and this is just the time of life when men start losing the rampant boners of their youth? Say it ain't so!

Vertically Yearning

Hey, VY:

Okay, breeders, here's how fags get condoms on our dicks without losing our erections: if you treat the putting on the condom as foreplay, and not an interruption of the sex act, it won't feel like an erection-busting interruption! Girls, put the condom on for him! Guys, there ain't no reason that rubber can't be on your dick for a half hour before you stick it in! The latex will heat up, your dick will get used to it, and when it comes time to fuck, you won't feel a sudden loss of sensation. Guys, if the act of putting a condom on is a turnoff, do something at the same time that's a turn-on: make out, bury your face in her tits. Girls, after it's on his dick, play with it! Guys, it's okay to touch your own cock during sex. Stroke yourself if that's what it takes to keep going. And, finally, if you know you're going to be fucking sometime soon, open the condom packet before things get hot and heavy—before your fingers are wet and slippery. Fumbling in the dark with a greasy condom packet is always a turnoff. Plan ahead!

Hey, Faggot:

I'm 32, straight, and female. My boyfriend and I have been together six months, and have been using condoms since we began having sex. We both got tested for everything, and we're both "clean," so I'm considering the possibility of going on the pill. I want to know how the side effects will be. Most of my girlfriends who've been on the pill say they love having large breasts and regular periods. I already have large breasts and regular periods. Also, what about the risks of cancer? Are there any other ways my boyfriend and I can make love skin-to-skin that don't involve the pill? Do you know anything about ball sinking/testicle bathing to kill the sperm through heat treatment? What about those superthin condoms?

Rubber Tired

Hey, RT:

To help answer your dozen questions, I enlisted the help of a biological female with what, in my opinion, are the best birth-control-advice credentials a person can possibly have: Mary Banecker works for Planned Parenthood. She's based in Philadelphia, and Mary has been helping girls who fuck boys who fuck girls plan their parenthoods for 17 years.

So what are the side effects of the pill?

"Minor side effects vary for each woman," according to Mary. "In the first three months, you may experience one or more of the following: nausea, slight weight gain, increase in breast size, bleeding between periods, light or missed periods, changes in skin complexion (i.e., acne), mood changes, fatigue, and decreased or increased sex drive. More serious, but rare symptoms may include abdominal pain, chest pain or shortness of breath, headaches, eye problems, and severe leg pain." Jesus, arsenic has fewer side effects!

But just because your friends may have developed larger breasts, or are having more regular periods "doesn't mean you will too—not every woman is the same," Mary added. You may get different side effects than the ones your friends taking the pill have had—acne, puking, mood swings—or none at all. And remember, the side effects of not using birth control are also pretty serious: nausea, vomiting, increased breast size, major weight gain, abdominal swelling, mood swings, missed periods, contractions, blinding pain, and children.

What about cancer? "Studies have shown that the pill does not cause cancer," said Mary. "In fact, the risks of developing ovarian or uterine cancer are actually reduced when a woman is on the pill, as are the risks of developing ovarian cysts or suffering an ectopic pregnancy." There has been some noise about a link between the pill and breast cancer, "but studies showing that the pill causes breast cancer have been inconclusive.

"Many [people] agree that the pill's benefits outweigh its risks," Mary continued. And by far the chief benefit—the main reason people take it—is that the pill taken correctly and consistently has "a pregnancy prevention rate of 99.6 percent. But it's important to remember that the pill does not protect you from any sexually transmitted infections, including HIV/AIDS."

The pill is not your only skin-to-skin option, however. "Some alternatives include the diaphragm, the IUD, Norplant, and Depo-Provera," most of which have mild-to-ghastly side effects of their own. "Less popular but highly effective skin-to-skin alternatives include sterilization and vasectomies," and, of course, anal sex and/or lesbianism. But, again, without condoms, "you are not protected from sexually transmitted infections." But if you've tested for everything, and he's tested for everything, and he's clean, and you're clean, and he isn't screwing around, and you aren't screwing around, or you are screwing around but neither of you is doing anything with other partners that would put your primary partner at risk of contracting a sexually transmitted infection—whew!—then you should be able to go skin-to-skin without having to worry. Much.

Finally, thin condoms may increase sensitivity, but they also "break much more easily," and "although increasing or decreasing the temperature of the scrotum and testicles may inhibit sperm production, [ball sinking/testicle bathing and other heat treatments] are not a reliable form of birth control." Unless you're sinking your boyfriend's balls into a deep-fat fryer.

Hey Faggot:

When are people like Mary Banecker from Planned Parenthood going to fess up on the best birth control option available to women: the fertility awareness method! It's not the rhythm method, and isn't just for Catholics. It is an empowering tool which provides women and their boy toys with the info they need—including when they are ovulating and fertile and when they are not—and therefore able to have clean, natural, skin-to-skin sex without drugs, pills, rubbers and all that other crap. It is perfect for women with regular periods, like Rubber Tired (if all other safe sex requirements are met, of course: monogamy, HIV, gonorrhea, etc. free). I've been using it successfully for 10 years without any negative side effects.

The positive side effects: No more urinary tract infections from irritating diaphragms; no more hemorrhoids from the pill; no more rubbers during infertile periods; a lot less lubricant consumption; a wealth of knowledge about my body and my fertility cycle. I have control over when I have children and when I don't, without taking drugs or damaging my body!

I get really pissed when I hear well-intentioned gals like Mary omit this option. When will professional family planners promote fertility awareness? As for the counter-arguments: It doesn't work for everyone. True, but neither does the pill or latex rubbers. People can make mistakes (user failure). Well, gosh, that's true. I might even have to get an abortion if I don't use it right! But I had to get an abortion at age nineteen because I didn't use a diaphragm right.

For more info about fertility awareness, I recommend *The Art of Natural Family Planning*, by John and Sheila Kippley, published by the Couple to Couple League.

                                                                Truth Girl!

Hey, TG:

"We don't promote one method of birth control over any other," Mary Banecker of Planned Parenthood told me, when I called and shared your letter with her. "We offer information about all methods. Fertility awareness is in our all-method fact sheets, we have pamphlets about it right beside pamphlets about condoms and diaphragms. We let people decide what's the best birth control option for them, and we give them the information they need to make that decision.

"As for fertility awareness, she's right that it shouldn't be confused with the rhythm method. The rhythm method was guesstimating when you were fertile and abstaining from sex, and it was not very effective. Fertility awareness is more complicated, more effective and it takes some training and commitment. It includes looking at your cervix, your vaginal mucus, your temperature, all of which change during the menstrual cycle, and tracking all three of those things over a long enough period of time to gain an awareness of your fertility cycle," and then abstaining from vaginal intercourse or using a condom or some other latex contraption when you're dropping eggs.

The book Mary recommends on fertility awareness is the creatively titled *Fertility Awareness* by Kay Whitlock and Regina Pfeiffer. And Mary wanted to emphasize that, so far as she knows, "the pill doesn't cause hemorrhoids."

Hey, Faggot:

I was wondering if you could research the bad effects of smoking marijuana while on the birth control pill. I've heard that cigarettes (which I don't smoke) can increase a woman's chance of heart disease by something like 10 times. I don't want to disclose my recreational drug use to my doctor, and I feel that this is a concern that would interest many of your readers.

DS

Hey, DS:

"There are no studies about the effects of smoking marijuana while on the pill," said Mary. "It does not mean that there are no negative effects; it just means that there are no data on what the effects are," negative or positive. I have personally undertaken studies on this subject, however: I have inhaled marijuana smoke, but for medicinal purposes only. (I suffer from a debilitating syndrome that, while not taken seriously by medical professionals, is good enough for dope pushers.) While I wasn't on the pill at the time, I did experience some side effects: watching too much television; confusion about location of apartment; no mood swings at all, even when called for; the demonstrably false impression that each fleeting thought was a brilliant revelation; and snacking between meals.

The risks of smoking tobacco while on the pill have been documented, however. "According to the American Cancer Society, women who smoke and use the pill are 10 times more likely to suffer a heart attack than non-smoking women who are not on the pill. Women who smoke also have an increased risk of stroke and blood clots in the legs, and these risks increase in women smokers who are on the pill and over the age of 35." But before you swear off your medicinal marijuana, remember that smokers with pack-a-day habits inhale much more smoke than dopers who smoke to get high. Dopers are also less likely to smoke every day, so the health risks to pill-popping dope smokers are probably less than those to pill-popping tobacco smokers.

Hey, Faggot:

Do you have any information on health problems from oral-anal encounters? I mean, what diseases might the partner using the tongue get from the partner offering the anus?

I'm not talking about AIDS—just diseases in general that might be carried by feces. I am female and my partner is male, and he is the one who very much wants to do it, though since he has been talking about it, I have developed some interest. My only concern is for his health.

Dolores

Hey, D:

Rimming is low- to no-risk for HIV transmission. There are, however, other risks: you could pick up hepatitis, and a myriad of no-fun intestinal parasites. Hep and parasites live in poop and rimmers may encounter microscopic "bits of shit," as a rather blunt Dutch AIDS pamphlet put it. But let's put these bits of shit in perspective, shall we? According to the FDA, you're likely to encounter microscopic "bits of shit" in the average hot dog. And that's not all: odds are any given hot dog also contains everything from rat hairs, to insects, to maggots, to plain old dirt.

Rimming—microscopic bits of shit. Hot dogs—bits of shit, rat hairs, insect pieces, maggots, dirt. Hm. Take the time to shower, scrub that butthole and you can pretty much eliminate your lover's chances of ingesting bits of shit. But what can you do about hot dogs? You can cook wieners—but cooking the bits of shit, insects, maggots, and dirt in hot dogs doesn't eliminate these contaminants, it only cooks 'em. Given a choice between snacking on your butt or eating a hot dog, I'd go with your butt.

Hey, Faggot:

These questions may seem dumb, but here goes:

1. If you are being fucked, then forced to suck the dick that fucked you, can you get sick from your own ass?
2. Can you get AIDS from watersports orally and anally?

TC

Hey, TC:

1. According to Barak Gaster, M.D., ingesting small amounts of your own feces probably won't make you sick. "The usual diseases that are transmitted fecally could be transmitted in that way, the most common being hepatitis A and some strains of E. coli. But if you are already colonized, then it means that you're probably immune. So, even though it's a really yucky idea, it is unlikely that being re-inoculated with these same strains orally would make you ill."
2. Dr. Barak: "Of all body fluids [in HIV-infected people], urine has among the lowest levels of HIV virus. So, the risk is much lower than it is for other body fluids, but a risk still exists."

Hey, Faggot:

I would like to react to your comments on rimming. I would no doubt be considered a tight ass for saying anything, but just because something feels good does not mean it's okay.

People have to face the facts: the asshole is meant for eliminating waste from the body. If you enjoy licking it or screwing around in it, don't be surprised when you get shit in your mouth. Here are only a few of the things a person can pick up from rimming: hepatitis, shigella, campylobacter, herpes I and II, gonorrhea, Epstein-Barr, cytomegalovirus, E. coli, streptococci, parasite eggs.

I don't care if people want to swing from the chandeliers while they have their fists up each other's ass, but I want people to realize that if they get anything from anal sex or rimming, which they will, they will be spreading it to everyone they have contact with. The consequences greatly outweigh a few minutes of pleasure that can be had. Get wise, assholes.

C.J.

Hey, C.J.:

Yes you can contract a whole bunch of nasty diseases rimming. You can also contract a whole bunch of nasty diseases from man-on-top-as-God-intended-cock-in-pussy het-sex. AIDS, gonorrhea, syphilis, chlamydia, herpes and all of its sequels, genital warts, trichomoniasis, hepatitis B, chancroid, crabs, scabbies, nongonococcal urethritis, to name just a few. Should straights give up vaginal intercourse simply because careless or unlucky folks have gotten the clap that way?

No, they shouldn't. What straights should do, what we all should do, is this: whether you're rimming, sucking, fucking, or swinging from the chandeliers, take precautions. If you're in a monogamous relationship, you can probably let your guard down, but you should still monitor your health, and your partner's.

And yes, our assholes were designed for poopin'—but we

use different parts of our bodies for uses unintended by our delinquent creator. Vocal cords were not designed for speech, our backs were not designed for walking upright, our noses were not designed to hold up our glasses. I suspect, like the vast majority of hets and homos, you engage in oral sex. Were mouths designed to give blow jobs? Or does your fucking and sucking original intent doctrine only apply to sex acts you disapprove of?

Hey, Faggot:

On the subject of rimming, you might want to inform your rimming readers about the hepatitis A vaccine, recently approved by the FDA. I got my first shot in May, and will get my second and final shot in November. It gives a person 10 years of protection. I'm already vaccinated against hepatitis B.

It's my practice, prior to rimming my partner, to thoroughly scrub his butt crack and anus with Betadine soap solution, leave it on for approximately five minutes, and then thoroughly rinse it off. Betadine soap solution is used by doctors and nurses to scrub up, prior to surgery. If it's good enough for them, it's good enough for me.

Rimmy Rimmer

Hey, Faggot:

My boyfriend and I are both in our late 30s and HIV-negative. I have used a diaphragm or condoms for over 20 years. I have tried two different types of birth control pills, and my body can't tolerate them. Contraceptive suppositories and foams give me vaginitis. I will not get an IUD or Norplant or any other invasive apparatus. My choices are barrier methods: the 'phragm or male or female condoms. All of my previous partners have been OK with this.

My present boyfriend dislikes these barrier methods intensely. He refuses to wear condoms—he says they're painful. He finds the female condom aesthetically disgusting. He is turned off by the "interruption" of his "style" of lovemaking when we have to stop for diaphragm insertion, and says he can "feel" my diaphragm when we're screwing. He doesn't want me to put in the 'phragm in advance because he won't go down on me when there's spermicidal jelly there. He bitches about the diaphragm nearly every time we get intimate. He says all his previous lovers have been on the pill and he doesn't understand why I'm not. He grimaces and pulls away when I put the 'phragm in. Sometimes he decides he doesn't want to screw after all.

We have discussed this ad nauseam and I am at my wit's end. I am ready to walk away from this relationship over this issue.

Frisbee of Love

Hey, FOL:

There's a relatively simple solution to the impasse you've reached with this idiot boyfriend of yours: if he hates barrier methods so much, he should get himself a vasectomy.

Birth control for breeders, like death control for gay men, is the responsibility of both partners. It is not up to the woman to "make" birth control happen any more than it is up to the bottom in gay sex to "make" condoms happen. It is wildly inconsiderate of your boyfriend to demand that you take birth control pills, which make you ill, because latex "interrupts" his lovemaking style!

Your boyfriend is being a weasel, lying about condoms "hurting" and being able to "feel" your diaphragm (have to admit I agree with him about female condoms: yuck). Ask the idiot what's going to interrupt his lovemaking style more—getting dumped for being a selfish prick, or your diaphragm? You say you're ready to walk away, and I encourage you to do just that. He's being such a prick about making love to you, I can't imagine he'll be any nicer when it comes to making a life with you. Move on.

Hey, Faggot:

This letter is in response to your criticism of the female condom in your reply to "Frisbee of Love." As the manufacturer and distributor of the Reality female condom, we would like to point out the many benefits of the female condom that you must have overlooked, given your comments. The female condom is the first and only woman-controlled contraceptive barrier method that also provides protection from STDs, including HIV/AIDS. Approximately 40 to 60 percent of men and women who try it continue to use it, and most find the female condom more pleasurable to use than the male condom. The device is less constricting and can be inserted several hours before intercourse, allowing a degree of spontaneity that the male condom can't provide. Also, a female condom is made out of a thin heat-sensitive material called polyurethane. Polyurethane is 40 percent stronger than latex and does not irritate people with latex allergies.

For samples and information, please call 800-274-6601, or visit our Web site at www.femalehealth.com.

Mary Ann Leeper, Ph.D.
President, The Female Health Company

Hey, Prez:

My comment regarding your firm's fine contraceptive product—"yuck"—was an informed, personal aesthetic judgment, which I have an absolute right to make. When the female condom first became available, my then-boyfriend and I gave 'em a whirl. While our "woman-controlled" condom worked just fine—no STDs were transmitted during the act, and no one got pregnant—it wasn't pretty. The female condom is basically a plastic bag with one hard plastic ring at the bottom of the bag (to anchor it in the vaginal canal), and a slightly larger, more flexible ring at the top. You work the bag into your partner's orifice—removing the inner ring for anal sex—and leave the flared base on the outside. Once the plastic bag was hanging out of my boyfriend's ass, it was about as appealing as . . . an ass with a plastic bag hanging out of it. Then I took my dick . . . and fucked the plastic bag.

The female-condom premise simply left me cold. A dick with a condom on it still looks like a dick. An orifice with a plastic bag hanging out of it looks like a . . . well, like an orifice with a plastic blah blah blah. And with male condoms, at least your dick is moving in and out of the orifice, not in and out of a bag.

Hey, Faggot:

I did not appreciate your dismissive comment about female condoms ("yuck"). It is not every day that we get a new contraceptive option, let alone one that is safe and relatively inexpensive. The female condom feels about the same to me as a male condom, and both male partners I've tried the female condom with for vaginal sex said it felt better than a male condom. Many stores don't carry the female condom, and many people haven't heard of it. Since lots of good options should ideally be what contraception is all about, I don't think you should be damning the female condom's future with a single word.

Dorian

Hey, Dorian:

I doubt it's within my power to damn the female condom, or keep it off store shelves, with a single word—even so toxic a word as "yuck." And while you may think female condoms are a good contraceptive option, not many folks seem to agree with you: of the 50 sexually active straight folks in my office, not one had ever used a female condom! And female condoms haven't exactly been flying off the shelves at condom emporiums.

Hillary, who works at Condomania in New York City, told me her store sells about a thousand male condoms in an average week. And female condoms? "If we sell five of those, that's a good week." What's the prob? "We used to carry them in boxes, $12 for a box of three," Hillary told me, "but people didn't want to spend that much, so now we sell them singly at four bucks a pop"—hardly inexpensive compared to other forms of birth control.

Hillary doesn't recommend female condoms to her customers. "Compared to regular condoms, female condoms are not very easy to use. Maybe women who've used diaphragms have an easier time with them, but most of the women I know who've tried them didn't like them."

Hey, Faggot:

I would like to point out a glaring omission in your response to "Frisbee of Love." In your reply, you completely ignored the issue of STDs and HIV/AIDS. Though the reader stated that both she and her partner tested negative for HIV infection, it is your duty as a sex counselor to advise her to protect herself from STDs.

Furthermore, where do you get off dismissing the female condom with a "yuck"? Your criticism of the female condom is not only unjustified but irresponsible. Currently the male and female condoms are the only effective protection from STDs. I would hate to think people would not use the female condom or another means to protect themselves from STDs and unplanned pregnancy because of your careless remark. As a sex counselor it is your responsibility to advise, not to promulgate your biased, unsubstantiated opinions.

                                    Fan of the Female Condom

Hey, FOTFC:

I am *not* a sex counselor. I am an advice columnist, and "advice," according to *The American Heritage Dictionary*, is an "opinion about what could or should be done." So, dope, promulgating my biased, unsubstantiated opinions is my sole responsibility. Don't like my advice? Get your own column.

Not that anyone would read a column you'd write. The advice you'd have me give, while popular with safe-sex absolutists, is near useless to anyone having sex in the real world. It is neither realistic nor necessary to tell people to use latex (or polyurethane) barriers at all times for two good reasons: first, folks don't want to use barriers if they don't have to; and second, lots of folks don't have to.

People in relationships with partners whose health and STD history they're familiar or comfortable with will sometimes assume a slightly higher level of risk in exchange for less hassle and greater intimacy. And guess what? That's their right—they're grown-ups. Grown-ups drive cars, ski, vote, eat sushi, take personality tests at Scientology Centers, and do all manner of risky, sometimes dangerous things. Frisbee's an adult making an informed, responsible choice about her sex life who sent me a question about birth control—not STDs—and that's the question I answered. Frisbee is free to disregard my advice, just as she has obviously opted to disregard the counterproductive STD-prevention white noise/dogma promulgated by morons like you.

Hey, Faggot:

Please print this, because no one can give me straight answers. I have a problem with birth control. Normally, I use rubbers when my girlfriend and I get at it. But I hate rubbers (so does she). She won't take the pill, and female condoms and diaphragms are gross. What I want to know is, how effective will it be if I just use spermicidal jelly and pull out before I come? Also, where can I get a vasectomy, how much will it cost, how effective is it, and could I get my balls fixed later on in order to have kids?

Need Help

Hey, NH:

According to a Columbia University survey, 21 percent of women who used only spermicide "experienced accidental pregnancy." And pairing spermicidal jelly with withdrawal isn't all that wise, as loads of girls get knocked up after boys put it in "just a little." You see, there's a steady stream of active sperms trickling out of your boy-dick even before you have your boy orgasm, and even the trace amount of sperm in your pre-come can be enough to knock some girly up. If your girlfriend is okay with combining spermicidal jelly, withdrawal, and the occasional abortion, then by all means proceed. But make damn sure she's okay with abortion before you throw away those "gross" male and female condoms and diaphragms—otherwise it's child support payments for you, or a New Jersey prom night for her.

As for vasectomy, now you're talking birth control, son. It'll cost you anywhere from $250 to $1,000—with family planning clinics costing much less than private docs. The procedure is relatively simple; it takes about 10 minutes. You'll have to go in for pre-snip counseling, and a follow-up spunk-check to make sure you're shooting blanks, before you get the blow-ahead. The snip will not impact the quantity, taste, or viscosity of your spunk. Reversing a vasectomy later in life, however—getting "your balls fixed"—is a much more expensive proposition. It'll cost you between $5,000 and $15,000, and it doesn't always work. Unless you're positive you don't want to have your own wee bio-kids, don't get a vasectomy.

(Oh, and let's not forget that killer jellies, abortions, and va-sectomies may protect you from parenthood, but will not protect you from herpes, warts, syph, HIV, etc. Only abstinence, proper/obsessive use of latex, or getting way too hammered to get it up in the first place will protect you from all STDs, and booze makes your date more beautiful, if only temporarily.)

Hey, Faggot:

I gotta throw my two cents in regarding vasectomy. I guess you have no direct experience getting your balls cut loose, and you spout the party line: no change at all! Good as new!

Check the fine print: as with any surgical procedure, a percentage do not get the desired results. For me, a breeder with two kids, I couldn't justify or afford more kids and I knew there was some subconscious magic that would probably make a future accident likely. I made an appointment. The pain was bad enough, but there was a deep sense of loss I wasn't prepared for. Then the pain grew. Can you say granuloma? The offered remedies were ibuprofen (ruined my stomach and didn't help my balls) and opiates (not so good for sleep). I finally found some Chinese herbs that helped.

As far as quantity, consistency, and frequency of spunk output: before getting cut, I was at 10–12 orgasms/week. A year later, I can manage 4–5/week of ¼ or ½ the volume, and the bang is nowhere near as big. One possibility I haven't tried is reversal—the vasocasostomy. It supposedly helps a percentage of us unfortunates. I haven't yet been able to face going back to the Doc.

RV

Hey, RV:

You might want to take your balls back to the doc. According to our ever-helpful friends at Planned Parenthood, sperm leaking from snipped tubes causes a small lump—granuloma—under the skin near the site of the operation in about 18 out of 100 cases. Sperm granulomas usually clear up by themselves. If not, surgical treatment can take care of that pain in your nuts.

As for your other "symptoms"—decreased sex drive, and lower spunk output—that's about what's going on in your head, not what's leaking into your sack; that "deep sense of loss" you mentioned. If shooting live rounds is important to your sense of sexual self-esteem, you shouldn't have had a vasectomy in the first place. Reversing a vasectomy is a much more expensive procedure, and not always effective, but if shooting blanks is wrecking you—and you can afford it—have that operation.

Hey, Faggot:

I'm dating this beautiful woman who has had a lot of partners and who hasn't been practicing safe sex. Save me the lectures about condoms, I'm all for them. I use them, and like the peace of mind they give me. We can both get tested (if I can talk her into that), but if she was infected recently, it could be months before her tests turns up positive. Here's what I want to know: Condoms are cool for fucking, but what about oral sex? Everything I've read says that an infected woman's vaginal secretions have lots of that nasty virus. Can I go down on her safely?

Cautious and Frustrated

Hey, C&F:

It's interesting that you don't name the sexually transmitted disease you're so concerned about contracting. In fact, your letter is written as if there were only one sexually transmitted disease going around. There are lots of 'em, and frankly, you should be more concerned about herpes or genital warts than dumb old HIV.

If you're using condoms, your risk of contracting HIV is very low. But you can still catch warts and herpes even if you are using condoms, though condoms do significantly lower your risk of contracting either of those bugs. As for oral sex, even assuming she does have HIV, your risk of contracting it is not all that great provided you have no cuts in your mouth. If she has herpes, however, you can contract that bug cuts or no cuts. If this woman was not sleeping with IV drug users and gay or bisexual men, odds are that if she does have an STD, it's not HIV. You, like most straight people, need to worry a bit less about HIV and a bit more about other less glamorous STDs, diseases that you are at greater risk of contracting. And, hey, if you're taking steps to protect yourself from the STDs you are actually at risk of contracting, you will have pretty effectively protected yourself from HIV as well.

Hey, Faggot:

I've had cold sores—oral herpes—since I was in elementary school. I was told they were contagious, and not to kiss anybody when I had an outbreak. By the time I was sexually active, I was informed by a very wise person that I could give someone genital herpes if I gave them oral sex during an outbreak or during my prodromal symptoms (when there's a strange ache and tingle, but no sore yet). So as long as I was symptom-free, I kissed, sucked off, and licked people to my heart's content, guilt-free.

Then I got genital herpes from oral sex with someone who didn't know cold sores were herpes, and ignored his prodromal symptoms. When I was diagnosed, it was drummed into my head that I must inform my potential partner before we have sexual contact whether or not I am anywhere near an outbreak, or I am an evil, disease-spreading bitch. No one I have ever kissed or sucked off has ever freaked out when they saw a cold sore on my lip a month later. But as I understand it, if someone were to find out I have genital herpes after sleeping with me, I'd be in for it.

I've had five breakouts in three years. I get no other symptoms (fever, swollen glands) that I've heard so much about (from people who don't have herpes). The supposed "public health announcements" on the radio and the Glaxo-Wellcome commercials on TV constantly emphasize that this is an "incurable" disease. I don't think this accurately describes a few days a year of a mild burning sensation on my labia. I'm hardly suffering, so why should I be stigmatized as disease-ridden? Why aren't people as terrified of oral sex with people with cold sores, which I hear is 90 percent of the population?

So what do you think? Does sleeping with people (using a condom, of course) when I don't have any symptoms and not telling them of my "herpes status" make me a dishonest slut?

Not a Leper

Hey, NAL:

If people with herpes are lepers, then there are a whole lot of lepers running around out there. The Centers for Disease Control recently released a study—to much apocalyptic fanfare—showing that one in five Americans over the age of 12 have herpes, a 30 percent jump since the late 1970s. But, the study went on to say, most people with herpes don't know they have it. Why? Because fewer than 10 percent of folks with herpes have ever had an outbreak; most infected folks have no symptoms at all—no sores, no symptoms. The way people carry on, you'd think the CDC discovered that one in five Americans are carrying the Ebola virus.

Like you, NAL, most folks with herpes who do get sores get them only very occasionally. For those with more severe cases—six or more outbreaks a year—there's a drug (acyclovir) that can help prevent outbreaks and lessen the severity of outbreaks that do happen. This is hardly Hot Zone stuff. People with herpes should be concerned about the fact that the presence of sores can make it easier for you to catch more serious STDs—like HIV—and that a severe case can complicate pregnancy; but they shouldn't be throwing themselves under buses.

While there's no cure for herpes—hence the freaked-out press herpes gets—it ain't Ebola, and it ain't HIV. Hell, it ain't hardly even "herpes" as we've been led to fear it. Yes, it's better not to have herpes than to have herpes, but what are you gonna do? Never have sex? Never kiss people? Not even the religious use of condoms can protect you 100 percent, as herpes sores aren't always in places covered by condoms, and sores don't have to be present for a person with herpes to be infectious (as you discovered, NAL).

All that said, NAL, I do think you should tell your partners before you go to bed with them that you have herpes. Explain how infrequently you have outbreaks, and what a minor deal they are when they do occur. If your partner's ignorant about the disease, clue him in. If he walks, well, better he should walk before you have sex than run afterward. If a guy is that terrified of dumb old herpes, you don't want to be having sex with him anyway, do you?

Hey, Faggot:

I'm writing about the nation's fastest-spreading STD: genital warts. Genital warts is a virus (HPV). It doesn't go away when the warts are removed. The virus stays in your blood, and is transmissible in the same ways as HIV. There are over 40 different strains of genital warts, and you can't ever screw someone who has had a wart without using latex.

This disease sucks. It makes you feel like a diseased fuck—which is the goddamned truth. As you women know, as soon as you get turned on, your juices start flowing. Casual sex and even casual make-outs are out of the question if you have genital warts. Someone could contract the virus from you just by touching your juices. I'm a good person, and I'm sexy, and men and women still risk their sexual health to be with me—and no one I've been safely intimate with has contracted the virus from me. But try not to get it in the first place.

Wish I'd Known

Hey, WIK:

Geez, maybe living under what for so many years seemed like an inevitable HIV infection and early death has made me jaded about stuff like herpes and warts. Somehow I've managed to avoid exposing myself to any of these three—herpes, warts, HIV—despite the fact that I've had sex on numerous occasions with men who had one or more of the above.

I had a boyfriend for years who had warts. He got one wart when we were together, had it burned off, and he never got another one—and I never got infected. I had similar experiences with boyfriends who had herpes and HIV: if you take reasonable precautions, and you have a partner you can communicate with openly, odds are you won't get infected.

But, WIK, the type of shame you're carrying around about warts—warts "makes you feel like a diseased fuck, which is the goddamned truth"—is the reason so many people with STDs have a hard time being open with their partners. If my boyfriend with warts was too ashamed of himself to tell me about it, we might have taken risks that could have resulted in my becoming infected too. Thankfully, he wasn't afraid to talk to me, we were able to take precautions, and I didn't get infected. Ta-da! See how that works?

P.S. It is especially important that women see their docs for regular Pap smears and speculum look-sees, as herpes or warts left untreated can have very serious consequences for women, including, in the case of warts, cervical cancer. See your puss doc regularly, ladies.

Hey, Faggot:

Don't laugh at this letter, because I'm completely fucking serious.

I'm a 17-year-old lesbian. My sister is an 18-year-old breeder. Her 23-year-old boyfriend wants to have a baby. My sister is not ready for a child—I'm ready to have a baby, but I cannot and will not fuck him. I'm ready to have a baby, as long as he and I don't have to fuck, and we don't get emotionally attached. Her boyfriend agreed to it, as long as he has no legal ties to me and the baby, it's all kept secret, and he can still see the baby. These conditions are acceptable to me.

So, we decided to have him jack off into a turkey baster. Then I can just impregnate myself with his sperm, right? My question is, do turkey basters really work? Or is there something else we should do? Any other tips you could give us?

Lezzie-Gonna-Be-Mommie

Hey, LGBM:

Don't laugh at this response, because I am completely fucking serious.

You're too young to have a kid; and anyone willing to have a baby under the circumstances you've described is too stupid to have a kid. And have you heard of "welfare reform"? The big, bad government is not as generous as it once was to single mothers and their dependent children, and no 17-year-old lesbian with her head stuck up her ass will be able to provide for a child.

Kids are expensive, time-consuming little monsters. They are not pets. So, I'd like to know, who's going to take care of you while you take care of this kid? Not the "father," as he wants "no legal ties," and presumably no financial obligations. Are you an independently wealthy 17-year-old lesbian? Here's hoping that you and your sister's idiot boyfriend are both sterile.

Hey, Faggot:

There seems to be an increase in the personals these days of men looking for a lactating female to help "fulfill a fantasy." A recent episode of NBC's *Friends* had the friends all tasting someone's breast milk. Doesn't ingesting breast milk pose a potential health risk? Shouldn't one check out the breast's HIV status first?

Carla

Hey, C:

If a woman is HIV-positive, her breast milk contains pretty much the same amounts of the virus as her blood, or the semen of an HIV-positive man. For this reason, HIV-positive mothers are advised not to breast-feed.

But here's an interesting little fact: HIV-positive mothers who breast-feed against doctors' orders increase their infant's risk of seroconverting (becoming HIV-positive) by only 15 percent. Considering that the children of HIV-positive breast feeders are exposed to their mother's breast milk (and the virus) several times a day for up to a year or more, a 15 percent seroconversion rate is pretty low—further evidence that oral exposure to HIV is less likely to result in seroconversion, or to "take," than other exposure routes.

So, while your concern for grown-up breast feedees, Carla, is commendable, the risks of a single, fantasy-fulfilling "taste," even if you happen to be taking a nip from the breast of an HIV-positive lactater, are slight.

Hey, Faggot:

Is the AIDS crisis over?

Just Wondering

Hey, JW:

Yes.

Hey, Stupid Faggot:

What kind of an idiot are you? How can you say that the AIDS crisis is over? Are you HIV-positive? Are you dying? I hope so. More than 30,000 people died in the United States from AIDS last year! The AIDS crisis is still going on, and it is getting worse—people are still dying!!

CR

Hey, CR:

Yes, people are still dying, and we shouldn't be complacent about that. We should push until everyone who needs them has access to new drugs and treatments, and push for better treatments. And we should push for a cure, and a vaccine. And while we're doing all this pushing, we should remember to avoid contracting HIV, or infecting others. And we can do all of this and still acknowledge that the AIDS crisis is over.

Declaring the AIDs crisis over is not the same as saying AIDS is over. People are still dying and will continue to die, drugs or no drugs, vaccine or no vaccine, cure or no cure. But is "people are dying" what we meant by "the AIDS crisis"?

Eric Rofes is a longtime gay community organizer, academic, and the author of *Dry Bones Breathe: Gay Men Creating Post-AIDS Identities and Cultures* (Haworth, 1998). " 'The AIDS Crisis' is a sociocultural construct," says Rofes, who as an academic is required to use pointy-headed jargon. This crisis construct "emerged from hard-hit gay male communities in the mid-1980s out of our experience of terror and panic at the arrival of AIDS. It was not a p.r. gimmick. It was our authentic psychological and cultural response as rumors of the disease circulated, lesions appeared, corpses piled up, and sex clubs closed."

Gay men in the United States, the first and hardest hit group in the Western world, created the AIDS movement, and our experience of AIDS—AIDS as crisis—defined the movement. As the first and (still) largest group of victims in the United States, how we experienced AIDS informed how most everyone experienced AIDS—and that was as crisis. It was a crisis because we said it was, and we said it was because that's how it felt.

"Yet by the mid-1990s," Rofes argues, "the majority of gay men no longer authentically experienced AIDS as a crisis. After 17 years, [we] have shifted out of crisis mode and created new, different understandings of AIDS. . . . [For many men] the crisis construct is a 'period piece' of urban, white, middle-class communities of the 1980s. While many men do not experience AIDS as a crisis, they still believe it's important to contribute to AIDS organizations, and believe HIV prevention is important. But they are neither terrorized nor panicked by AIDS. While some individual gay men may be in personal crisis (men with HIV whose health is precarious, for example), the overarching cultural experience of AIDS as crisis which emerged for gay men in the 1980s is over. Quite simply, [gay men have] incorporated the realities of AIDS into their world view and gotten on with their lives."

Compelling stuff—read Rofes's book for more. But "the AIDS crisis" as I understood it when I was getting arrested at ACT UP demonstrations was different. My idea of what "the AIDS crisis" meant is nicely summed up by Gabriel Rotello in his book, *Sexual Ecology*: "Perhaps the most fundamental complaint of AIDS activism has centered on what everyone else did, or rather failed to do . . . when the epidemic first exploded. How the government failed to warn, the media failed to report, the scientific establishment failed to produce remedies or vaccines. . . . 'They,' the mainstream world, could have saved us during this crucial period and did not."

Call it the "we die, they do nothing" AIDS crisis, after the early ACT UP chant. If I'm reading my worn-out copy of *Reports from the Holocaust* correctly, this "construct" of "crisis" is the one ACT UP founder Larry Kramer was operating under. Yet tremendous progress has been made: the government does warn (if imperfectly, and primarily by pouring money into imperfect AIDS organizations), the media do report, and the scientific establishment has produced results, if not vaccines or cures. Can anyone chant "we die, they do nothing" these days with a straight face?

I stumbled over another interesting definition of "crisis" in *The Gay Almanac.* In an interview with a young academic, which brings us back to jargon land, a careful distinction is made between AIDS and the AIDS crisis: "The AIDS virus is something empirical and real, that causes biological deterioration and suffering. The AIDS crisis, on the other hand, is an epistemological formation, specifically modern, that designates people with AIDS as ultimate others, therefore eliminating the possibility for empathic response." By this definition, the AIDS crisis was a lack of empathy. But empathy is nowhere in short supply these days—we practically have to pick it from between our teeth every night before we go to bed, so violently is empathy stuffed down our throats.

So what do we mean, in 1997, when we say "the AIDS crisis"? Do we simply mean that people are dying—39,000 last year in the United States? Forgive me for banging this gong, but what about breast cancer? About 45,000 women died of breast cancer last year in the United States, yet few people talk about the Breast Cancer Crisis—we talk about breast cancer. More than a million people died of AIDS worldwide last year, but according to the World Health Organization, tuberculosis killed more than three million, malaria more than two million (half children), and hepatitis B another million. Yet we don't talk about the Malaria crisis, or the TB crisis, or the Hep B crisis— three communicable diseases for which science has produced remedies, and in the case of Hep B, a vaccine. Three million children die after drinking contaminated water every year, but no one describes this as a "crisis," or makes an issue of "access" to clean drinking water.

So if "crisis" isn't about "people are dying," and it isn't about how we're experiencing AIDS anymore, and it isn't about "we die, they do nothing," and it isn't about a lack of empathy, then what is "the AIDS crisis" about?

"The AIDS crisis" has become a slogan, like "AIDS: The Quicker Picker-Upper," or "AIDS: The Un-Cola." Some of us hold on to it because we're afraid to let go of the moral authority that living in crisis lent us; others because they're trying to sell us something. But selling terror and panic—promoting a crisis mentality, requiring gay men who no longer feel they're in crisis to fake it—will backfire: terrorized people cannot make informed, rational choices about their health. Continuing to promote a crisis mentality harms those who fall for it, and destroys the credibility of AIDS organizations in the eyes of those who don't. And this, in the long run, is worse for HIV/AIDS prevention and service efforts than admitting the obvious: The crisis is over, even while the epidemic continues.

Hey, Faggot:

The AIDS crisis is over? In case you missed the papers last week, here are some clippings you might find interesting: the new drugs are already failing half the people taking them. Nothing has changed, idiot.

HIV-positive Gay Man

Hey, HGM:

Thanks for the clips. I do read the papers, so I caught the "New AIDS Drugs Fail Many" stories when they first came out. But I appreciate your taking the time to send them.

Last week I devoted an entire column to the end of "the AIDS crisis" without dwelling on—without hardly mentioning—the new drugs and treatments. The new treatments are not the sole reason AIDS is no longer a "crisis." The crisis was a particular set of circumstances, and circumstances have changed. While the new treatments are one of the changes, they are not the only one.

But let's look at these new treatments—protease inhibitors and triple-drug cocktails—in light of this study "demonstrating" that they're failing half of all people on them. Docs at the San Francisco General Hospital AIDS Clinic looked at 136 "real-world" HIV patients, as opposed to HIV patients enrolled in

clinical trials (where failure rates have been in the neighborhood of 10 to 20 percent). Of these 136 people, 47 percent
"achieved durable suppression" of HIV, while 53 percent "had
evidence of ongoing viral replication." Those failing the new
drugs weren't dropping dead, but their viral loads—the amount
of HIV in their blood—were rising.

Now, if one merely glanced at the headlines, one could get
the impression that the drugs are failing half of all those taking
them. But as everyone working in AIDS insisted earlier this
year—when the headlines were good—one needs to read
more than just the headlines to get the full story.

"The mainstream press is always going to go to one extreme
or another," said Dr. David Spach, AIDS clinician and coeditor
of *The HIV Manual*, a guide for clinicians working with people
with AIDS. "Last year they said this was a cure, which was not
correct. Likewise, to give the impression now that all the thera-
pies are failing half the time, well, that's equally wrong."

Why is that? "Most of the people in the San Francisco study
were heavily pre-treated [with less sophisticated AIDS drugs],
had advanced HIV disease, or were drawn from patient popu-
lations that have a lot of problems with adherence to the medi-
cation regimens." Since the introduction of these drugs, we
have known that not taking them properly can result in failure,
and that the sicker someone is the greater the chance the drugs
won't help him. "So with this particular sample," Dr. Spach
said, "these kind of success/failure rates should be expected."

Dr. Spach sees almost as many "real-world" patients as the
number tracked by the San Francisco study, and oversees the
treatment of hundreds more. How are his patients doing? "Extremely well. I have a handful of people who are not adhering
to the medications, and they are not doing as well. But our success rates overall have continued to be as high as those in the
clinical trials."

Not even Dr. Steven G. Deeks, author of the San Francisco
study, attributes the results to the "failure" of the drugs. On the
HIV Insite Web site (http:hivinsite.ucsf.edu), Dr. Deeks writes:
"In an attempt to determine why some patients fail potent protease therapy, baseline characteristics of this group were ana-

lyzed. Adding only a protease inhibitor to a pre-existing nucleoside regimen was highly predictive of a poor outcome [the pre-treated]. Initiating therapy with a low baseline CD4 T-cell count and/or high baseline viral was also predictive of drug failure [the very sick]. Finally, documentation in the medical records of difficulty adhering to medical regimens was also predictive of drug failure [folks not taking the drugs properly]."

As Jim Puzzanghera wrote in the Knight-Ridder newspapers (under the headline "AIDS Drugs Fail Many"), "The reasons for the failures stem not so much from the drugs as from the people taking them, according to the study." You included this clip with your death threat—did you not read it? To test the failure rates of the drugs themselves, as opposed to the failure rate of the people taking them, you would probably have to factor out the group who could not "adhere" to the treatment.

The other two "failing" groups—the very sick, the "pre-treated"—should not be factored out: the drugs are indeed failing them. But barring the emergence of new treatments that can help them, these two groups are going to be "factored out" eventually by AIDS—and that is tragic and I pray new meds come along that can help them. But if we make sure that everyone who needs these drugs has access, there will be fewer people "too sick" to be helped, or "pre-treated" with other medications, and this lethal "factoring out" will ultimately result in there being fewer people "failed" by the drugs.

As for the failure of the cocktails to help those who have "difficulty adhering to the regimen," all that proves is that the drugs don't work if you don't take them correctly. The same can be said of any drug or treatment: aspirin won't work if you don't take it; chemo won't work if you skip appointments. If working for people who don't take them correctly is the standard by which AIDS treatments are to be judged—a standard applied to the treatment of no other illness—then there will never be an AIDS treatment that can't be shown to fail at an alarming rate.

Protease inhibitors and drug cocktails are not aspirin, of course. Folks have to take handfuls of pills daily; some with food, some on empty stomachs. Messing up even once or twice can have serious consequences. The protease bar is set cruelly high. Personally, I can't keep track of my asthma inhaler, so I can't imagine what it must be like to juggle all those pills. If I had AIDS and was enrolled in the San Francisco study, I would be among the 53 percent. The drugs are too complicated, and we need simpler, easier-to-follow regimens.

And they are on the horizon. "Right now, these drugs are very complicated," said Dr. Spach. "But in two or three years, it will be a lot easier. AZT and 3TC," two cocktail drugs, "just came out in a combination pill. What used to be eight pills a day is down to one pill twice a day. And there are drugs being developed now that will be twice-a-day or once-a-day regimens—probably all the new drugs that come out in '98."

Finally, it is important to emphasize that these are new drugs. They may yet fail. People should not construe them as "permission" to get infected: the best clinical trials have failure rates of 10 percent—better to be uninfected than face those odds. But even if the drug cocktails ultimately fail, or drug-resistant strains of HIV emerge, the psychological importance of the "protease moment," as writer Eric Rofes calls it, cannot be overstated. We have now seen that HIV is not invincible, that science can attack the virus itself, and not just play a losing game treating the infections that kill people with compromised immune systems. Are we so in love with death that we are incapable of seeing this moment—this protease moment—for what it is?

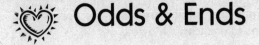 # Odds & Ends

Some of the best Q&A from "Savage Love" over the past seven years didn't fit into any of the previous six categories. Where do you put bizarre questions that aren't necessarily about a fetish or a turn-on or a relationship or a disease? One of my personal favorites is a question I received about whether female cats have orgasms—where would that go? Or what to do if your chocolate chip cookies are comin' out of the oven all flat and greasy? Or if it's possible to make cheese from human breast milk? Or what to do when you're caught peeing in your girlfriend's shower? Or the column I wrote about the sudden use of dead first ladies as a plot device in major Hollywood films after the Clintons were elected?

Some would argue—including my editor—that these questions could be left out of this collection altogether. This is supposed to be a sex and relationships kinda book, and sex is the angle I'm working, not cookie recipes or kitty clits. But even the most sexually obsessed folks in the world, myself included, sometimes think about other stuff besides sex. Or have questions about sex that aren't necessarily all that sexual. I've included nonsexual questions and sex questions that aren't necessarily about sucking and fucking in my column over the years to make a couple of points: first, sex isn't the only thing I know about or can look stuff up about; and second, sex isn't the only thing I think about. Sometimes I think about movies.

Hey, Faggot:

My friends and I were making fun of a cat in heat when we began a heated argument. Do cats have orgasms? Do they appreciate sexual pleasure akin to that of humans?

Except for one dissident, we all agreed that they must have sexual pleasure. The dissident argues that it is a simple matter of instinct for animals, and they just want to reproduce. Is it even possible to tell? Can you measure their brain waves or something?

Concerned About Cat Orgasms in Wisconsin

Hey, CACOIW:

Since there's not much difference between big kitties and little kitties—tigers are basically enormous house cats—I thought a zookeeper could offer a stimulating perspective on cats in heat. Perhaps a death-defying perspective: house cats in heat will take on pencils, furniture, your leg, anything at all—God alone knows what a tiger in heat might do to an unsuspecting zookeeper.

So I called the zoo my parents took me to on Sunday afternoons; the zoo my grade-school classes went to on sunny-day field trips; the zoo where I once threw up three times my own body weight in cotton candy, hot dogs, ice cream, Milk Duds, and French fries. I wanted to be true to my zoo.

"I don't know anything about that," said my childhood zoo's director of communications, when asked about big-cat orgasms. When I asked her if I could speak with someone who might know something about it, someone who maybe jerks off the boy cheetahs for the breeding program, someone like a zookeeper, she said no. "We can't help you. You can't talk to the zookeepers." Why not? "I'll ask them your question for you, and then I'll get back to you, but the answer is no." Pretty please? "I'll ask them for you. If there's something pertinent to the zoo, or some light they can shed on this, I will call you back." If I promise not to tap on the glass, can I pretty-please talk to one of the actual zookeepers? "You're not a very good listener, Mr. Savage." No, I guess I'm not. But you're not a very good director of communications.

Stonewalled, I called a rich-kids-on-field-trips zoo, the big flashy suburban zoo.

"All male mammals have orgasms, because that's how they ejaculate," said the helpful, good-humored rich-kids librarian. "When it comes to male mammals, you can see they're having orgasms. It's obvious—they ejaculate. But with the females, it's a more difficult question."

Unfortunately, the librarian wouldn't let me talk to one of the actual zookeepers either—why can't people talk to zoo-keepers? are they easily startled? hard to breed? what?—but since she was a zookeeper herself for nine years before becom-ing a zoo librarian five years ago, she could tell me all I needed to know:

"Some animals experience pleasure from sexual activity. It has been shown that bonobos [a rare species of pygmy chim-panzee] use sex to forge social bonds. But when it comes to sexual pleasure, with female cats it's harder to say. Female cats go into estrus—a fancy word for heat—and they can't ovulate until they've been mated with, and they don't leave estrus until they ovulate. One way to bring female house cats out of heat," short of taking #2 pencils to our pusses' pusses, "is to bring her to a vet and let him stimulate her, by inserting a rod." (Which is exactly how I stimulate my boyfriend, who is not a cat.) What do zookeepers do with great big cats in heat? Does someone have a three-foot-long #200 pencil? "We don't do that with big cats. They're dangerous, they'd hurt you. And since all the big cats are endangered species, we don't spay them—so all our females go into estrus. If we don't want to breed her, she just has to live through it."

So when they do get bred, do the females get off? "That's a difficult question. For the male there's definitely pleasure, but it's grayer for the female. When she mates, she's fulfilling some-thing inside herself, a deep urge, but it is actually painful for the female. The male has barbs on his penis, and when he pulls out, the barbs scratch the vaginal canal, which stimulates ovulation." Barbed penises sound like a disincentive—why does the female cat do it? "Every hormone in her body is telling her to. You can call it 'instinct,' but that's an overused, catchall term. All animals, including humans, do things because of instinct, and many of them are pleasurable."

Do human females have an estrus cycle? "We're one of the few mammals where females don't go into estrus." Why not? "The current evolutionary theory is this: it was better for human children and females to have males around hunting for them, providing protein, protection from other males. And one good way for females to keep the guys around was to always be ready for sex," and not just when they went into heat.

Well, gee whiz! Wasn't she helpful? Let's hear it for all the good folks at the suburban zoo!

Hey, Faggot:

I'm an over 40 gay man who stays young-looking through serious exercise and dieting. However, there is an aging problem I don't know how to deal with: as I get older my nipples are losing their color. I think nipples are the sexiest part of a man's body and I don't want to have unattractive ones. Is there anything I can do?

Andrew

Hey, Andrew:

You could get your tits tattooed. "It would work," said Eric Eye of Mind's Eye Tattoo in Seattle. "There are tattoo artists who specialize in cosmetic work; some work with women who have had mastectomies. They can re-create the tone of ariola and nipple." A woman who gets tattooed after a mastectomy isn't having her nipples tattooed though—her nipples have been removed—she's getting plain old skin tattooed. You would be getting nipple skin tattooed, and, Eric says, "nipple skin is funky, it's not the same as working with regular skin. First off, it would hurt like hell for obvious reasons. He'll need to be touched up with some degree of frequency, and it would hurt like hell each and every time." Eric wanted me to stress how important it is you go to somebody who has been doing cosmetic tattooing for years. "Call a reputable tattoo shop and find a reputable tattoo artist, or get a referral. There are a lot of fly-by-night cosmetic tattooists around who do a lot of crazy shit to people."

Hey, Faggot:

Come (sperm) is spell c-u-m.

SB

Hey, SB:

Of all the words with a second, sexual meaning, why does only this one require an alternate spelling? We don't "suk dik," eat "pussee," sit on "kocks," get "blohjahbs," or nuzzle "juggs," do we? "Cum" is an adolescent, *Hustler* magazine affectation.

And the fact that "cum" can be a noun or a verb further complicates the matter. As noun, it's always cum: "Look, there's some cum lying there." "Oh, I have cum in my eye." Not so when used as a verb: "Cum on me, baby." "He [came] on me." If in the present tense, the slang verb for ejaculate requires an alternate spelling, why not in its past tense? Why don't we say, "She cam/caam/camme/caim/c@me when I ate her out"? Because it's a stoopid thing to do, that's why!

And what if you need to use both the noun and verb forms in one sentence? Writing "He came in my mouth, so I swallowed his cum" is inconsistent, don't you think? Looks sloppy. How much simpler it is to use the standard four-letter spelling and allow the word to have, as so many words do, more than one meaning.

Hey, Faggot:

What is the correct preposition to be used after the word "masturbate"? Does one masturbate "to," "at," "about," "on," or "of" someone or something? I was composing a steamy note to someone and I wrote the following sentence: "I masturbated to you last night." It almost sounds like I meant to send some sort of communication signal by my actions. It's hard not to sound too academic/syrupy/wordy (i.e., I masturbated to my mental image of you last night). None of my dictionaries or grammar references were any help. Which do you think is best?

JW

Hey, JW:

You masturbate "to" porn videos, "on" someone who is lying underneath you, "at" a specific location, and "about" a person, action, or thing. You may think "of" someone while you masturbate, but you don't masturbate "of" them, you masturbate "about" them. So, it goes like this: "Last night I masturbated to a porn tape, at home, on my boyfriend, but I was thinking of you the whole time—I was masturbating about fucking you, darling."

Hey, Faggot:

I'm a faithful reader of your column, but something keeps bothering me. I know to criticize or challenge risks incurring your savage wrath, but . . .

You and your contributors constantly refer to heterosexuals as "breeders" and I resent that. Yeah, I'm straight. So what? I was born this way. But I never, and I mean never, have had any desire whatsoever to breed. I resent being lumped into a stereotype of mindless reproduction just because I happen to fuck the opposite sex.

I have been adamantly pro-choice and anti–population growth since I was a girl, and I have remained childless by choice and design, despite the inadequacies and failures of a variety of methods, hormones, and devices. I am offended by the arrogance of breeders who inflict their out-of-control screaming ego machines on everyone, and the insane behavior of the murderous and dangerous Christian Right and anti-choice maniacs.

"Breeders" think squirting come in someone and producing a baby is some kind of miracle, unique in the history of humanity. It is not, and it is obvious any two fools can make a baby. Meanwhile all the world's ills are really about one thing: there's too many goddamned people. So please leave me out of this insulting and degrading category.

Fed Up Het Non-Breeder

Hey, Breeder:

Once upon a time, "breeder" was an insult—our little derogatory term for you heterosexuals. We whispered "breeder" behind your breeder-backs, made fun of your bi-level haircuts, Jordache jeans, and "spare tires." But, hey: you guys were calling us names too: faggot, dyke, queer, sissy, nancy-boy, butt-pirate, cocksucker—the list goes on and on. We made a few of those words our own, and I suggest you do the same. Some people are going to call you "breeder" whether you like it or not—I know I am—so why not learn to live with it? If we could get used to fag, dyke, and queer, you can get used to breeder. And be comforted: "Breeder" does not mean "those-who-make-babies" but rather "those-who-have-the-kind-of-sex-that-can-result-in-babies-if-they-ain't-careful." And, hey, not all sissies are sissies, and not all dykes are dykes, but that never stopped breeders from calling gay men and lesbians those names. And the fact that you've opted not to breed is not going to stop me from calling you breeder, breeder.

Hey, Faggot:

My new lover does not want my come "staining" her sheets, her clothes (sometimes she's partially dressed during the act), her mattress, the rug, whatever. She's not anal retentive, and can be quite the animal when it comes to getting down, but she insists that we put a large beach towel underneath us or in any other strategic area where my come might land. So what's the poop? Does come stain? Can it ruin a mattress, a rug, her skirt? I want to respect her needs, but no woman has ever made such a demand before.

Curious About Come Stains

Hey, CACS:

I took your concerns to Michael S. Peru, proprietor of Noble Dry Cleaner and Laundry Services in Seattle, Washington, and an authority on the subject of come stains. "The pH [acidity] of the individual in question is the issue. Come is a bodily secretion, and everyone's pH is different," said Michael. "Some people's secretions stain more quickly than others. Typically, if you clean the garment within a week, there shouldn't be any problem, unless it's some pretty potent stuff.

"Bodily secretions are water based. You can make bodily secretion stains easier to remove by diluting them, by soaking the garment or the stain. But this usually isn't necessary." What if your girlfriend is too shy to take a come-stained garment to the dry cleaner? " 'Albumin' is the technical dry-cleaning term for bodily secretion. She should simply indicate to the dry cleaner that this garment is 'albumin' stained if she's too shy to say, 'My boyfriend shot on this.' "

But tell your girlfriend not to be shy: "A dry cleaner," Michael says, "is like a doctor—you can tell us anything."

Hey, Faggot:

What is the secret to making great Toll House Cookies? My cookies always come out flat and greasy.

Amateur Cook

Hey, AC:

Flat, greasy Toll House cookies? Sounds like a shortening issue to me: are you melting your butter? Well don't! The directions call for "1 stick butter softened." You soften butter by letting it come to room temperature. But sometimes folks in a hurry slam the butter in a pan or throw it in the microwave and melt it, assuming it makes no difference. Ah, but it does! My friend Becka suggests you use Crisco, which comes soft, in place of butter if you can't wait for the butter to soften. But Crisco is for wimps.

And my pal Richmond, a baker, cautions you to mix your ingredients thoroughly. "If you undermix, you may wind up with pockets of butter in your batter." Whatever cookies those butter-pockets wind up in will emerge from the oven flat and greasy. Good luck.

Hey, Faggot:

I don't know where else to turn with this problem, and I've never seen it mentioned anywhere: I have hair that grows halfway up my penis on the top, and two thirds of the way up on the bottom. It's gross and embarrassing, and there seems to be more of it every week. I've been shaving for a couple of years, but within hours, I have unsightly and uncomfortable stubble on my cock. What I need to know is if electrolysis will work on the sensitive skin of the penis. Will it damage the skin? Could the electricity impair normal functioning? Do the home electrolysis machines advertised on TV work? If not, is there any place in New York that does this kind of work, and how much does it cost? Help!

LS

Hey, LS:

On your behalf, I spoke at length with two professional electrologists; one in San Francisco, one in New York. Unfortunately, after these conversations I didn't understand the process any better than I did before I picked up the phone. So I called the person I probably should have called in the first place for the jargon-free dope—my transsexual pal Judith.

Judith has undergone 36 hours of electrolysis, all on her face. Does it hurt? "Yes, it hurts like hell—unless you have the area being worked on deadened with an injected anesthetic like lidocaine. Some people take a kind of heavy-duty aspirin, others try topical creams. But the people I know that have done the pills and creams say it's still very painful. Go to a place where they can give you an injection, just like at the dentist. You won't feel 95 percent of the zaps."

The zaps? "Yes, zaps. A tiny little thread of metal—you can barely see it—is inserted into a hair follicle. The 'probe' delivers a very brief, very intense little electric blast to the root. The zap kills the root, and then you lift the hair right out. And because you've killed the root, the hair doesn't grow back."

What about weenies? "The place I go to doesn't do them. They had trouble with a couple of clients early on who made the electrologist uncomfortable." How so? "They were getting hard-ons, and one guy came. They didn't want to deal with that kind of stuff, so they stopped doing genital work." The electrologist I spoke with in San Francisco doesn't do weenies either. "I don't know who's calling me for an appointment, you know? It could be some weirdo."

When I asked Aaron Bernstein, a certified clinical electrologist in Manhattan, about the reluctance of some electrologists to do weenie work, he was shocked. "This man's problem is really very common. I've done many cases like his." Has he encountered pervs, customers in it for weenie-zappin' thrills? "Hardly. People don't do this for the 'thrill,' believe me." Mr. Bernstein rejects the term "zapping." "We insert a sterile probe into the follicle, a natural skin opening. Then we release a radio frequency which causes the tissue of the papilla [the root] to oscillate at a high rate of speed, destroying the hair-growing cells in the follicle." Sounds like zapping to me, but Mr. Bernstein reassured me that "the tip of the probe never gets hot."

And all three assured me that electrolysis will work on your weenie's sensitive skin. "The most sensitive skin on a person's body is on the face," said Judith, "and most electrolysis is done on faces." Nor will the zapping impair your weenie's normal functioning. Judith's sensitive face, after a full 36 hours of zapping, is lovely, hairless, and fully functional.

Both our NYC and SF electrologists had low opinions of home electrolysis machines—as one would expect them to. Lawyers have low opinions of home "last will and testament" kits; sex advice columnists have low opinions of "professional psychotherapists." But Judith, who is not a provider but a consumer, had an even lower opinion of home kits than the professional hair-zappers. "Trained electrologists do better work than untrained ones," she said. "Unless you've been trained, you may damage or scar your skin." And should you choose to DIY, you won't have access to those lidocaine shots—so that home machine is guaranteed to hurt, "hurt lots."

Judith pays $88 an hour for her treatment, a fee at the high end (Mr. Bernstein charges $80 an hour), so her 36 hours of treatment have set her back over $3,000. "You can find cheaper, even half as cheap, but they're probably not very experienced, or they're using substandard equipment," she warns. "You'll save money, but it will hurt more, and you may end up with scars. Electrolysis is nothing to scrimp on."

Finally, you ask if I know of anyone in New York who does this sort of work. Well, yes, Mr. Bernstein. How did I make his acquaintance? *I looked him up in the motherfucking phone book.* E comes right between D and F in the Yellow Pages, just like in the alphabet. There are about 200 other electrologists listed in the Manhattan Yellow Pages, if you and Mr. Bernstein don't hit it off. Geez.

Hey, Faggot:

I've been trying to change since I was a kid: no luck thus far. I'm now in college and there's no way I'm coming out anytime soon. The social, psychological, and theological conditionings are just too strong. I'm a 21-year-old male (virgin) too afraid to initiate direct contact. I'm somewhat handsome, height-weight proportionate, so appearance isn't a factor whatsoever, but I'll be damned if I'm not a prisoner of my mind, my fears, my peers, etc. Yet I live vicariously through the gays I see on the street. I imagine what it would feel like just to kiss another guy, be cuddled and embraced. Do any of your readers truly understand the impossibility of my situation?

Not only am I in the closet, but I'm hidden deep within the clothes, and even if someone were to search the closet carefully, I would simply sequester myself to the inner chamber of the closet, deeper still. Nevertheless, I love boys, all boys: Asians, Latinos, white and Black, green and purple. I have a lot of love to offer. But reality sets in: I don't want to lose my heterosexual friends, for I care for them also. I say this with sadness, but I'm afraid I have no choice but to gaze upon male beauty from afar; full of longing, desire, and unfulfilled fantasies.

No Name, No Game, No Flame

Hey, Dumbfuck:

I'm guessing you left No Clue, No Spine, and No Guts off your list because they don't rhyme with Name, Game, and Flame. But they belong on your list, Miss Self-Pity.

Does anybody understand what you're going through? Yes, anybody who's queer does: we've all been there, done that. You aren't special, and to be perfectly frank, at this point in history, you aren't all that interesting. If you're miserable "deep within the clothes," whatever that's supposed to mean, then come the fuck out. If you're happy "sequestered in the inner chamber," then stay there. I have no sympathy for guys who know they're gay, have access to urban gay institutions, can articulate their desires, and yet choose to remain in the closet out of sheer *chickenshittedness*.

One word of advice: your pathetic, poetic posturing won't be nearly as alluring at age 40 as it is now—other 21-year-olds are much likelier to fall for the angle you're working. So you might not want to wait until you've got a drinking problem, a potbelly, and child support payments to make before you finally screw up the courage to come out. In the meantime, spare us your bullshit whining. Don't have the balls to come out, now or ever? Fine. Don't. Rot in the closet.

Hey, Faggot:

Believe me when I say that had I not felt shitty about myself before I got married, it never would have happened. I think about killing myself all the time. I don't know where people get the courage to come out. Maybe I'm not going to change. So now what? I'm 33.

Closet Fruit

Hey, CF:

It'll take more courage to pull that trigger, or swallow those pills, than it'll take to open your mouth and start telling the truth. Yes, you've gotten yourself into a fix. Yes, it's going to be a long, hard road. Yes, people are going to get hurt. But what are your other options? A lifetime of misery? A loveless, hostile marriage? A messy, unnecessary suicide? C'mon—there is no other option. You've reached the point where the misery of being in the closet outweighs the imagined misery of coming out—all pre-coming-out queers had to reach that point. Eventually we say to ourselves, "Coming out can't possibly be more painful than hiding here in the closet," and out we come to discover that, yes indeed, being out hurts lots less than being in. And every last one of us wishes we'd done it sooner. Your soon-to-be ex-wife will get over it one day, your family will get over it, *you* will get over it. You're 33 years old, you're a grown-up: it's your life—live it.

Hey, Faggot:

From the bottom to the top of my heart, I truly adore your style of writing advice columns. Man, you are all that and then some. I'm not stroking your ego either, because I want something from you. This compliment is sincere. Never give people sympathy when they come to your door with sad, sad songs! I like that! No, I love that!

Hopefully, my story does not seem to be sad. My "problem" is that I am incarcerated, and although I've recently placed a personal ad, I can't find someone who'll accept my imprisonment. I didn't get a response at all! Can you give me a list of publications that I can purchase (or whatever!) where I can place an ad in for a man who is bisexual? Heterosexual? Homosexual?

Thank you for your advice column and your help in search of love.

Lonely in Prison

Hey, LIP:

Here's something I've never understood about those prisoner-seeking-boyfriend ads you see in gay papers all the time: if you're in prison, how come you can't find a boyfriend? Judging from personal ads, American prisons are stuffed to the rafters with convicts looking for a boyfriend. If you date "in-house" you'll probably have better luck finding a bisexual/heterosexual/homosexual man who understands your situation.

Hey, Faggot:

Since porno flicks became available, I have watched thousands of them. One thing I note is that guys rarely play with and/or suck on gals' breasts. It seems most guys head for the final act without even noticing gals' breasts. Why should gals be so concerned about their breast image, as most are, when their breasts are often neglected in lovemaking?

Curious

Hey, C:

I have a sneaking feeling that breeder boys in real life may pay more attention to gals' breasts than breeder boys in porn. Just to be sure, I called a lifelong expert on women's breasts, my older, straighter brother, Billy. "Any man who isn't paying attention to his partner's breasts is not paying attention to his partner," he said, sounding an awful lot like . . . me. "I mean, the best thing in the world is to be inside a woman and have a nipple in my mouth," he concluded, sounding like himself again. Wake up, straight boys: porn features highly stylized, ritualized performance-sex, and is not meant to be taken literally.

Hey, Faggot:

I am a 41-year-old woman puzzled by the tendency of men I've gone to bed with lately to dictate what I say during sex. I've always been enthusiastically vocal in bed, both on a volunteer basis and in response to sweet inquiries, and I have no objection to dirty words. However, I don't like being scripted, particularly in a harsh fashion ("Say you love my cock! Say it louder!"). The first time this happened, the guy also wanted to bite and spank me, so I chalked it up to an SM tendency. But it keeps happening, even with men who are not otherwise kinky—most recently with an old flame, with whom I first went to bed 16 years ago. When he was 24, he whispered sexy things in my ear; now at 40, he's barking out orders like the rest of them. Is this an aging thing, or what? It doesn't happen with younger men.

Prefer Spontaneity

Hey, PS:

This sounds a bit Dworkinish, but maybe your aging partners have been consuming a lot of porn over the past fifteen years. While I don't believe pornography makes men into rapists, I have observed that every other guy I've been to bed with in the last five to ten years speaks fluent porno—"Suck that big cock, yeah." The last time I watched a breeder porn, I seem to recall hearing "I love your cock!" over and over again. . . .

Hey, Faggot:

I hope you can answer a question that has intrigued me for some time. I am a straight male. I know that the quantity of every man's amount of come varies. However, the actors in X-rated films seem to come a lot more than I do. My question is: Is it possible for a man to increase the amount of his ejaculate, with diet, vitamins, etc.?

Anonymous

Hey, A:

Like you said, the quantity of every man's come varies—as does its thickness, hue, and flavor. Some people claim you can increase the amount of your come by drinking more fluids, eating more fruit, or saving it up. Give it a whirl. Guys in porno videos come more than you do for the same reason porno guys generally have bigger cocks, nicer asses, and bigger tits than you do: viewers want to see big cocks, nice bodies, and high-volume orgasms. Guys who fit the bill get cast, guys who don't, don't. Think of it as unnatural selection, Porno-Darwinism.

Hey, Faggot:

My entire life I have felt self-conscious over the size of my dick. I'm 5'8", 150, and my erect dick is, well, I'd rather not say. Flaccid you can hardly see it. I've tried everything, but will not consider surgery. If it matters, I'm gay and 24. Interesting: I can write that I'm gay but find it difficult to say my cock measures 3¾" hard.

At first I thought I couldn't be gay because my dick does not measure up to porno magazines or videos. I don't need a shrink but was wondering if you knew of any support organizations that cater to small men?

I have so much love to give but hold back because I fear rejection. The whole world looks bigger than me. Am I the only one in the world like this? Please help me. I cannot discuss this with friends and feel so alone. I'm fairly nice-looking and often get offers. My fear of rejection or ridicule forces me to turn down many hot-looking dudes. This question might seem trivial but, believe me, it has affected all avenues of my life.

Steve

Hey, Steve:

If you were the "only one in the world" with your problem, three thousand American men wouldn't have gone in for penis enlargement surgery in the last few years. You said you've tried "everything"—which means exactly what? ten-pound weights? cock-enhancing crystals?—and that surgery was the only option you wouldn't consider. But why not surgery? If you're seriously miserable, why not invest some serious money in pumping the little feller up?

There's been a spate of articles in the smelly press (Vanity Fair, Esquire, Vogue) about penis enlargement. According to these articles, most men going in for penis enlargement are of "average" length and "extremely body conscious and narcissistic," and may "need psychological help, not surgery." But not you. You have, forgive me and brace yourself, what is technically termed a "microphallus." It was specifically for guys like you that the penis enlargement pioneer—a Chinese physician named Dr. Long (not making it up)—began experimenting with snipping what's known as the "suspensory ligament," the ligament that not only holds the penis up (attaches it to the pubic bone, actually), but also holds about two inches of penile "root" inside your body. Snip this ligament and the penis "drops"—

one to two inches emerge from inside the body to join those inches outside the body.

Thickening "techniques"—shooting fat extracted from the butt or abdomen into the shaft—are more problematic and controversial. Fat is often reabsorbed by the body, "lumps up" or hardens into cysts, and repeated "attempts" may be necessary. The ligament snip is not without problems either: without being attached to the suspensory ligament, the angle of your erect penis may not be what it was: it may point straight forward, or even down. The snip seems, in my reading of the scant literature on the procedure, analogous to pulling your arm out of its socket. It's longer than it was, but you don't have the control over it that you once did.

As for support groups, I couldn't find one for you. Which doesn't mean they don't exist—you can't swing a dead cat in this country without hitting a support group for survivors of swung dead cats. Maybe someone reading this knows of a support group for short-dicked men and will write in. Failing that, for the cost of a small ad in the classified section of a weekly newspaper you could start a support group of your own.

Hey, Faggot:

You asked for it, you got it! In your response to Steve, the 24-year-old gay man who was ashamed of his small dick, you asked people to write in about support groups for small-endowed men. There is such a group: Small, Etc. I think you were unduly harsh on Steve. I hope you'll help him by publishing information about Small, Etc.

GH

Hey, GH:

Information? I'll give you the novelization:

Chapter One. Our Hero Meets Adversity Head On, and Triumphs Over the Forces of Largeness. Tired of the contempt and ridicule he encountered on account of his four-inch penis, J decided to form a club/support group for small guys. What had J suffered? "There were times people ran out on me: we got undressed and they took one look at my cock and bolted. Or people got into bed and saw my dick and said, 'I thought you were bigger than you are, let's have sex, but I'm not going to be interested in anything permanent.' " Was J scarred by these exchanges? "Yes! I still can't urinate in a public rest room without going into a stall. I don't change or shower at the gym. I go in gym clothes and return home to shower."

Without anyone to discuss his troubles with, J got a P.O. box, placed an ad in *The Advocate*, and Small, Etc. was born. "I never really expected it to grow," J said (about his, er, club). "In seven years, we've grown to 600 members—mostly from the U.S., but we also have members in Canada, Germany, the Netherlands, Jamaica, and Australia." Members pay $30 a year and receive *Small Gazette*, a quarterly newsletter. "It's up to about 80 pages and has over 400 personal contact ads." Personals are free to members, and apparently pretty effective: J met his lover of six years through an ad in *Small Gazette*.

Chapter Two: J Realizes His Club Is Discriminatory, and Does the Right Thing. Shortly after he started the club, well-endowed guys began contacting J in order to meet small men. "It was mind-boggling. Why would someone who's good-looking, well built, muscular, attractive, and well endowed want to be with a small guy? They can have anyone they want, and yet here were guys requesting guys who are small-endowed!" J opened the club to all: "I felt I didn't have the right not to let them join. I understand discrimination."

Chapter Three: Small Straight Men Contact Our Hero. "*Penthouse* magazine mentioned us, but didn't say we were a gay club. I got letters from straight guys all over the country. I wrote everyone back personally. Even though we're a club for gay and bisexual men, the problems and the rejection are similar."

Chapter Four: J Reads an Advice Column and Gets Angry. J saw Steve's letter, and didn't much care for my advice. "I was upset you focused on operations, which I frown upon. I've looked into those operations, and what the doctors don't tell you is that they have lots of side effects: It desensitizes the head of the penis; you can't control the direction of your erection; added girth goes away after a while. People I know who've had the operations wound up having problems. And it's not like you're going from having a four-inch cock to having an eight-inch cock: you grow maybe an inch. To go through all of that surgery and pain and expense for one inch is just not worth it. The key to solving the problem isn't surgery, it's self-esteem," said J. "To feel wanted by others in the same situation, or wanted by others who are bigger than you, that's what helped me get over it. And that's what my club does for men like me." Heartwarming, ain't it? The End.

Hey, Faggot:

This is a note for Shrinky Dink. Quit fixating on your little friend! Dick size is nothing in the grand scheme of life. I for one don't like big dicks. Gag me! My current semi-significant other has a long one. After I've done all I can do, there's part of him left over, untouched! I feel like I went to the buffet and left a lot of food on my plate. Waste, waste, waste. I've been with small guys, and they were great in bed. Shrug off the unavoidable rejections, just like average-sized guys do. Rejection is not reserved for the wee ones. Good luck!

John

Hey, John:

Makes sense to me, but your letter pissed J off. "If dick size isn't important, why does he have to tell us about his lover being so big?" As for your sympathy, J felt sure Steve would feel worse for having read your letter: "I know it would make me feel worse. 'Shrinky Dink' is support? Look, we're not looking for sympathy. We want acceptance." If J's organization is really interested in acceptance, Small, Etc. needs to serve notice that small men are mad as hell and not going to take it anymore! I suggest a Million Small-Man March. Wee shall overcome!

Hey, Faggot:

I have a question that seems diametrically opposed to your usual questions on this subject: How can I, a mostly sexually satisfied husband, convince my wife to let me give her *more* oral sex? She has many excuses: "It's not clean," or she "just urinated," or "It's not real sex like intercourse." She denigrates the practice as "hooligan behavior" and allows me a lick or suck very sparingly.

I have tried every means of convincing her that I can think of. I've tried to tell her that women's nerve endings for sexual pleasure receive more stimulation from oral sex than from regular intercourse. I've begged her to let me be a part of any fantasy she might have on the subject: I'll gladly lick her in the car, while hiking in the forest, while she watches TV or talks on the phone, even in a darkened (uncrowded) movie theater.

Salivating in SF

Hey, SISF:

Get her to talk to some of her lady friends who like oral sex or something. And be sure to tell her it's really important to you. Okay?

Hey, is everybody as excited as I am about *Independence Day*?! I don't usually fall for Hollywood hype, and I don't like action movies much, and I hate science fiction. But I have fallen for the hype this time—and I can't get up! It's the trailer that did it. Oh, my God—it is so amazing. These big motherfucking alien spaceships start blowing shit up, and the people of Earth—our defenses lowered after a steady stream of "nice" alien propaganda, from *E.T.* to *Alf* to *Third Rock from the Sun*—are, understandably, a little shocked by this bad behavior. Pro-alien propagandists would have us believe that aliens are our friends, but no way, man: they're comin' here to blow shit up first, anal probes second!

320 — SAVAGE LOVE

Hey, Faggot:

Recently at my job (at a brokerage house) we got a new manager who has taken away our casual-dress Fridays. Now, it's no big deal, but his memo referred to dressing casual as somehow indicative of "declining personal standards and social decay." This is ludicrous! It's so typical of management to focus on the petty-ass shit rather than focusing on running the office more efficiently or maintaining good morale. Please let me know your feelings on this.

Questioning Authority

Hey, QA:

You work for a brokerage house. Don't like dress codes? Go get a nose ring and pull espresso somewhere.

By far the way coolest part of the trailer for *Independence Day* is when the aliens blow up the White House! And, rumor has it, the first lady is inside! This is the second film to come out of Hollywood during the Clinton era in which the first lady dies or is already dead. Did you see *The American President* with Michael Douglas and Annette Bening? Michael Douglas is basically Bill Clinton, but fictional Bill comes complete with a spine, principles, a conscience, ideals, scruples, honor, etc., *and his wife is dead*. Watching *The American President*, you get the creeping feeling that the filmmakers are saying Bill Clinton would be a terrific president if only Hillary would drop dead. Not even President Michael Douglas's Chelsea knockoff teenage daughter seems to miss Mom much!

I can't recall a single dead cinematic first lady during either Reagan administration. Did anyone ever suggest that Bush would've been a better president if Barbara had died of a gin-and-tonic-induced stroke? What is up?

Hey, Faggot:

I'm 21 and I am a college student. My college life is completely separate from my life at home. I am gay. I have nothing against gay people. But I don't want to be gay! It has been my life goal to get married and have children for as long as I can remember. I will never be happy with a man. I would never be able to tell my family, and I don't want them to know. I am having a real hard time dealing with this and I'm taking it out on my friends. I think that my friends would accept me, but I don't know for sure.

My problem is that I can't keep this to myself anymore. I don't want to "come out," I never want to be considered "out." But I can't deal with this alone. Counselors won't be any help—this is too personal to talk to a stranger about. What can I do?

Deeply Depressed

Hey, DD:

Um, come out—you'll be really glad you did. And, hey, if your friends freak out or your parents disown you, well, there's nothing like a Hollywood blockbuster to take your mind off your troubles. Just pretend your family and all your homophobic friends are on a tour of the White House with the first lady when . . . BOOM!!!

There are a lot of stars in *Independence Day*, just like there were in all those big '70s disaster movie ensemble pictures like *Earthquake* and *The Towering Inferno*. Will Smith is the lead—he's a top-gun fighter pilot—and Jeff Goldblum, Bill Pullman, and Randy Quaid are in it too. Unfortunately Shelley Winters isn't in *Independence Day*, and that's a shame. I just finished her autobiography—what a great lady! But you know who's in it that you probably wouldn't expect? Harvey Fierstein! *Independence Day* is the first-ever aliens-attack-the-earth picture with an openly gay actor in it—another milestone!

Hey, Faggot:

If one were to make cheese from human breast milk, what commercially available cheese would be its closest relation in taste and texture?

SF

Hey, SF:

Most commercially available cheeses are made from plain old cows' milk, so we can infer that cheese production—what you do with the milk, not its origins—largely determines taste and texture.

To test this hypothesis, I called a cheese shop in San Francisco with the cringe-inducing name Say Cheese. According to Joe, "Taste depends on the shape of the cheese, and the amount of time it's aged, what the cows are fed, what kind of bacteria you introduce into the milk." And texture? "The older a cheese is the harder it is, the younger a cheese, the creamier." Why is that? "As cheese ages, it dries, salts calcify, making for a harder, denser cheese."

When I asked Joe to recommend a cheese that would come close to breast milk, he balked: "I've never tasted breast milk." Was he bottle fed? "I don't remember." When pressed, he offered that "maybe it would look like sour cream, or cottage cheese," but Joe doesn't think human breast milk would taste very good. "Sheeps, goats, and cows don't eat meat, they don't eat onions or garlic, they don't drink coffee. The flavor of human cheese would depend on what you were feeding your human. Considering our diets, human breast milk would probably taste pretty awful." Does Say Cheese stock human breast milk cheese? "No we don't." Why not? "It's a disgusting idea, and no one makes it." But if it were available, would you? "I don't think so."

Looks like the way to find out what human breast milk cheese might taste like is to make some. According to Dale

Baumgartner, head cheese-maker at the Tilamook Creamery in Oregon, it takes ten pounds of milk to make one pound of cheese. A dairy cow makes more than that in one day, but the average lactating woman needs almost four days to produce ten pounds of milk, and that would be a problem: "When you're making cheese," said Dale, "it's really important to use fresh milk," especially if your milk is unpasteurized.

When I asked Dale about making cheese from human breast milk, he said, "The department of health might have something to say about that." But is it possible? "You could probably do it, I don't see why not—provided you could get your hands on the milk."

Hey, Faggot:

Where do you get off advising heterosexuals about their problems? Where do you get off advising men about women, or even worse, advising women when you don't even fuck them?

Heterosexuals, take my advice: don't take advice from someone who doesn't have sex with women. He doesn't know what he's talking about. I don't know what your credentials are to advise homosexuals, but you have no credentials to advise heterosexuals. So go walk down Castro Street with your faggy friends, be sure to wear a condom before you stick your dick in another guy's shit, but don't you dare advise heterosexuals on their love lives!

Pissed

Hey, P:

Where do I "get off advising heterosexuals" about their sex lives? Because I'm gay. The average gay person knows more about sex than the average straight person, and we're usually better at it. And I'm qualified to comment on heterosexuality by virtue of my exposure to the phenomenon: I was raised by heterosexuals; most of the people I work with, went to school with, meet at parties, read about in books and magazines, see in movies, watch on television, etc., etc., are heterosexuals. And most gay people, myself included, have had breeder sex.

Post-puberty and pre–coming out, I identified as straight. I had girlfriends, we fucked: I lost my virginity to a girl name Wanda. The first blow job I ever got was from a girl named Sue. Have you given a blow job, Pissed? I've had vaginal intercourse; have you had anal intercourse? Well, then who's the expert here?

Hey, Faggot:

If it's wrong for a person from one group to tell another group what to do, perhaps Pissed thinks it's equally wrong for Hets to make laws that affect homos. Where do men get off making laws that affect a female's reproductive rights? Perhaps Pissed should also write a letter to the Pope, that 12-language-speaking Polish guy who tells lots of monolingual non-Poles what to do. Go after some of those overweight, old, straight, white, rich males making laws in Washington, D.C., and leave Dan alone.

All Clogged Up

Hey, Pissed:

Breeders who read "Savage Love" believe that complete acceptance and understanding of alternative lifestyles actually enhances life as we know it, including our own sexuality. Most of Dan's hetero advice is right on the money—do you think he'd get any hetero mail if he didn't hit us where we lived? Get out of your hole. Better yet, stay in it and keep your piss with you.

Mt. Tam

Hey, Faggot:

Your response to Pissed was full of shit.

Being gay does not make you a "sex expert," it does not make you good at sex. Being gay may give you a different perspective than some, but it does not, in and of itself, mean much. You have your nerve assuming that straight people never agonize over who they are, or why they wanna fuck the people they do. People who are gay can be just as insensitive as anybody else. You included. I'm disappointed.

CW

Hey, CW:

Gay people insensitive?! We are so sensitive! In fact, my female friends tell me that all the time. "Dan," they say, "you are so sensitive."

Hey, Faggot:

Pissed suffers from the same disease that most of our world suffers from: ignorance. Pissed says that Dan Savage isn't qualified to give advice to heterosexuals because he is gay. Why is it so difficult for Pissed and people like him to understand how much a comment like that hurts? What makes you think, Pissed, that pain, love, sharing, hopes, and dreams are things that only heterosexuals share in common? We share the same world. Your ignorance blinds you. Blinds you to the fact that we are everywhere.

We designed the clothes you wear, the computer you use. We built the car you drive and the home you live in. We made the movies and music you enjoy. We grow, harvest, deliver, and cook the food that feeds your family. We care for you when you're sick, protect you, and go out of our way to make sure you get to where you are going, on time and safely. And like it or not, we teach your children.

So, Pissed, you think Dan Savage is not qualified to give advice? think again. Think about how much we have in common and how much we share.

DF

Hey, DF:

Your "We Are Everywhere" speech makes the gays and lesbians sound like Amway or something. While it's very touching, people who hate queers, hate queers—knowing that "we make sure you get where you're going on time and safely" (what are we? an airline?) won't change 'em a bit. Popes have been working their Catholic hocus-pocus under the ceiling of the Sistine Chapel for hundreds of years. That collective queer "we" that painted that masterpiece hasn't altered the church's homophobia one eensy, weensy, altar-boy-buggerin' bit. Homophobia and the enjoyment of an individual homosexual's contributions to art, culture, and commerce can coexist quite nicely, and have done so for centuries. Convincing a bigot that a fag short-order cook fried his eggs, or a dyke air traffic controller kept his plane from slamming into the Everglades ain't gonna change shit. But it's a lovely, if syrupy, sentiment.

Hey, Faggot:

There is an operation to enlarge or enhance almost all our body parts, but I never heard of ball or scrotal enlargement. I would love to have a large set to enhance my sexual pleasure and fill out a pair of Speedos. Is there an operation, implants or injection to increase their size? Please let me know if there is. Thanks.

JS

Hey, JS:

Until a couple of years ago, you could've called the good folks at Dow Corning, ordered yourself a couple of silicone nuts, hopped a flight to Mexico and paid a no-questions-asked doc a couple of hundred bucks to implant them for you. A little poolside R&R in Puerto Vallarta, and then you're Stateside with a tan and impressively packed Speedos.

But when Dow's breast implants were yanked off the market so were their little brothers, testicular implants. Even if they were still available, no one I spoke with had ever actually performed a cosmetic nut implant: when I asked the secretary at a cosmetic surgeon's office if she'd ever heard of a cosmetic testicular implant, she said, "No, and I've worked with surgeons in California." And if they're not doing nut implants in California, they're just not being done.

So, what are your options? You could inject saline—sterile salt water—directly into your scrotum, a process known as "scrotal infusion." The results are impressive—you can blow your scrotum up to the size of a basketball—but short-lived: Your balls will deflate in a few hours as the saline is absorbed into your body. Another option might be collagen injections. If they can fill Goldie Hawn's lips with the stuff, why not your scrotum?

"Collagen is the most common protein in the human body, or any mammal's body," said Dr. Gerald Bernstein, a dermatologist and dermatologic cosmetic surgeon. "It's a very hard fibrous material, used as a volume expander, to fill up spaces that are depressed or absent. We can fill in wrinkles with it, and make lips bigger."

What about having collagen injected into your scrotum? "I have never heard of anybody doing that. I would not do that, even if requested to. You're running the risk of putting pressure on the testes [never a good plan], and the collagen is temporary, it only lasts three to six months. And collagen is expensive, about $200 a cc, and to fill an area that large, it would take 10 cc at least. That's an awful lot of money to spend for three months' discomfort."

Hey, Faggot:

How does one measure one's penis? I hear that the average erection is 5½ inches, but am not sure how they arrive at that figure. Depending on what starting point or method I use, I get different results.

Six?

Hey, Six:

An honest measurement is taken from the top of the shaft—where cock meets tummy—to the tip. Some guys measure from the underside of the shaft—where cock meets scrotum—and some apparently measure from behind the balls for all the "that can't be nine inches!" stories I hear. These men are deluding themselves and misleading others: Measure only what you can work into someone else's body. "Insertable" inches are the only inches that count, guys.

Hey, Faggot:

I am a married heterosexual woman, living in San Francisco. Recently a lesbian friend and her girlfriend came to visit. The night they arrived, my husband and I didn't feel like going out, but they wanted to. They expressed a desire to go to a dance club that was gay friendly. While looking through our local weekly paper, my husband made a comment about one club being a "dyke bar." We didn't think anything of it, because we have so many friends that are gay, who refer to themselves as "fags" or "dykes." We are obviously not homophobic and were only using the term the club used to describe itself.

The next day my friend told me that she thought my husband "crossed boundaries" and used a term that "he hadn't been given permission to use." She compared his using the term "dyke" to a white person using the term "nigger." I think she's full of shit. She thinks we can't understand how she feels because "we're not lesbians." So do we have permission to use the word "dyke"? If a person refers to him or herself as a dyke or fag, do we actually have to ask their permission to refer to her/him in that way?

Not Straight and Not Narrow

Hey, NSANN:

If someone gives you permission to call them dyke or fag—like I do—then you have every right to use the word when speaking with or referring to that person. It follows that since the dance club in question lists itself as a "dyke bar," you have the club's permission to call it a friggin' dyke bar. Your husband called the bar "dyke," he didn't call your friends dykes. If they're uncomfortable with his using the word in reference to the club, they need to take it up with the club owner, not your husband. We can't expect straight people to read "dyke bar" in club listings and say "lesbian establishment" out loud.

Hey, Faggot:

I am a 36-year-old male, approximately 30 lbs. overweight. I have always battled with my weight and have learned to live with the ups and downs. However, no matter how much weight I lose or how often I work out I *always* have a big, flabby chest— a source of discomfort and shame to me that I have not learned to accept. In a word, I hate my tits. I envy flat-chested guys who stay that way, fat or skinny.

I know there are surgical procedures to correct this problem. What do you know about these? What do your readers know? How expensive is it, and what, if any, are the side effects?

Ashamed of My Tits

Hey, AMT:

This may or may not have anything to do with your boobs, but according to a long, scary piece in last week's *New Yorker*, and a medium scary piece in last month's *Esquire*, everything we eat, drink, wear, and sit on is slathered in estrogens (female hormones), and/or industrial chemicals that mimic estrogen in our bodies. Consequently, girls are hitting puberty earlier, and boys aren't pumping out sperm at anything near the rate we once did. There's other spooky, potentially estrogen-exposure-linked shit going down: increased rates of testicular cancer, higher rates of breast cancer in men and women, increasing numbers of young boys with malfunctioning testicles, and . . . men with enlarged breasts. If the scientists studying dropping sperm counts are correct, the extinction of the human race is two generations off. Meanwhile, what are we going to do about your tits?

Most men with large boobies suffer from either pseudo-gynecomastia, or actual gynecomastia. The pseudo variety is merely a concentration of fat in the chest, and a little liposuction goes a long way toward taking care of the prob. Men who have gynecomastia, on the other hand, suffer from . . . an imbalance of hormones. In other words: *too much estrogen* (see above) (!!!), resulting in a buildup of "glandular breast tissue." If your large titties are at all sore, or tender to the touch, see a·doc! Gynecomastia has been linked to several kinds of cancer (testicular, lung, adrenal, liver, kidney), and mostly afflicts men over age 50. But 30 percent of all gynecomastia cases have no apparent cause—except maybe all that estrogen in the environment!

Over 5,000 American men get breast-reduction surgery every year. A cosmetic surgeon I spoke with—who did not wish to be identified—told me the cost varies, but you can expect to pay anywhere from $3,000 to $5,000 for a boob job. If the brainiacs are right about this estrogen-poisoning thing, the numbers of men going in for boob jobs may rise sharply. This increased demand could very well drive up the price—so don't delay! Get your boobs done now!

Hey, Faggot:

My boyfriend got a so-called boob job as a teenager because he was embarrassed by his "breasts." What a waste! He has no sensation in his nipples. Oh, what I would give for a little bit of breast on him and the chance to suck a responsive nipple! He says that if he'd known nipples were a source of erotic pleasure for men, he never would have done it. Now we both feel cheated, but the damage cannot be undone. Men, leave your boobs alone!

Save the Tits

Hey, Faggot:

Three weeks ago, I was at my girlfriend's apartment taking a shower. The urge to release my pressurized bladder hit me and I dutifully whizzed into the bathtub's drain. At the same time, my girlfriend tiptoed into the bathroom and, in an attempt to surprise me, jerked open the shower curtain. My urine stream was particularly apparent, as I had been beefing up on B-complex. She became incensed when she caught me pissing in her shower. We haven't spoken since.

Is it unreasonable for me to stick to my guns on this one? Am I such a heinous bastard for urinating in the shower? It's not like I bathed in urine, or pissed in her shampoo bottle, but if I'm in the shower and gotta piss, I'm going to point toward the drain and let fly. A little bit of pee-pee never hurt anyone, did it?

Umlar in Ballard

Hey, UIB:

Women have a different relationship with urine than men do. Men break up cigarette butts in urinals, draw in the snow, swing it back and forth, see how high we can piss up into the air before the stream breaks and arcs into the toilet bowl: for us, piss is a toy. Women, as they must squat or foul themselves, don't play with their pee. For the ladies, urine is not a toy, and pee-time is not playtime, it's sit 'n' think time. Women piss and ponder, men piss and play.

Deprived of a festive relationship with piss, women are likelier to be squeamish about their own and others' urine. Hence the shower freak-out. As for the dispute, I'm on the girlfriend's side. There ain't nothing wrong with peeing in the tub so far as I'm concerned, but it's her bathtub—hers. Not yours, not mine. An apology is in order, and a solemn promise to never, ever pee in her bathtub again. Follow up your promise with a sincere effort not to get caught the next time you pee in her bathtub—lock the door, face the wall, and lay off the B-complex.

Hey, Everybody:

If you haven't bought a box of Girl Scout cookies this year, I suggest you pick up a few boxes of Tagalongs peanut butter patties pronto—these boxes are sure to be collector's items one day.

Pictured on the front of the box are two Girl Scouts up to their chins in water, nose to nose, looking deep into each other's eyes. "Go for it!" is written above their heads. I ♥ subtle and subversive homoeroticism, and despite the braces one of the girls has in her mouth—sure to get in the way of any late-night "going for it" back at the cabin—this photo qualifies as teenage lesbian erotica in my book.

If unsubtle homoeroticism is more to your liking, you need only flip the box over. Let me read you the text from the back of the box: "I just love water sports! Our teachers are complete pros! Jamilia and I actually synchronized our strokes. . . ."

Okay, let's stop and examine the first three lines: the Girl Scouts pictured on the box are only shown swimming—no one is shown on water skis, playing water polo, or snorkeling. Swimming isn't water sports, plural, it is a water sport, singular. So why doesn't the copy read, "I just love swimming!" Why "water sports"? "Pro" is slang for prostitute, and "strokes," well "strokes" has a vaguely sexual vibe. Now the appearance of water sports, pros and strokes on the back of a Girl Scout cookie box could be a completely innocent coincidence, but, ladies and gentlemen of the jury, I submit to you line four from the copy on the back of the Tagalongs peanut butter cookie box—"We did the whole length of the pool *on our backs.*"

On Our Backs, as any dyke worth her strap-on can tell you, is the grandmammy of lesbian porno magazines—this month's issue features lesbian nuns. Not interviews with members of the lesbian nun community, not an article about lesbianism in medieval convents—but big, glossy black-and-white photos of two humpy young women in habits munching each other's cookies. (I'm guessing these girls aren't really nuns—unless genital piercings were recently approved by Rome.)

"Go for it!" "Water sports." "Pros." "Strokes." "On Our Backs." Someone, some deep-cover operative of the International Homosexual Conspiracy (IHC), has clearly infiltrated whatever agency designs Girl Scout cookie boxes. Like the IHC plant who designed Mattel's Earring Magic Ken—Ken came complete with a cock ring on a chain around his neck—the Girl Scout operative succeeded in slipping a completely queer product past his or her completely clueless hetero supervisors and struck a blow for lesbian visibility.

When Mattel realized they'd been had, Cock Ring Magic Ken was quickly pulled off the shelves, and Mattel's press spokesperson denied they were in the business of "putting cock rings into the hands of little girls." The Girl Scouts, once they realize what's actually going on in that pool pictured on the back of the peanut butter cookie box, will probably do the same. Get a box of Tagalongs while you still can.

Hey, Faggot:

I am always alone on Valentine's Day. No romance, no relationship. It's depressing.

So, do you have any ideas on what to do, where to go, any neat things I could do for myself or others that day? A onetime volunteer opportunity might be nice, but where?

I'd like to make plans ahead of time to do something more constructive on February 14th than feeling sorry for myself. No more whining, nor more pity parties!

B

Hey, B:

Valentine's Day sucks.

It's one of those two or three days a year when everyone and everything conspires to heighten our expectations to absolutely unrealistic levels, assuring us a miserable letdown of an experience. If we dare watch TV, or pick up a paper, or *leave the fucking house* anytime around Valentine's Day or Christmas or Thanksgiving or New Year's Eve or Mother's Day we're barraged with images of impossible-to-attain levels of material and/or emotional comforts, images that force us to draw unflattering comparisons with our own piddling less-than-hallmarked lives.

And you know what, B? Valentine's Day sucks whether or not you have a squeeze. If you don't have one, you feel like a loser. If you do, they forgot to send you flowers, or they were too busy to see you, or you couldn't get reservations at a decent restaurant, *or whatever*. But something invariably happens that makes you feel like "your" Valentine's Day, the Valentine's Day promised you by every goddamned Hallmark card commercial and every fucking florist from here to the Arctic Circle, was ruined.

Valentine's Day seems to exist solely to make us feel like our relationships are less than perfect, in the same way Christmas seems to exist to make us feel like our families are less than perfect. I loathe the whole nasty business.

So, what to do if you're single? You could go out on Feb 14th in hopes of running into other squeezeless types, who may be a little more vulnerable, and therefore makable, due to VD's cruelest premise: if you don't have a Valentine on Valentine's Day to send you cards and suddenly overpriced flowers, you are a loser.

But matches made in desperation aren't usually matches worth making, so I advise you to bow out of the whole ugly business. Go with your altruistic impulse: spend the day at a hospice, an old folks home, or a homeless shelter—there are plenty of people out there in need of a valentine, even (or especially) platonic ones.

Or you could go to Vegas for three days, hole up in a suite with a case of scotch, a stack of Dean Martin CDs, and order up yourself a boy from one of those classy modeling agencies that serve the hotels. It'll cost ya, but you won't be alone—there'll doubtless be plenty of other folks there doing the exact same thing.

Hey, Faggot:

Since arriving in your country over a year ago, I have experienced an ongoing problem. As soon as I arrived, I was immediately struck by the unusual number of very attractive people. The two thirds of your population who are not grossly obese seemed to be blessed with an exquisite physique, and while a baseball cap and university sweatshirt is not a universal fashion statement, were also reasonably well turned out.

Unfortunately, I quickly discovered that looks are not everything (a lesson often relearned many times). My heart sank further and further as person after person turned out to be either incredibly superficial, selfish, plain stupid or more commonly a mixture of all three. The ability of people to deceive themselves seems to have developed to an extraordinary level here.

I am sure the letters you read expose you to these phenomena in doses which I could not even begin to imagine. I feel confident that you will be able to advise me. Forced by circumstances beyond my control to stay here for at least another eight months, I desperately need to find some companionship. Please help me!

Sick of Your Twisted Country

Hey, SOYTC:

O, j'ai attendu depuis longtemps d'avoir un ami en qui je pourrais confier mon secret. Moi aussi, je suis français! Comme je déteste ce pays et les imbéciles laids, gros, et parresseux qui habitent ici et qui ne couchent pas avec moi. Et ces garçons américains! Si stupides. Je sais exactement ce qui t'arrive, car quand je suis arrivé aux États-Unis, ceux qui n'etaient pas obèses m'ont impressionés. Alors, j'ai flirté avec eux: "Hello, I am better than you, but I will condescend to stick my dick in you for a moment. Please return with me to apartment now." Mais hélas! Ces américains bêtes avec leurs chapeaux de baseball! Ô, mon ami, visite-moi et nous pourrons tuer deux de ces oiseaux proverbiaux avec un petit caillou: je peux enfoncer mon petit 'Chirac' dans toi, et ni toi ni moi ne serrons plus jamais seuls!

Hey, Faggot:

I read your column every week, and it seems like all your mail is from people who think you're evil incarnate. You must hate going to work in the morning if all you ever get are complaints! Doesn't anyone ever send you a well-deserved compliment?

I guess not, so here's a bunch: I'm a straight guy who loves your column. All my straight friends love your column—even my straight old Republican dad loves your column. I've learned so much reading your column, and picked up tips on lots of new sex things to try. You're funny, and your advice is right on. Don't let the bastards get you down.

EKG

Hey, EKG:

Don't you worry your pointy li'l breeder head about me, sweetness: I get lots of complimentary mail from people who think my column is absolutely all that. But I don't run those letters because, well, (a) compliments aren't very interesting, and (b) unlike some advice columnists I could name, I am not an insecure bag o' slop.

Hey, Faggot:

I read your column in *The Village Voice*. You are a very honest and intelligent man. I am a heterosexual female, happily married with lots of single friends, both male and female, gay and straight, who could use reading this column every morning! There are plenty of men and women out there, but people these days don't have realistic ideas. You set them in the right direction.

Keep up the great work!

Toni

Hey, T:

Letters like yours make it all worthwhile! And while you and your friends can't read me every day, as "Savage Love" runs exclusively in weekly publications, let's face facts: Ann Landers and that good-for-nothin' copycat sister of hers aren't going to live forever. A couple of brain aneurysms, a stroke or two, and there's going to be a gaping hole in a lot of daily newspapers right where "Dear Abby" used to be.

So don't despair, Toni, I'll be running in the dailies soon enough. Not that I plan on abandoning weekly papers when Hearst and Knight-Ridder come crying for me. I will keep writing butt sex/bondage/bestiality columns for weekly papers even after I've moved seamlessly into Ann and Abby's old markets with a slightly tamer version of "Savage Love"—all rotten kids/cheatin' husbands/nosy neighbors.

Hey, Faggot:

I read in a book of sex facts that a male will ejaculate approximately 18 quarts of semen during his lifetime. How much of this do you think ends up in Kleenex™?

RM

Hey, RM:

It depends on two things: how much of a man's semen is ejaculated while masturbating as opposed to during sex (when semen is likelier to wind up in an orifice, a condom, or on the sheets); and how many men use tissues, specifically Kleenex™ brand tissues—a Kimberly-Clark product—when wiping up after masturbating.

Some very rough, rounded numbers: the average American male has sex once a week, and masturbates three times a week. There are two to five milliliters of spunk in the average ejaculation; 105 million men in the United States over the age of 12, prime ejaculatory years. We polled 16 male subjects over the age of 18 here at Savage Labs, and of the 16, eight reported using tissues to wipe up after masturbating, followed by towels (four persons), T-shirts (three), and "my girlfriend's hair" (one). And, finally, Kleenex™ brand tissues account for 50 percent of the "facial" tissue market.

Here's what we can pull from these numbers: if a man produces a lifetime ejaculatory output of 18 quarts, ¾ of which is produced while masturbating, that equals 13.5 quarts on a guy's stomach over the course of his life. If a guy's a tissue user, there's a 50 percent chance he's using Kleenex™ brand tissues. So the answer to your question, how much of an individual male's 18 quarts winds up in Kleenex™ is just that: 13.5 quarts, provided he's using Kleenex™ tissues. This is, of course, a high estimate, as even men who prefer tissues don't always have access to them, and sometimes must resort to other things, such as socks, towels, *The New Republic*, girlfriend's hair, etc.

The grand totals are more interesting: one man masturbating three times a week produces 624 ml of ejaculate in a year (3 × 52 × 3.5 ml = 546 ml), or a little more than half a quart. Which, on its own, may not sound like much, but multiply that 546 ml by 105 million men, and we're talking about a tsunami of spunk crashing across the country: 57,330,000,000 ml, or nearly 61 million quarts! If half the men in this country, like our sample, prefer tissues, and half of those men use Kleenex™, that means 15,250,000 quarts of ejaculate winds up on Kleenex™ brand tissues per annum!

Hey, Faggot:

So, like, how many boxes of Kleenex is that?

John & Jason

Hey, JJ:

There are 105 million men over the age of 12 in the United States who masturbate an average of three times a week, producing 60,582,684 quarts of spunk per annum; half of all men we surveyed used facial tissues to wipe up, so we estimated that 30,291,342 quarts per annum winds up in crusty balls of tissues every year. Kleenex controls 48 percent of the facial tissue market, so roughly 15,150,000 quarts per year wind up specifically in Kleenex brand tissues.

And now you want to know how many boxes of Kleenex it takes to soak up those 15-ish million gallons? Well, it depends. First, on how many tissues the average tissue-using male consumes when cleaning himself up. Four, by our estimates. And what type of Kleenex are men using? Unfortunately, this question throws a major wrench into our research efforts: Kleenex's Family Size box ($1.99) contains 250 two-ply tissues; a box of Cold Care tissues ($1.89) contains 144 three-ply tissues; a box of Cold Care Extra Large ($1.39) contains just 60 three-ply tissues; Cold Care Ultra Comfort ($1.69) contains 108 three-ply tissues; and Cold Care with Menthol ($1.59) contains 60 three-ply tissues to a box. With so many variables—thickness of ply, the size of the tissue, the number of tissues per box—it's nearly impossible to determine exactly how many boxes of Kleenex American males go through per year.

But we can work out some averages: going off the numbers above, the average box of Kleenex has 124.4 2.8-ply tissues. The average American male masturbates three times a week, or 156 times a year; half of the 105,000,000 men over the age of 12 wipe up with tissue, and half of all tissue users buy Kleenex brand tissues, so 26,250,000 men out there wipe spunk off their tummies with Kleenex products. As the average tissue-using male consumes four tissues during cleanup—a conservative estimate—he'll need 624 tissues per year (3 × 52 = 156 × 4 = 624), which works out to slightly more than 5 boxes (624/124.4 = 5.02). Multiply those 5.02 boxes by 26,250,000 men, and that works out to 131,775,000 boxes of Kleenex per year, just to wipe up all that jizz.

Hey, Faggot:

So, uh, like how many trees is that?

Tree-Hugger Tim

Hey, THT:

Will this never end? A couple of weeks back, we estimated that American men use 131,775,000 boxes of Kleenex per year to wipe up the 15,150,000 quarts of semen they ejaculate during masturbation (that's one out of every six boxes of Kleenex sold). Another 15 million quarts are wiped up with non-Kleenex-brand tissues, and another 30 million quarts are wiped up with towels, socks, girlfriends' hair, etc.

Now you would like to know how many trees go into those 131,775,000 boxes of Kleenex? Well, according to Dr. David Brink, professor emeritus at the University of California, Berkeley, Forest Products Lab, we simply can't know "how many trees are in 131,775,000 boxes of Kleenex." There are just too many variables for Dr. Brink, who has been studying forests since 1936, to slap a number on this. For instance, are we talking about just the tissues, or the tissues and the box? We'd need to know the weight of all those boxes, figure out how much of the tissue and the box are made from recycled paper, and subtract this percentage (because if it's recycled, it's not a tree, and it's already been counted).

We'd have to figure out which "fiber" Kimberly-Clark uses to make their tissues. Brink said, "It's probably soft wood, because hardwood is more dense and not as absorbent" and wouldn't make good tissue. And finally, we'd need to know if the pulp was lightened by a bleaching method. If so, only 50 to 70 percent of the wood that went into the bleaching process is used. Unfortunately, Kimberly-Clark wouldn't return our phone calls, and we were unable to get answers to any of these questions.

"You see, there is no simple way of figuring this out," said Dr. Brink. "And I assume the person is asking this for some sort of environmental reason. I don't want to lend any weight to the specious argument that we shouldn't manage our forests and use wood product," said Dr. Brink, before he hurried off the phone and back to the lab.

Hey, Faggot:

I have a sad concern. I am a smelly guy. It goes beyond bad b.o.: I suffer from badly timed and barely controlled bouts of flatulence. Embarrassing, you may think, but surely tolerable. No, sir. The whole honking and hissing affair is compounded by the shocking stench of these evil, rotten, lingering farts. Amorous encounters with women are often interrupted by a leap from the bed and a race to the nearest unoccupied room. The whole thing has made me miserable, and as you can imagine, it isn't charming the hell out of the chicks.

My question is this: Other than finding an understanding girlfriend who'll love me gas and all (which won't do a damn thing for me when I'm shifting from foot to foot about to blow in the supermarket checkout line), what can be done about my b.o., the frequency of my wind, and its odious character? This is not a joke, but feel free to laugh at my unfortunate condition.

That Wasn't Me

Hey, TWM:

Laugh? You have all my sympathy, Mariah. I take your problem very seriously, and my first thought upon reading your letter was that the root cause of your problem must be your diet: what you put in your mouth largely determines the odor of what comes out your pooter, pores, and pits. Actually, that was my second thought. My first was relief that your letter was postmarked from a distant state, making it unlikely that I will ever find myself trapped behind you in line at the supermarket.

But back to your troubles. On your behalf, I called a diet doc. "That guy has got a nutritional problem, all right," said John Hoeber, M.S., R.D., a registered dietitian in San Francisco, confirming my diagnosis. "Probably too much cabbage and sausage washed down with skunky beer. I'd say he needs a good colonic and a cleansing fast." The colonic and fast will get the gunk out of your guts. (A "colonic," by the way, is like an enema.) "Obviously he's eating something that's not agreeing with his system. Most likely he's got a food allergy or intolerance. 'Evil, rotten, lingering farts' are well-known symptoms of food allergies.

"When foods are not digested properly in the gut," Doc Hoeber elaborated, "the normal flora of the intestines [gut bacteria] snack on the partially digested matter, creating gas. Normally this isn't overly odoriferous, but perhaps his normal flora has gotten a bit abnormal from abuse. The obnoxious body odor can also be a symptom of food allergy, as the body attempts to metabolize food particles that have entered the bloodstream through a damaged intestinal wall."

So, Mariah, what should you do? Get yourself a good-paying job and a gold-plated HMO, cuz you're gonna be shelling out some dough. "He should see a gastroenterologist, allergist, registered dietitian—and while he's at it, a little aroma-therapy couldn't hurt. I believe this is a very serious problem, and he should not hesitate to get a definitive diagnosis. If it's food allergies, he should probably do an elimination/challenge diet, where the most commonly offending foods are avoided for a few weeks, then one by one added back in. He should be able to find out which foods to avoid and how to get proper nutrition from the ones that are left." To find a registered di-etitian, call the cheapskate American Dietetic Association, whose hot line—(312) 899-0040—isn't an 800 number. Tell 'em Doc Hoeber sent ya.

Hey, Faggot:

I'm a model. I want to meet you. What do you say?

Tim

Hey, Tim:

Thanks for sending me a page ripped from a fashion maga-zine—am I to assume the model in the Versace ad is you? But if you included your phone number cuz you wanted a date, I'm afraid it wouldn't work out. I know you've never seen me, but trust me on this: I don't have the word "imbecile" tattooed on my forehead—and not because it wouldn't fit. Anyone can mail me a Versace ad ripped from a magazine and claim he's the model in the picture. If you wanna convince me that's your fine self in that expensive suit, you should've sent some Polaroids of your fine self in your birthday suit along with the ad ripped from the magazine. It's not too late, though: you could still send me a couple of Polaroids—and if you include a self-addressed stamped envelope, I'll send them back to you immediately after my research assistant posts them on the Internet.

Finally . . . how can I put this? This may come as something of a blow, as rejection isn't something Versace models—provided you *are* a Versace model—find themselves on the receiving end of very often, but . . . you're just not my type, Tim. Look on the bright side, though: you can always use this painful experience in your craft. The next time you have to create the illusion that there's a thought trapped in your pretty head—desperately searching for a door—just remember this moment. Your brow will knit, the photographer will snap.

There's an advice columnist out there for you somewhere, Tim; you're just going to have to keep looking for him.

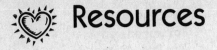 # Resources

Magazines

Adult Video News
AVN Publications
8600 West Chester Pike #300
Upper Darby, PA 19082
(215) 789-2085

Anything That Moves
Bisexuality
2404 California Street #24
San Francisco, CA 94115
(415) 703-7977 ×2
www.anythingthatmoves.com

Bound & Gagged
Gay male bondage
The Outbound Press
P.O. Box 2048
New York, NY 10116-2048
(212) 736-6869
www.boundandgagged.com

Cross-Talk
Cross-dressing
P.O. Box 944
Woodland Hills, CA 91356

Girlfriends
Lesbian
3415 Cesar Chavez #101
San Francisco, CA 94110
(415) 648-9464
(800) grl.frnd [475-3763]
www.gfriends.com

Hair to Stay
Hairy Women
Winter Publishing
P.O. Box 80667WWW
Dartmouth, MA 02748
(508) 994-2908
www.hairtostay.com

In Uniform
A.M. Publications
P.O. Box 3226
Portland, OR 97208
(503) 228-6935
www.teleport.com/~uniform/

KPPD
Kinky people, places,
and things
DM International
P.O. Box 16188
Seattle, WA 98116
www.blarg.net/~dmi/home/
home.html

Libido
Literary erotica
P.O. Box 146721
Chicago, IL 60614
(312) 275-0842

On Our Backs
Lesbian erotica
3415 Cesar Chavez
Suite 101
San Francisco, CA 94110
(415) 648-9464

Taste of Latex
Fetish
DM International
P.O. Box 16188
Seattle, WA 98116
www.blarg.net/~dmi/home/
home.html

TV Connection
Transgendered
DM International
P.O. Box 16188
Seattle, WA 98116
www.blarg.net/~dmi/home/
home.html

Women in Power (formerly Bitches with Whips)
Female domination
DM International
P.O. Box 16188
Seattle, WA 98116
www.blarg.net/~dmi/home/
home.html

Books

Anal Pleasure and Health
Jack Morin, Ph.D.
1986, Yes Press

The Black Book
"The guide for the erotic
explorer"
Bill Brent, editor
1996, Black Books

The Bottoming Book: Or, How to Get Terrible Things Done to You by Wonderful People
Dossie Easton and
Catherine A. Liszt
1995, Greenery Press

Cunt Coloring Book
1989, Naiad Press

Encyclopedia of Unusual Sex Practices
Brenda Love
1992, Barricade Books

Fetish: Fashion, Sex, and Power
Valerie Steele
1996, Oxford University Press

The Good Vibrations Guide to Sex
Cathy Winks and Anne Semans
1994, Cleis Press, Inc.

A History of Men's Underwear: from Union Suits to Bikini Briefs
Gary M. Griffin
1991, Added Dimensions

A Kid's First Book About Sex
Joani Blank
1983, Down There Press

Learning the Ropes: A Basic Guide to Safe and Fun S/M
Race Bannon
1992, Daedalus Publishing

Leatherfolk: Radical Sex, People, Politics, and Practice
Mark Thompson
1991, Alyson Publications

Leatherman's Handbook II
Larry Townsend
1989, Carlyle Communications

Lesbian Sex
JoAnn Loulan
1984, Spinsters/Aunt Lute

Lesbian Sex Book
Wendy Caster
1993, Alyson Publications

Men Loving Themselves
Jack Morin
1988, Down There Press

New Joy of Gay Sex
Charles Silverstein and Felice Picano
1992, HarperCollins

A New View of a Woman's Body
Federation of Feminist Women's Health Centers
1991, Feminist Health Press

The New Our Bodies, Ourselves
Boston Women's Health Collective
1992, Simon and Schuster

Penis Power: A Complete Guide to Potency Restoration
Gary M. Griffin
1991, Added Dimensions

Sex Over 40
Saul Rosenthal
1987, Putnam

Sex for Dummies
Dr. Ruth Westheimer
1995, IDG Books

Susie's Sexpert's Lesbian Sex World
Susie Bright
1990, Cleis Press

Solo Sex: Advanced Techniques
Dr. Harold Litten
1992, Factor Press

The Topping Book: Getting Good at Being Bad
Dossie Easton and Catherine A. Liszt
1996, Greenery Press

Education

Kinsey Institute
Information and User Services
Morrison Hall 313
Bloomington, IN 47405
(812) 855-7686
www.indiana.edu/~kinsey/

Planned Parenthood
810 Seventh Avenue
New York, NY 10019
(212) 541-7800
www.plannedparenthood.org

San Francisco Sex Information
P.O. Box 881254
San Francisco, CA 94188-1254
(415) 989-7374 (SFSI)
www.sfsi.org

Sex Information and Education Council of the United States (SIECUS)
130 West 42nd Street
Suite 350
New York, NY 10036
(212) 819-9770
www.siecus.org

Retail

Centurian/Spartacus
Fetish
P.O. Box 459
Orange, CA 92666
(714) 971-1113

Condomania
Latex
www.condomania.com

351 Bleecker Street
New York, NY 10014
(212) 691-9442

7306 Melrose Avenue
Los Angeles, CA 90046
(213) 933-7865

Gauntlet Piercing
870 Huntley Drive
Los Angeles, CA 90069
(310) 657-6677

2377 Market Street
San Francisco, CA 94114
(415) 431-3133

144 Fifth Avenue, Second Floor
New York, NY 10011
(212) 229-0180

Good Vibrations
Toys, books, video, novelties
1210 Valencia Street
San Francisco, CA 94110
(415) 974-8980
www.goodvibes.com

Good Vibrations Mail Order
938 Howard Street,
Suite 101 GB
San Francisco, CA 94103
(415) 974-8990

Pleasure Chest
Toys and clothing
7733 Santa Monica
Boulevard
West Hollywood, CA 90046
(213) 650-1022 (retail)
(800) 75-DILDO (mail order)

Stormy Leather Inc.
Leather, toys, clothing
1158 Howard Street
San Francisco, CA 94103
(415) 626-1672
www.stormyleather.com

Toys in Babeland
Toys, books, video, novelties
707 E. Pike Street
Seattle, WA 98122
(206) 328-2914
www.babeland.com

SM/Fetish/Kink

American Association for Nude Recreation
1703 N. Main Street,
Suite E
Kissimmee, FL 34744-3396
(800) TRY-NUDE
[879-6833]
www.aanr.com

Eulenspiegel Society (S/M)
P.O. Box 2783
New York, NY 10163
(212) 388-7022
www.tes.org

Foot Fetish and Fantasy Society
P.O. Box 24866
Cleveland, OH 44124
(216) 449-4114

Girth & Mirth
Big gay men
for local chapters visit
www.chubnet2.com/abc/

Military and Police Uniform Association
P.O. Box 69A04-BLK
West Hollywood, CA 90069
(213) 650-5112
www.members.tripod.com/
~mpua

National Leather Association International
3439 NE Sandy Blvd.#155
Portland, OR 97232
www.nla-i.com

Red Hankies
Fisting
P.O. Box 3988
San Diego, CA 92163
(619) 688-8668

STDs

American Social Health Association
P.O. Box 13827
Research Triangle Park,
NC 27709
(919) 361-8400
www.sunsite.unc.edu/ASHA/

CDC National HIV/AIDS Hot Line
(800) 342-AIDS [2437]
(English)
(800) 344-7432 (Spanish)

CDC National STD Hot Line
(800) 227-8922

Herpes Resource Center: National Herpes Hot Line
(800) 230-6039

Gay and Lesbian Organizations

Gay and Lesbian Alliance Against Defamation
1875 Connecticut Avenue
NW, #800
Washington, DC 20009
(202) 986-1360
www.glaad.org

Human Rights Campaign
1101 14th Street NW
Washington, DC 20005
(202) 628-4160
www.hrcusa.org

National Gay and Lesbian Task Force
2320 17th St. NW
Washington, DC 20009-2702
(202) 332-6483
www.ngltf.org

Parents and Friends of Lesbians and Gays (PFLAG)
1101 14th St. NW, Suite 1030
Washington, DC 20005
(202) 638-4200
www.pflag.org

Women

National Abortion and Reproductive Rights Action League
NARAL
www.naral.org

National Organization for Women (NOW)
P.O. Box 96824
Washington, DC 20090
(202) 331-0066
www.now.org

National Women's Health Network
Suite 400
514 10th Street NW
Washington, DC 20004
(202) 347-1140

Health

American Urological Association/Prostate Health Council of the American Foundation for Urologic Disease
1128 North Charles Street
Baltimore, MD 21201
(410) 727-1100
www.prostatehealth.com

The National Breast Cancer Coalition
1707 L Street NW,
Suite 1060

Washington, D.C. 20036
(202) 296-7477
www.natlbcc.org

Youth

The Hetrick-Martin Institute
Gay, lesbian, and bi youth at risk for HIV/AIDS
2 Astor Place
New York, NY 10003
(212) 674-2600

National Child Abuse Hot Line
(800) 422-4453

National Runaway Switchboard
3080 North Lincoln Avenue
Chicago, IL 60657
(800) 621-4000

National Youth Crisis Hot Line
(800) 448-4663

!OUTPROUD!
The National Coalition for Gay, Lesbian & Bisexual Youth
P.O. Box 24569
San Jose, CA 95154-4589
(408) 269-6125
www.cyberspaces.com/
outproud/

Tran/Cross-dressing

American Educational Gender Information Center
P.O. Box 33724
Decatur, GA 30033
(770) 939-0244

The Renaissance Transgender Association, Inc.
987 Old Eagle School Road, Suite 719
Wayne, PA 19087
(610) 975-9119
www.ren.org

Good Advice

Ann Landers
www.creators.com/lifestyle/landers/lan.asp

"Dear Abby"
Abigail Van Buren
www.uexpress.com/ups/abby/

Dr. Ruth Westheimer
www.drruth.com

"Savage Love"
Dan Savage
c/o *The Stranger*
1122 East Pike, Suite 1225
Seattle, WA 98102
www.savageonline.com

Bad Advice

American Family Association
www.afa.net

"Ask Isadora"
Isadora Alman
3145 Geary Boulevard #153
San Francisco, CA 94118
www.askisadora.com

Dr. Laura Schlessinger
Author and call-in radio show host
www.drlaura.com

Focus on the Family
P.O. Box 35500
Colorado Springs,
CO 80935
(719) 531-3400

PENGUIN PUTNAM

online

Your Internet gateway to a virtual environment
with hundreds of entertaining and enlightening
books from Penguin Putnam Inc.

*While you're there get the latest buzz on the best
authors and books around—*

Tom Clancy, Patricia Cornwell, W.E.B.Griffin,
Nora Roberts, William Gibson, Robin Cook,
Brian Jacques, Catherine Coulter, Stephen King,
Jacquelyn Mitchard, and many more!

Penguin Putnam Online is located at
http://www.penguinputnam.com

PENGUIN PUTNAM NEWS

Every month you'll get an inside look at our
upcoming books and new features on our site.
This is an ongoing effort on our part to provide
you with the most interesting and up-to-date
information about our books and authors.

Subscribe to Penguin Putnam News at
http://www.penguinputnam.com/ClubPPI